NOBLE PURSUITS

SENIOR AUTHORS
Virginia A. Arnold
Carl B. Smith

LITERATURE CONSULTANTS
Joan I. Glazer
Margaret H. Lippert

LTX
7-01-103

READING
EXPRESS
MACMILLAN

Macmillan Publishing Company
New York

Collier Macmillan Publishers
London

ACKNOWLEDGMENTS

The publisher gratefully acknowledges permission to reprint the following copyrighted material:

"Across the Great Divide" is adapted from ACROSS THE GREAT DIVIDE by Simon James. Copyright © 1978 by Maverick Films, Inc. Reprinted by permission of Scholastic Inc. By permission also of The Hutchinson Publishing Group Ltd.

"Apple-Pie" by Ivy O. Eastwick is reprinted by permission of Hooper & Wollen, Executors of Miss I. E. O. Eastwick.

"The Art of the Ndebele" from NDEBELE: *The Art of an African Tribe* by Margaret Courtney-Clarke. Copyright © 1986 Margaret Courtney-Clarke. Used by permission of Rizzoli International Publications and the author.

"Artichoke" from NO ONE WRITES A LETTER TO A SNAIL by Maxine Kumin. Text © 1962 by Maxine W. Kumin. Reprinted by permission of Curtis Brown, Ltd.

"The Audition" is adapted from STARSTRUCK by Marisa Gioffre. Copyright © 1983 by Highgate Pictures, a division of Learning Corporation of America. Reprinted by permission of Scholastic Inc.

"Bravado" is from THE POETRY OF ROBERT FROST edited by Edward Connery Lathem. Copyright 1947, © 1969 by Holt, Rinehart and Winston, Inc. Copyright © 1975 by Lesley Frost Ballantine. Reprinted by permission of Henry Holt and Company, Inc. Permission also of Jonathan Cape LTD. By permission also of the estate of Robert Frost.

"Castaways on the Sea of Time" is adapted from NEW FOUND LAND by John Christopher. Copyright © 1983 by John Christopher. Reprinted by permission of the publisher, E. P. Dutton, a division of New American Library. By permission also of the author.

"The Citadel" is an adaptation of Chapter 11 from BANNER IN THE SKY by James Ramsey Ullman (J. B. Lippincott). Copyright 1954 by James Ramsey Ullman. Reprinted by permission of Harper & Row, Publishers, Inc. By permission also of Harold Matson Co., Inc.

"El Condor Pasa" by Paul Simon. Copyright © 1970 Paul Simon. Used by permission.

"Diet, Exercise, and Good Health" is an abridgment of Chapter 2 from TOO FAT? TOO THIN? by Caroline Arnold. Text Copyright © 1984 by Caroline Arnold. Abridged by permission of William Morrow & Company. By permission also of the author. The figures in the chart are adapted from *THE LEARN Program for Weight Control* by Dr. Kelly D. Brownell of the University of Pennsylvania School of Medicine, 1987. Used by permission.

"Dinah" is an adaptation from the complete text of DINAH AND THE GREEN FAT KINGDOM by Isabelle C. Holland. Copyright © 1978 by Isabelle C. Holland. Reprinted by permission of Harper & Row, Publishers, Inc. By permission also of JCA Literary Agency Inc.

"Dream Variation" is reprinted from SELECTED POEMS OF LANGSTON HUGHES. Copyright 1926 by Alfred A. Knopf, Inc. and renewed 1954 by Langston Hughes. By permission of Alfred A. Knopf, Inc.

"The Dream Watcher" from THE DREAM WATCHER by Barbara Wersba. Copyright © 1986 by Barbara Wersba. Reprinted by permission of McIntosh and Otis, Inc.

"Fat Men From Space" is from FAT MEN FROM SPACE by Daniel Manus Pinkwater. Copyright © 1977 by Manus Pinkwater. Reprinted by permission of Dodd, Mead & Company, Inc.

Macmillan Publishing Company
866 Third Avenue
New York, N.Y. 10022
Collier Macmillan Canada, Inc.

Printed in the United States of America.

ISBN 0-02-172890-9

9 8 7 6 5 4 3 2 1

Contents

BODYWORKS

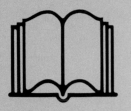

PREPARING FOR READING

Learning Vocabulary

1. Jason felt that by going out for track he would be grooming himself for the baseball team.
2. During practice, he could tell the coach was upset by the expression on his face.
3. Marceline passed the other runners with a confident stride.
4. The searing pain in Jason's chest was an unexpected result of his effort to pick up speed.
5. After almost colliding with two other runners, Jason finally reached the finish line.

grooming	expression	stride
searing	colliding	

Developing Background and Skills
Figurative Language

Writers use language in different ways—sometimes in surprising ways. When writers use **figurative language,** they often come up with unusual ways to say things. The paragraph below includes examples of several different kinds of figurative language. Read it carefully to see if you can understand the meanings.

For the first few laps, the miler ran like the wind. He was an engine going at full speed. The crowd in the stands went bananas. But suddenly, fortune ceased to smile on the runner. He just could not keep going. He died in the last lap.

The phrase *the miler ran like the wind* is an example of a simile. A **simile** is a comparison between two things of unlike nature, using the word *like* or *as*. The intended meaning of the phrase is "the miler ran very fast."

An example of a metaphor is the sentence *He was an engine going at full speed*. A **metaphor** is another kind of comparison. In a metaphor, one thing is said to be another thing. In the sentence above, the runner is said *to be* an engine. Of course, he is not an engine. The intended meaning of the sentence is that the runner is acting in a mechanical way.

An example of an idiom is the sentence *The crowd in the stands went bananas*. The intended meaning is that the crowd became very excited. An **idiom** is an expression whose meaning cannot be understood from the individual words that make it up. Idioms are so common that we don't even think about using them. They include such expressions as "saved by the bell" and "straight from the horse's mouth."

In using **personification**, a writer gives personalities to things, ideas, or qualities. In the phrase *fortune ceased to smile on him*, smiling, a human characteristic, is given to something non-human.

Hyperbole is intentional exaggeration. When the writer says, "He died in the last lap," we know that the miler did not really die: he merely slowed down and fell behind the other runners. The use of hyperbole emphasizes the difference between the way the miler ran in the first and last laps of the race.

The story you will read next includes many examples of figurative language. Think about how the author's use of these expressions makes his descriptions more interesting.

THE MILER

JERRY SPINELLI

I didn't make the baseball team.

The coach said he already had a ninth-grader for shortstop, and an eighth-grade second-stringer, and I wasn't quite good enough to beat them out. I said I'd be willing to play another position. He said he had veteran ninth-graders at all the positions. I told him I wanted to be a major leaguer someday. I told him I hit almost .330 in Little League last year. He looked impressed. He said that's the kind of spirit he likes to see. He said it's not that I don't have the talent, it's just that I need another year to grow. To mature. In the meantime, he said, he wants me to stay in shape. He said he'd like to see me go out for track. It'd be good for me, he said, and nobody gets cut from track.

I tried out the sprints. I figured that would help me be a better base-stealer. But I was too slow for the sprints.

I tried the half mile. It was too long to run full speed, and too short to run slow. I couldn't figure it out.

That's how I became a miler.

At first I wasn't too excited about it. I didn't see how running the mile was going to help me be a better shortstop. I was only doing it because the baseball coach was grooming me for next year.

Then I saw a mile race on TV. Some great miler from England was running, and as he finished each lap the announcer was screaming: "He's on a record pace! He's on a record pace!" Each lap the people in the stands went crazier. On one side of the screen they showed the world record time and on the other side they showed the runner's time. The whole stadium was standing and screaming, like they were pushing him with their voices, and even though it was the last lap, instead of going slower he was going *faster*. I couldn't believe it. The stadium was going bananas, and he was flying and the world record time and his time were getting closer and closer and he broke the world record by 3/10 of a second. And even then he didn't collapse, or even stop. He just kept jogging another lap around the track, holding his arms up and smiling and waving to the cheering crowd.

Even though it was Saturday, I went outside and ran ten times around the block.

I turned out to be a pretty rotten miler. We had our first time trials, and I came in dead last. My time was 6 minutes and 47 seconds. The guy that broke the world record did it in less than 3 minutes and 50 seconds.

But that was nothing. It was all just peaches and cream compared to the worst part, the really, *really* bad thing: one of the people that beat me was named Marceline McAllister. The girl.

"I'm quittin'," I told Peter Kim, who was on the track team too. A half-miler.

"Why?" he said.

"*Why*? You see who I lost to in the time trials?"

"I wasn't watching."

"The girl."

"Which one?" he said. There're other ones on the team too, but she's the only miler.

"McAllister," I said.

He shrugged. "So?"

"So?" I hollered. "Waddaya mean, so? She's a girl, man! You ever lose to a girl?"

He said maybe I had a cramp.

"I didn't have any cramp."

"Maybe you just had a bad day."

"So what?" I screeched. "How bad could it be? She's still a girl. I got beat by a girl. I'm quittin'."

Then he started talking to me. He reminded me that some of the other girls on the team were doing better than last too. In fact, one of them was the second-fastest sprinter in the one-hundred-pound class. He said he heard that at our age a lot of girls are better than boys, because they mature faster. He said that in another couple years I'd beat her easy. And he reminded me that the baseball coach had his eye on me.

"He's really gonna be impressed, watching me lose to a girl."

"He didn't tell you to beat anybody," Peter said. "He just said to keep in shape."

I tried to explain. "Peter, all that stuff doesn't make any difference. The thing is, she's a girl. And a girl's a girl. You know what I'm saying? A *girl*. G-I-R-L. You understand me?"

Peter's expression changed. "No," he said, "I don't understand. Do what you want." He turned and left.

"Okay," I said. "I won't quit." He kept walking. I called, "Just don't tell! Peter? Hear? Don't tell anybody!"

It was a long, long track season.

Every day we started with calisthenics. Then most days we ran around the whole school grounds. *Five* times. Some other days we did intervals. That's where you run real fast as hard as you can for a while, then walk for a while (a little while), then run fast again. Run-walk-run-walk. You just listen for the whistle to tell your legs when to start or stop. You'll never know how cruel a whistle is until you're walking after your tenth interval, and you hear it blow again.

As much as I hated practice, there was one good thing about it: you weren't running *against* anybody. There were no places. No first. No last.

That's why I dreaded the first meet. It was at Mill Township. I came in last. By a lot. But the thing was, it didn't really bother me. That's because on the bus over to the meet I all of a sudden realized something: even though I was running, I wasn't really in the *race*. If all I was supposed to be doing was staying in shape for baseball, there was no use getting all uptight about where I finished. I was actually running for the baseball coach, not the track coach. I was a baseball player disguised as a track runner. I didn't really want to break the world's record. I was no miler. I was a shortstop.

It was a big relief when I thought about all that. It still might look to some people like I was losing to a girl. But inside I knew the truth. You can't lose if you're not racing.

After the mile the coach called to me. I was still jogging. I was hardly puffing. I thought I'd do another couple laps around the grass. Really get in shape.

"Hold it," he said. He came over, and we walked back to the locker room together. "Nothing wrong? Muscle pull? Dizzy?" he asked.

"I'm okay," I told him.

He looked at me funny. "So why were you taking it easy?"

I told him the whole thing, which I probably should have done the first day of practice. I told him about the baseball coach. About being groomed for next year. About wanting to be a major league shortstop.

He was nodding his head while I said these things. When I finished, he still kept nodding, looking at me. Then he stopped. He bent over so his face was right opposite mine. He didn't blink. His voice was hoarse. Almost a whisper.

"What's your first name?"

"Jason."

"Jason? Jason, when you're on my team, you run. And you run as well as you can. I don't care if you're slower than a turtle, you'll try your best when you're on my team. You will run as hard as you can. Every step of the way. Do you understand?"

I nodded.

"And next time I see you dogging it, you are no longer on my team. Understood?"

I understood.

So much for taking it easy.

So I did my calisthenics and ran my five times around the school and did my intervals and I tried harder.

In the second meet I brought my time down to 6:30. I was still last. McAllister's time was 6:15.

In the next couple meets I kept improving. But so did she. Then something happened that made me try even harder. We were racing Shelbourne, and they had a girl miler too—and *she* beat me.

The next day at practice I ran around the school six times. I did my calisthenics perfectly. Even after fifteen intervals I dared that whistle to blow again.

Next meet, for the first time, I didn't come in last. I beat somebody. A kid on the other team.

Peter saw I was trying harder. He started running with me at practice. (He takes track seriously, like I take baseball.) During my races he would stand at the last turn with a stopwatch, and at each lap he would call out my time and yell, "Go, Jason! Go! Go!" And on the last lap, coming off the final turn, he would yell at me, "Sprint! Now! All out! Sprint! Now! Now!" And he would be sprinting along the grass with me.

My times got better. I broke the six-minute barrier with a 5:58. McAllister kept getting better too. I was closing the gap on her, but the closer I got, the harder it got.

Then, on the next-to-last meet of the season, going down the backstretch, I got closer to McAllister than ever before. I was so close I could feel little cinder specks that her spikes were flipping back. Her hands were tight fists. Her hair was flapping like mad from side to side and slapping her in the neck. I could hear her breathing. She was kind of wheezing. Grunting. And all of a sudden, right there on the backstretch, it came to me: *Marceline McAllister wasn't faster than me.* Not really. She was just trying harder. She was trying so hard it scared me.

I practiced hard in the days before the final meet. But not super hard. The problem wasn't in my legs. It was in my head. I knew I could beat her now, but I didn't know if I wanted to pay the price. And the price was pain. I found that out following her down the backstretch that day. I was really hurting. My legs felt like they were dragging iron hooks through the cinders. My head was flashing and thundering. But the worst part of all was my chest. It felt like somebody opened me up and laid two iron shotputs inside me, one on top of each lung, and each time I breathed out, the shotputs flattened the lungs a little more. By the last one hundred yards there was only about a thimbleful of air to suck from.

When I remembered all that pain, and realized it would have to get even worse for me to go faster, I wasn't sure beating her was worth it. I felt like somebody, somewhere, double-crossed me. I couldn't believe I would have to try so hard just to beat a girl.

When they called the milers to the start, me and McAllister, as usual, being seventh-graders and the slowest, lined up at the back of the pack. Only this time somebody else lined up with us. It was Pain. He was grinning. *O-h-h-h no*, I thought. I swore right there this would be the last race I ever ran in my life.

In all my other races, what I did was stay pretty far behind McAllister for the first two or three laps. That way I could save my energy and sprint after her on the last lap. But this time I stuck with her right from the start. Like a wart.

By the end of the first lap I was already blowing hard. My legs were getting a little heavy. Pain didn't touch me yet, but he was right beside me, still grinning. We were really smoking.

We kept it up the second lap. Didn't slow down at all. Her spikes were practically nicking my knees. Our breathings had the same rhythm.

At the half-mile mark things started to get a little scary. Never before, this far into the race, were we this close to the leaders. I was almost as tired as I usually was at the end of a whole mile. Something had to give. Pain was right there, stride for stride, grinning away. Something was going to happen.

It did. Coming off the first turn into the backstretch of the third lap. The leaders started to go faster. McAllister speeded up too. She was trying to stay with them. *Oh, no!* I thought. *She's crazy!*

I had no choice. I had to go too. I stepped on it, and all of a sudden Pain wasn't alongside me anymore. He was *on* me. He was beating up on my head. He was pulling on my legs. He speared a cramp into my side. He opened up my chest and dumped in those two iron shotputs.

Little by little McAllister pulled away: three yards . . . five yards . . . ten yards . . . When she leaned into the far turn I got a side view of her. She was running great. Long strides. Arms pumping. Leaning just a little forward. Keeping her form. Everything the coach told us.

A feeling I never expected in a million years came over me: I admired her. I was proud of her. I knew she was hurting too, maybe even as bad as me, but there she was, gaining on the guy in front of her. I wanted to be like her.

The gun went off: last lap. Four hundred forty more yards and my racing career would be over.

I reached out, like my own breath was a twisted rope, and pulled myself along. My lungs sagged under the shotputs. I tried to forget that. I shook my arms to relax. *Stride long. Head steady. Keep your form. . . .*

I don't know whether she slowed down or I got faster, but the gap between us closed: ten yards . . . five yards . . . three yards. We were on the final backstretch, and I was where I started, nipping at her heels. *Now!* I thought. I pulled alongside her. Some others were already sprinting for the tape, but we were in our own private race, crunching down the cinders, side by side. We never turned to look at each other.

Then, going into the final turn, she started to edge ahead. A couple inches. A couple feet. I went after her. My lungs disappeared. Only the shotputs now. And now they were doing something. They were getting warm. They were getting hot. They were burning.

I caught her coming off the final turn. Side by side again. There was no form now. No nice fresh strides. With every step we staggered and knocked into each other like cattle coming down a chute. I wished I had the shotputs back, because in my chest now was something worse: two balls of white-hot gas. *Stars!* A pair of stars in my chest. A billion degrees centigrade. And they were expanding. Exploding. Searing hot gas scalding into my stomach and arms and legs into my head. My eyes were star gas. Faces on the side lurched and swayed. The track wobbled under my feet. Elbows, shoulders, hips colliding. If Peter was running with me I didn't know it. I couldn't see. I couldn't hear. I couldn't breathe. I was dying.

I don't know when I crossed the finish line. I only know they stopped me and helped me up and dragged me around with my arms draped over their shoulders.

Then there were hands coming down from everywhere. I did my best to hit them all. "Way to go," they kept saying. "Way to gut it . . . Way to run . . . Good race . . . Good race . . . Good race . . . "

Finally I plopped to the ground. Little by little I got my shoes off. My chest was returning to normal. The star gas must have gone out through my eyes: they were burning.

Another hand, palm up, in front of me. I slapped it. I looked from the hand to the face. It was McAllister. She looked sick. Her lips were bluish and wet and her mouth was crooked. But then it smiled.

"Good race," she said.

Questions

1. Why did Jason decide to go out for track?
2. Why did Jason adopt the attitude that although he was running, he wasn't really in the races?
3. How might the story have ended if the coach had not threatened to put Jason off the team?
4. Do you think it is important to try your best, even in something you don't care about? Explain your answer.

Applying Reading Skills

Copy each sentence below and underline the phrases that are examples of figurative language. Tell whether each is a simile, a metaphor, or an idiom, or an example of personification or hyperbole.

1. Coming in last was just peaches and cream compared to the fact that I had been beaten by a girl.
2. The coach said he didn't care if I was as slow as a turtle as long as I tried my hardest.
3. Peter reminded me that the baseball coach had his eye on me.
4. He was about as sympathetic as a fencepost.
5. You'll never know how cruel a whistle is until you hear it blow after the tenth interval.
6. My legs felt like iron hooks dragging through the cinders.
7. By the last hundred yards, there was only a thimbleful of air in my lungs.
8. Pain was right there, stride for stride, grinning away.
9. McAllister's hair was slapping her in the neck.
10. As I went after her, my lungs disappeared.

The Women's 400 Meters

Skittish,
    they flex knees, drum heels and
    shiver at the starting line

    waiting the gun
    to pour them over the stretch
    like a breaking wave.

Bang! they're off
careening down the lanes,
each chased by her own bright tiger.

Lillian Morrison

PREPARING FOR READING

Learning Vocabulary

1. For some athletes, the <u>motivation</u> to win comes from a need to work out an inner, or mental, <u>conflict</u>.
2. Success for other athletes comes from a desire for <u>status</u>.
3. Sports psychologists think that athletic performance is related not only to physical <u>competence</u> but also to several mental <u>aspects</u>.
4. Through <u>imagery</u>, athletes can mentally rehearse their skills while seated, calm and relaxed.

motivation	conflict	status
competence	aspects	imagery

Developing Background and Skills
Main Idea

Careful writers organize their material so their readers can understand it. Sentences are grouped into paragraphs, each of which has a **main idea.** The main idea is the most important information in the paragraph. Sometimes the main idea is stated in a single sentence at the beginning, in the middle, or at the end of the paragraph. See if you can find the main idea in the paragraph below.

Pierre de Coubertin (kü bãr tan') organized the modern Olympics. He believed that international sports activities would lead to better understanding among nations. The first modern Olympic Games took place in Athens in 1896. Since then, the games have been held every four years except in wartime.

In this example, the main idea is stated in the first sentence. The other sentences give further information about the main idea. They provide what we call **supporting details.**

In many paragraphs, however, the main idea is implied, or not directly stated. All of the information given makes up the supporting details. Here is an example.

In a recent survey, the school's athletes were asked to give their opinion on the following question: *Is winning more important than playing a good game?* About 10 percent said "yes." About 75 percent said "no," indicating that the opposite is true. About 15 percent felt that winning and playing a good game are of equal importance.

If you can't find a sentence that states the main idea, list the details. The diagram below includes a list of the details. It also includes one way to state the main idea.

SUPPORTING DETAILS

10%—winning more important
75%—playing a good game more important
15%—winning and playing a good game equally important

Most of the school's athletes agreed that playing a good game was more important than winning.

MAIN IDEA

As you read the next selection, look for the main ideas (stated or implied) that the author presents.

IMPROVING SPORTS PERFORMANCE

MELVIN BERGER

Just before the 1976 Winter Olympics, one cross-country skier was performing so badly that he was expected to be a failure in his event. At the Games, though, he came close to getting the best time of all the competitors in his part of the relay race. His success moved the United States team from twelfth to eighth place.

In midseason, a varsity high school basketball player lost her confidence because she wasn't making any of her shots. After only a few days, she was playing as well as ever and went on to lead her team to win the league trophy.

A placekicker on a college football team was nearly perfect at practice. During games, though, he missed several game-winning kicks. One season later, this kicker was doing as well at the games as the practice sessions. In fact, he set a national record for the longest kick in college football.

In each case, a sports scientist turned things around for the player. How was the change made? Not by bettering the athlete's physical condition, but by improving his or her mental state. The scientists who helped these players are called psychologists. They are experts and specialists in human behavior. Those who deal mostly with mental aspects of athletes and athletics are known as sports psychologists.

Dr. Richard M. Suinn of Colorado State University is an outstanding sports psychologist. He has been the team psychologist for the U.S. Nordic ski team and for the Women's Track and Field team. He is best known, though, for helping athletes overcome stress and nervousness. This lets them perform at their peak.

Dr. Suinn teaches the athletes progressive relaxation. In this system, Dr. Suinn first shows the athlete how to feel both tension (tightness) and relaxation (looseness). He seats the player in a comfortable chair and instructs him or her to raise a wrist and make a very tight fist. This creates tension in the arm and hand. Then he tells the athlete to open the fist, relax, and let the hand rest on the chair.

"Can you feel the difference?" Dr. Suinn asks the player.

Most can easily feel the change. Then Dr. Suinn teaches them to create tension and relaxation in different muscles around the body. After a short period of training, the athletes do not need any more help. They are able to relax their muscles at will, even before stress.

Dr. Suinn has another plan to improve athletic performance. It is called visuo-motor behavior rehearsal, or VMBR, for short. This approach to training has three basic steps.

The first is to give the athletes lessons in progressive relaxation. The next step is for the player to call to mind mental images of the sport. Dr. Suinn calls this "body thinking." The goal is to create vivid images of taking part in the sport. Swimmers feel the water on their skin and smell the chemicals in the pool. Skiers see the slope in front of them and hear the wind whistling as they speed along. Runners sense the buildup of tension before the race and the burst of energy as the starter's gun explodes.

Last, the athlete mentally rehearses the skills of the sport, while seated calm and relaxed. The ice skater adjusts her body balance as she goes through her figures. The pitcher winds up and throws a fastball smack into the center of the catcher's mitt. The football halfback twists and turns while running for a touchdown.

Before one major race, skiing champion Jean-Claude Killy could not practice on the slopes because of an injury. The only way he could prepare for the race was through the use of mental imagery. Killy later reported that it was the best race he ever skied!

By now, a number of other psychologists have adopted Dr. Suinn's approach. Through progressive relaxation and VMBR, they have helped many athletes. Players report sharper skills, increased confidence, and improved performance.

Still, there is little hard scientific evidence that the system works. It is very difficult to carry out experiments to prove that athletes really get better as a result of sports psychology.

Dr. Suinn's first experimental study of VMBR shows what can happen with such tests. Dr. Suinn divided the Colorado State University ski team into two groups. Both were about equal in size and ability. He gave one group VMBR training. The other got the ordinary training.

The VMBR group, though, improved so much that it actually ruined the experiment. The coach would not allow members of the untreated group to take part in the events. This made it impossible to compare results. But the fact that the VMBR group won the league trophy and got many individual honors surely points up VMBR's usefulness.

To do well at sports, an athlete needs special skills and talents for the game. But what is also important is a strong will to excel, sometimes called sports motivation.

Dr. Dorcas Susan Butt of the University of British Columbia, Canada, has a special interest in sports motivation. Once she was a champion tennis player. Now she is well known as a sports psychologist.

Dr. Butt finds that an athlete's motivation stems from a number of different basic drives. Her main research goal is to understand and explain the various types of athletic motivation. She is also trying to discover which of the motivations are most helpful to the athlete's personality.

According to Dr. Butt, there are four levels of sports motivation. The basic level is the life force. This biological energy, she says, is part of every human's drive to live and will to win.

At the next level are the psychological motivations. They are aggression, conflict, and competence. All three of these motivations may be present in the same athlete. Usually, however, one of them is stronger than the others.

Aggressive athletes have a great deal of energy. Much of this energy is directed against their opponents. They also tend to be very active and eager. Althea Gibson, the Wimbledon tennis champion in 1957 and 1958, is an example of an aggressive athlete. Miss Gibson always played a hard, strong game. She once said that she felt like attacking her opponents physically at times.

Conflict-motivated athletes are often unhappy and moody. They use sports to work out conflicts within their personalities. One young man who was well developed physically but very shy had a strong need to show himself off to others. He took up weight lifting as a way of improving his self-image. Ultimately he became an Olympic gold medalist.

Many of the top athletes, too, are motivated by the competence drive. These players perform to the best of their abilities because it fulfills their own inner needs. They are less interested in whether they win or lose.

Roger Bannister, the first runner to break the four-minute mile, was a competence-motivated athlete. He set himself high goals and then worked to meet them. When racing, he was satisfied if he ran well, even if he did not win the race. In 1965, Bill Rodgers, a leading marathon runner, ran the mile in 4:18:8. Fifteen years later, "just to see if I could do it," he cut two seconds off his record.

Competition and cooperation make up the two social motivations on the third level. Competition, says Dr. Butt, is the "win at all costs" attitude. It springs from the aggressive and conflict motivations. Competitive athletes focus their attention on doing better than the others. Cooperation is just the opposite. It comes from the competence motivation. Cooperative athletes work well with others and put the team's success above personal gain.

Most individual sports, though, stress competition. To win, you have to beat, or do better than, someone else. Dr. Butt believes that even here there is room for cooperation. Athletes can be friendly and helpful, even though they are working hard to win.

The final level affects both psychological and social motivations. Dr. Butt calls it the rewards of sports motivation. Part of this motivation comes from others. It includes praise, attention, prizes, and status. But another very important part comes from within. It centers on such factors as pride, confidence, and a good sense of self.

Dr. Butt's findings are changing sports. They show that competence and cooperation can improve an athlete's chances of succeeding in sports. Players with these drives are happy and fulfilled people. Competition and aggressiveness may be bad for some athletes, and bad in some sports.

Improving sports performance and understanding motivation are only two lines of study in sports psychology today. There are many others. Among them are these:

Can psychological tests be used to predict athletic success? (One study showed that a standard test was 70 percent correct in picking those who would do well in Olympic competition. When combined with records of past performances and physical exams, it proved to be 90 percent correct.)

How can staleness in training be avoided? (Leave time between practice sessions, and don't overcoach.)

What is the psychological makeup of a typical athlete? (Athletes tend to be outgoing, enthusiastic, confident, aggressive, and have a strong will to succeed.)

Is there any value to the before-the-game pep talk? (It does not help. There seems to be more value in a talk after the game between athletes and coach.)

The one thing that all research in sports psychology does show—there is more to winning than just learning the rules of the game.

Questions

1. Describe the two methods used by Dr. Suinn to help athletes perform at their peak.
2. Why was it impossible to draw any conclusions from Dr. Suinn's ski team experiment with VMBR?
3. Do you think the methods of sports psychology are a "fair" way to improve performance? Why or why not?
4. In what other fields or activities might the methods of sports psychology improve performance?

Applying Reading Skills

Read each paragraph below. Write the main idea—stated or implied—for each. For an implied main idea, you may want to list the supporting details first.

1. According to Dr. Butt, the four levels of motivation are life force, psychological motivations, social motivations, and "reward" motivations. Life force, or biological energy, is the basic level. Psychological motivations include aggression, conflict, and competence. Competition and cooperation, which often work together, describe the third level. "Reward" motivations include praise, attention, prizes, and status.

2. No one would deny that physical condition plays a vital role in athletic performance. But studies show that an athlete's mental state also affects the way in which he or she performs. Improvement of "self-image" can have amazing results.

3. Through "body thinking," swimmers create images that allow them to feel the water on their skins and smell the chemicals in the pool. Skiers see the slopes and hear the wind. Runners sense the buildup of tension before a race and the burst of energy at the sound of the starter's gun.

Foul Shot

With two 60's stuck on the scoreboard
And two seconds hanging on the clock,
The solemn boy in the center of eyes,
Squeezed by silence,
Seeks out the line with his feet,
Soothes his hands along his uniform,
Gently drums the ball against the floor,
Then measures the waiting net,
Raises the ball on his right hand,
Balances it with his left,
Calms it with his fingertips,
Breathes,
Crouches,
Waits,
And then through a stretching of stillness,
Nudges it upward.

The ball
Slides up and out,
Lands,
Leans,
Wobbles,
Wavers,
Hesitates,
Exasperates,
Plays it coy
Until every face begs with unsounding screams—
And then

    And then

       And then,

Right before ROAR-UP,
Dives down and through.

Edwin A. Hoey

WRITING ACTIVITY

WRITE A SUMMARY

Prewrite

The article "Improving Sports Performance" gives information on a topic of interest to many teenagers. Suppose you were asked to write a summary of the article for the sports page in your school newspaper. Your summary will be a brief report explaining the most important main idea and supporting details of the article.

Before you begin to write, review the information on finding the main idea and supporting details on pages 30 and 31 and reread the article. Writing an outline will help you identify and organize the main ideas from the article. Complete the following outline.

IMPROVING SPORTS PERFORMANCE
I. Stress and Performance (Dr. Richard Suinn)
   A. Progressive relaxation
   B. ____
      1. (Steps)
      2. ____
      3. ____
II. Motivation and Performance (Dr. Susan Butt)
   A. Life force
   B. ____
      1. (Kinds)
      2. ____
   C. ____
      1. ____
      2. ____
   D. Rewards
      1. (Outside)
      2. (Inside)

Write

Try this organization for your summary.

1. **Paragraph 1**

   Open with a sentence that gives the topic of the article. Continue with a sentence that tells why sports fans and athletes may want to read your summary. Also include in this paragraph the name of the article and the author.

2. **Paragraph 2**

   Focus on Part I of the outline, Dr. Suinn's work.

3. **Paragraph 3**

   Focus on Part II of the outline, Dr. Butt's work.

4. Write a headline for the article to attract your readers.

5. Use your Glossary or dictionary for spelling help.

Revise

Read your summary. It should be a brief description of the important ideas in the article. Check your outline to see if you omitted any main idea or detail. An example or quote from a person adds interest. Try to include such an example in your summary.

1. Proofread your summary for spelling and for the use of correct punctuation at the end of each sentence.

2. Check the exact words, punctuation, and spelling in all direct quotations from the article.

3. Rewrite your summary to share.

PREPARING FOR READING

Learning Vocabulary

1. To retrieve the golden apples, Heracles (hār′ ə klēz) had to overcome a dragon by force.
2. Atlas, who held the inverted bowl of the sky on his head, gladly transferred the burden to Heracles.
3. Atlas taunted Heracles by saying he thought he would never take on his burden again.
4. Atlas was deceived by the trick Heracles played on him.

overcome	inverted	transferred
taunted	deceived	

Developing Background and Skills
Figurative Language

Writers use language in two different ways. They may use words and phrases in their exact meanings. An example of this literal use of language is *Heracles was afraid he would fail in his task.* Often, however, writers use expressions that mean something different from what is exactly stated. They use language in a figurative way. An example is *The threat of failure hung over Heracles' head.* Both sentences mean about the same thing. But you would probably agree that the second is more colorful and more appealing to the imagination.

There are several different kinds of **figurative language,** often referred to as figures of speech. Let's review them by using the following chart.

FIGURATIVE LANGUAGE	DEFINITION	EXAMPLE (AND MEANING)
simile	a comparison of two things unlike in nature using *like* or *as*	Heracles was as strong as an ox. ("Heracles was very strong.")
metaphor	a comparison of two things unlike in nature without using *like* or *as*	Heracles was an ox. ("Heracles was very strong.")
idiom	an expression whose meaning cannot be understood by the individual words that make it up	The king had to keep his word. ("The king had to do as he had promised.")
personification	giving human feelings, motives, or actions to non-human things	The arrow found its mark. ("The arrow hit the mark the bowsman intended.")
hyperbole	intentional exaggeration	A thousand thoughts came to Heracles' mind. ("Heracles thought of a great many things.")

As you read the next selection, think about how you might substitute different figures of speech for the words and phrases that describe the characters, their feelings, and the events that take place.

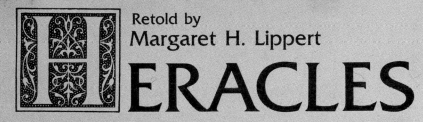

Retold by
Margaret H. Lippert

HERACLES

The story of Heracles (hār' ə klēz), who is often called by his Roman name Hercules, has been told and retold for more than two thousand years. According to the ancient Greeks, Heracles was the son of the great god Zeus (zūs), king of all the gods. However, the mother of Heracles was not a goddess. She was a mortal, or human being. Heracles was born a man with the godlike strength of his father.

From the time he was an infant, Heracles could do remarkable things. When he was eight months old, he strangled two sea serpents.

When Heracles grew up, an angry goddess made him temporarily insane and caused him to kill his wife and three sons. To work through his grief, Heracles agreed to do twelve labors for his cousin King Eurystheus (ū rēs' thē əs). The King was jealous of Heracles because he was so strong. He ordered Heracles to do more and more dangerous labors, hoping that Heracles would be killed. Over eight years, Heracles completed ten of the labors successfully. Now he is about to be given the eleventh labor.

ing Eurystheus looked up. The mighty hero stood before him. Heracles was back, again. And again he had performed his task. King Eurystheus was filled with rage. "I will get rid of this man forever," he thought.

"Heracles," he began, "you have killed ferocious beasts. You have overcome gruesome monsters. But you have not yet visited the land of the gods themselves. I have heard that the gods have a beautiful garden, planted around a tree which bears golden apples. I wish to have three of these golden apples to give to my daughter. Your eleventh labor is this: bring me three golden apples from the garden of the gods."

Heracles lowered his head. He knew that Eurystheus was desperate. No mortal had ever been to the garden of the gods, which lay at the far western edge of the world. Furthermore, it was said that the golden apples which grew there could be picked only by the gods themselves. If a mortal plucked one, he or she would die. Heracles was silent. He knew he must accomplish this labor, as he had accomplished all the others before it. But he was filled with dread.

Heracles set out with his lion skin over his shoulders and his bow and arrows at his side. He traveled over land and sea. At last he came to the far western edge of the world and approached the garden of the gods.

The singing of birds, beginning so softly that it could hardly be heard, became more distinct as he got closer. The sweet smell of flowers in bloom grew stronger. In front of him loomed a high stone wall. Behind the wall was the garden. Heracles walked along the wall until he came to an open gate.

The first sight of the garden took his breath away. Flowers of every color lined grassy walkways. Trees with ripe fruit arched over the paths. In the center of the garden grew a tree lovelier than the rest. Its branches were bending under the weight of golden apples.

"I am standing where no human has ever been," Heracles thought, "seeing what humans were not meant to see. I want to turn back, but I cannot. I must complete my labor, though I do not know how to begin."

A low hiss broke through his thoughts. "What can that be?" he wondered, turning toward the tree hung with golden apples. At the base of the tree he saw a huge dragon head, then another, and another . . . dozens and dozens, more than Heracles could count. The hundred-headed dragon, which was chained to the tree to guard the golden apples, had become aware of the presence of a stranger. It roused itself to protect the treasure. Heracles drew back behind the wall to plan his next move.

At that moment, his eye was caught by a sight more wondrous than the garden, and more frightening than the dragon. A giant stood in the distance, outside the stone wall. His knees were as high as Heracles' head. Without looking up, Heracles turned to run. But he heard no heavy footsteps behind him. Heracles looked back and was astonished to see that the giant had not moved.

Heracles shaded his eyes against the sun to see why the towering giant had not come after him. He was amazed to see that the giant was supporting the inverted bowl of the sky on his head and uplifted hands.

"That must be the god Atlas," thought Heracles. "I heard he was ordered by Zeus to hold up the sky forever." An idea

began to take form in Heracles' mind. "I will die if I pick the golden apples. Only a god can do so and live. Atlas is a god. Perhaps I can persuade him to help me."

Heracles walked toward Atlas. He cupped his hands around his mouth to make his voice louder. Lifting his head, he looked up at Atlas and shouted, "Atlas, I am Heracles."

"What business have you here?" challenged Atlas.

"I have been sent by King Eurystheus to get three golden apples for his daughter," responded Heracles politely. "I will take your burden from you for a moment if you will pick them for me."

Atlas could not believe his good fortune. He looked down, almost toppling the whole sky. Below him stood a man. He was a big man, eight feet tall, with muscular shoulders and a back almost as broad as it was long. His arms were massive, and his hands looked strong enough to overcome man and beast. Yet in spite of his extraordinary size and build, Atlas did not think that the man beneath him could hold the sky. He did not think that any human being could be strong enough to do that. However, no one had ever offered to take his burden, even for a moment. So Atlas could not resist Heracles' offer.

Atlas looked over the wall into the garden and saw that the hundred-headed dragon had wakened and was alerted to danger. "I will be happy to pick the apples for you, Heracles," he said, "if you will kill the dragon."

The hundred-headed dragon did not frighten Heracles. He had killed beasts and monsters much more dangerous than the dragon. He stepped into the garden through the gate and crouched on the grass. He carefully fitted a poisoned arrow to his bow and took aim. Dozens of hissing heads with

open mouths stretched out toward him, but because the dragon was chained to the tree Heracles was out of its reach. The dragon shrieked with helpless rage. Streaks of flame shot toward Heracles from the open mouths. Heracles took aim at the closest head and loosed his arrow, which sank deep into the neck. The dragon's hundred heads roared with agony as the poison took effect. Then the writhing body slipped down to the ground and lay motionless.

Heracles returned to Atlas and stood at his feet. Atlas had witnessed the death of the dreaded dragon. Without another word, he carefully leaned over and transferred the weight of the sky to the shoulders of Heracles.

Heracles could not believe what was demanded of his body. Only the sheer force of his will kept him pressing his hands up against the overpowering weight of the sky. His legs began to buckle, and he knew that his strength would soon give out. He struggled to steady his arms, and pain ripped through his shoulders. Salty sweat pouring down his forehead stung his eyes, but forcing them open he called frantically, "Atlas, have you picked the apples? Bring them to me."

Atlas was enjoying his unexpected freedom. He stretched and looked around. He had never really noticed how beautiful this garden was, how sweet the flowers, how lovely the songs of the birds, how luscious the fruit. He stepped over the wall and helped himself to three golden apples. Then he returned to Heracles.

"Heracles," he taunted, "what a fine job you are doing. I have the apples, and I believe I will deliver them to King Eurystheus myself. Then I will return to take up my burden again."

Heracles knew that Atlas had no intention of returning. He knew that if Atlas left, he would be imprisoned until the end of time under the unbearable weight of the sky. He was in so much pain that he could barely think, but through his distress came a glimmer of a thought.

"Atlas," he gasped, "I will be glad to share this burden with you. However, I cannot survive unless I place a pad on my shoulders. Take the sky until I can fold my lion skin to cushion the weight."

Atlas was deceived. He put down the apples and reached up to take the sky for a moment. Heracles relaxed his shoulders, and the full weight of the sky rested once again on the head and upstretched hands of the mighty Atlas. Heracles picked up the apples and ran as fast as his aching body could go.

Heracles returned to King Eurystheus with the golden apples safely hidden in his tunic. When the king saw him approaching, empty-handed, he was delighted. "Heracles, my cousin, have you failed? Where are the golden apples I ordered you to bring back for my daughter?"

Without a word, Heracles drew forth the apples and held them out to the king. Eurystheus glanced down at them and was overcome with fear. Surely the gods would punish anyone in possession of their golden apples. Suddenly he wished he had never requested them for his daughter. He was afraid to present them to her. "Take them, Heracles," he said. "They are yours."

Heracles was too wise to keep the lovely shining apples. He returned them to the shrine of a goddess, so that she could take them back to their rightful place in the garden of the gods.

For the twelfth labor, King Eurystheus ordered Heracles to go to the land of the dead and bring back the fierce three-headed dog that guarded the underworld. No human had ever returned from there alive. But after challenging the king of the dead and capturing the vicious dog, Heracles came back.

The twelve labors prepared Heracles for a life full of further adventure and glory. At his death, he was lifted by the gods to join them in their palace on the top of Mount Olympus. Heracles was the only mortal ever to be so honored.

Questions
1. What was the eleventh labor Heracles was asked to perform? What was the twelfth?
2. Why did King Eurystheus give the golden apples back to Heracles?
3. Why do you think Atlas didn't just put down the sky and forget about his burden?
4. Describe a present-day labor that even Heracles would find difficult to do.

Applying Reading Skills
A. Copy the sentences below. Underline the figure of speech in each sentence and tell whether it is a simile, a metaphor, an idiom, or an example of personification or hyperbole.

   1. The sight of the garden took Heracles' breath away.
   2. The apples beckoned to Heracles, but he was afraid to pick them.
   3. King Eurystheus could not defeat Heracles in a million years.
   4. King Eurystheus was a tower of rage when Heracles produced the apples.
   5. The apples were like golden mirrors in the sunlight.

B. Use the figurative language suggested to describe each of the following.
   1. the strength of Heracles (simile)
   2. the beauty of the garden of the gods (simile)
   3. the chain holding the dragon (metaphor)
   4. the weight of the sky (metaphor)

PREPARING FOR READING

Learning Vocabulary

1. By <u>diligently</u> following exercises that develop the muscles, a bodybuilder may achieve a powerful <u>physique</u>.
2. <u>Devotion</u> to the <u>principles</u> of bodybuilding—weight training and good nutritional habits—can lead to amazing physical results.
3. Champion Arnold Schwarzenegger was the star of a famous <u>documentary</u> film about bodybuilding.
4. Today, both men and women bodybuilders display their muscles and demonstrate their strength in <u>competition</u>.

diligently   physique   devotion
principles   documentary   competition

Developing Background and Skills
Context Clues

What do you do when you come across an unfamiliar word in your reading? You can, of course, look it up in the dictionary or ask someone for help. But there is something else you can try first.

You can use **context clues** to figure out what a word means. Context clues can be found in nearby words, phrases, and sentences. You can find clues to the meaning of words you *don't* know by paying attention to the words you *do* know.

Read the paragraph below. Pay special attention to the underlined word.

Athletes who took part in the ancient Olympic Games trained by lifting <u>halteres</u> (hôl′ tərz). Halteres, made of lead or stone, were the origin of today's dumbbells.

You're probably not sure what a haltere is. But if you think about the context clues, you can come close to a definition. What context clues were given in the two sentences?

• Athletes trained by lifting halteres.
• Halteres were made of lead or stone.
• Halteres were the origin of today's dumbbells.

Would you agree that a haltere is a kind of weight? You can check in a dictionary to be sure.

Writers can provide many different kinds of clues to meaning, or semantic context clues. Sometimes writers use synonyms and direct definitions as semantic context clues. Read the examples below.

The <u>biceps</u> are large muscles in the front of the upper arm. The word *biceps* comes from Latin words meaning "two headed." Biceps have two heads or origins. They are attached to two bones.   DIRECT DEFINITION

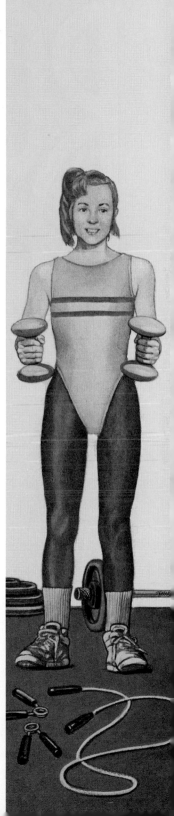

The gymnast was extremely <u>lithe</u> as she moved through her routine. Her body was limber and flexible.   SYNONYMS

What are biceps? Where can they be found?

What two synonyms are given for the word *lithe*?

You may find enough semantic context clues in one sentence to figure out a word's meaning. In many cases, however, you will have to read more than one sentence to be sure you really understand what a word means.

As you read the next selection, you will probably come across some unfamiliar words and terms. See if you can figure out their meanings by using context clues.

BODYBUILDING

ARTHUR PORETZ

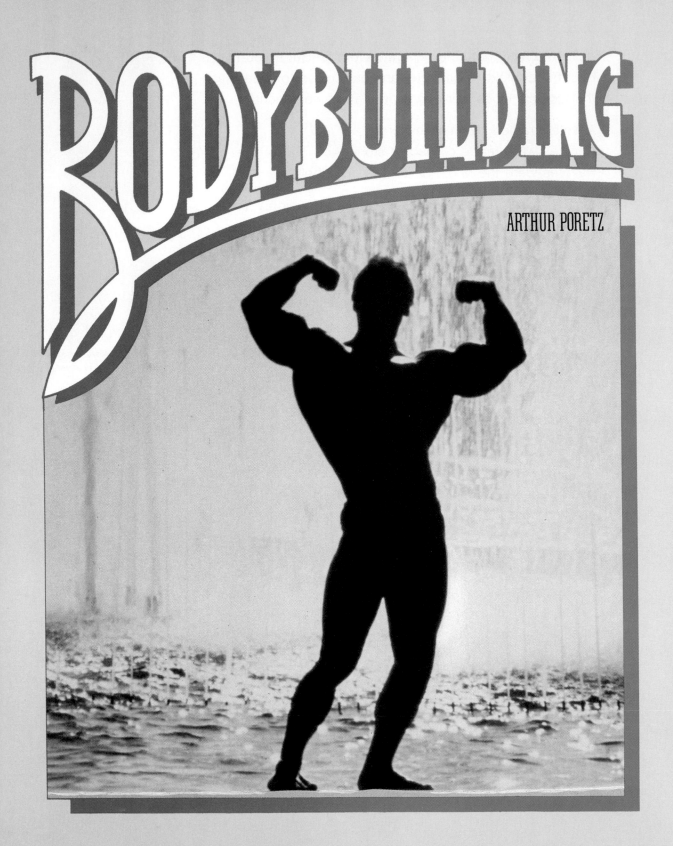

Bodybuilding. Even the word sounds strong and powerful. Today, bodybuilding is the seventh most popular sports activity in the world. Men, women, and teenagers train hard to become bodybuilders. Many of them build their bodies to compete in contests. Others train to change their appearance, improve their stamina and coordination, or even to build their confidence.

Yet not many years ago, bodybuilding was not a sport at all. Few people took it seriously. Then along came Arnold Schwarzenegger. A European-born bodybuilder, he caught the imagination of the world. His personality, intelligence, and muscular body helped to change the world's opinion about bodybuilding.

He was a winner of the Mr. Olympia bodybuilding title six times. Five times he won the Mr. Universe crown. When he was featured in the 1977 documentary film *Pumping Iron*, Arnold became a famous movie star. His success inspired millions of men, women, and teenagers to become serious bodybuilders.

WHAT IS BODYBUILDING?

Bodybuilding is a sport in which men and women try to develop muscle groups and body bulk through a strict program of physical exercises. This is done by increasing stress on the muscles through lifting weights. As the exercises are repeated using gradually heavier weights, the size and strength of the muscles being stressed are gradually increased.

Weight training is at the heart of bodybuilding. However, weight training is not for everyone. It is the most intense form of exercise ever developed. The rewards of weight training can be great. But along with the rewards come pain and fatigue. All bodybuilders know the meaning of the motto: "No pain, no gain."

WHEN DID BODYBUILDING START?

Thousands of years ago, bodybuilding was practiced by the ancient Babylonians. Warriors knew their muscles would grow by the constant lifting of heavier and heavier stones. Larger muscles meant greater strength on the field of battle.

The idea of building the body for competition as well as for strength developed in the fifth century B.C. Athletes who took part in the Olympic Games of ancient Greece trained by lifting weights made of lead or stone. These weights, known as *halteres* (hôl' tərz), were the origin of the dumbbells used in bodybuilding today. Olympic athletes exercised with halteres to create a powerfully built physique.

The history of the sport in this country can be traced to two people, Bernarr McFadden and Charles Atlas. In 1903, Bernarr McFadden staged the first physique contest in the United States. Judges named the winner "The Most Perfectly Developed Man In America." Charles Atlas won the title in 1922. He became well known for his program of body-building lessons sent by mail to millions of Americans. Many still remember his mail order ads with the headline that asked: "Are you a 98-pound weakling?"

Chris Dickerson

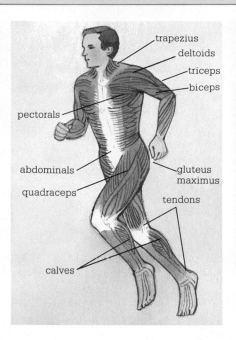

THE BEGINNING BODYBUILDER

It's never too early to become interested in the principles of bodybuilding. These include weight training programs and good nutritional habits. But working with heavy weights is not recommended for junior high students unless they are supervised by a trained instructor.

Lou Ferrigno, who played the Incredible Hulk, weighed 135 pounds when he began training with weights at the age of fifteen. He was very shy and lacked confidence in himself. In five years of serious weight training, he developed an immense amount of muscle mass. In time, he grew to 265 pounds of championship-winning muscles and non-fat bulk.

"I owe everything to bodybuilding," Lou Ferrigno says today. The self-discipline of training taught him how to work toward a goal with great dedication. He also learned to keep trying no matter how hard the training program became. And he felt better about himself as a person and no longer shy with other people.

Arnold Schwarzenegger

Carla Dunlop

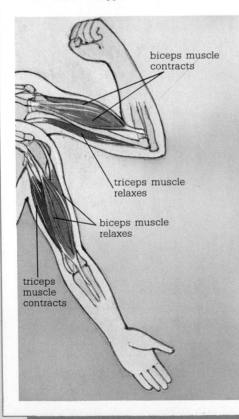

biceps muscle
contracts

triceps muscle
relaxes

biceps muscle
relaxes

triceps
muscle
contracts

Arnold Schwarzenegger was also fifteen when he began his life-long dedication to bodybuilding. His devotion to the sport was intense. Bodybuilding dominated his teenage life. Training diligently six days a week, his body developed gradually at first, and then dramatically. He won his first contest at age eighteen. At the age of nineteen, Arnold entered and won the Mr. Europe Contest. He was the best-built man in all of Europe. Soon he would win his first Mr. Universe title to become the best-built man in all the world. He was on his way to fame and fortune!

PUMPING IRON — NOT FOR MEN ONLY

Until the 1970s, very few women "pumped iron," or lifted weights for the purpose of bodybuilding. Today, many thousands of women flex, or display, their muscles in competition. In the mid-1980s, a documentary film called *Pumping Iron II: The Women* was made. It was about women bodybuilders and how they trained.

In the film, an Australian named Beverly May Francis displayed the biggest muscles ever seen on a woman. At 5 feet 5 inches and 130 pounds of solid bulging muscles, she was able to lift a 476-pound weight off the floor! In her native country, she was called the Female Arnold Schwarzenegger.

Carla Dunlop, a former Ms. Olympia, feels that bodybuilding means much more than big muscles. "Bodybuilding," she says, "makes you feel strong, so you're capable of doing a lot . . . and that changes how you feel about yourself."

Rachel McLish, two-time Ms. Olympia, says, "Just three 30-minute bodybuilding sessions each week will begin to reshape a woman's body. Her energy level will improve, and her sense of self-worth will increase."

BODYBUILDING EXERCISES

If the idea of bodybuilding appeals to you, here are some exercises you can do to prepare yourself for weight training.

Bent-Leg Sit-Ups

Lie on your back on the floor, with your knees bent and your feet under a bed or sofa. Keeping your hands on your waist, slowly sit up, then lie back down. It is not necessary to lie back fully. Let your stomach muscles do the work, and keep your movements smooth.

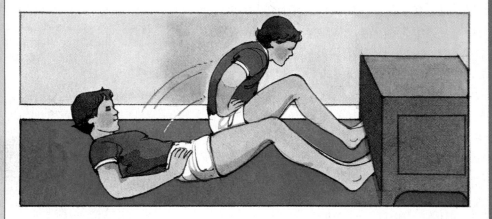

Bent-Leg Raises

Lie on the floor with your legs straight out, your hands under your buttocks, and your chin touching your chest. Then pull your knees all the way to your chest.

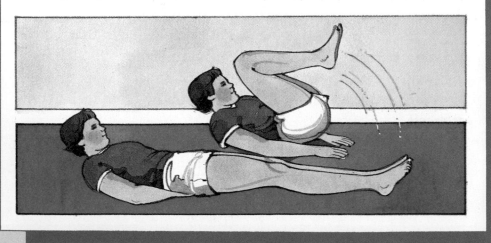

Questions

1. What do Arnold Schwarzenegger, Bernarr McFadden, Charles Atlas, Carla Dunlop, and Rachel McLish have in common?
2. Why do you think Lou Ferrigno turned to bodybuilding?
3. What does the bodybuilding motto "No pain, no gain" mean?
4. Does bodybuilding appeal to you? Explain why or why not.

Applying Reading Skills

Use context clues to figure out the meaning of each underlined word in the sentences below. Write the word and its meaning.

1. In slow stages, the man raised the great weight above his head and held it for three minutes. His <u>stamina</u> was amazing.
   a. courage   b. endurance
   c. slowness   d. a kind of muscle

2. The contestants turned, flexed their muscles, and assumed different positions as the seated judges watched closely. The judges <u>scrutinized</u> each performance.
   a. felt   b. spoke to
   c. ignored   d. observed carefully

3. In bodybuilding, a strict program of physical exercise develops muscles and body <u>bulk</u>. As weightlifting exercises are repeated, the size and strength of the muscles are gradually increased. At the same time, the overall size and weight of the body becomes greater.
   a. fat   b. physical condition
   c. strength   d. size, especially great size

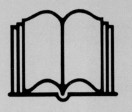

PREPARING FOR READING

Learning Vocabulary

1. Taking drugs for reasons other than health is drug <u>abuse</u>.
2. Many people feel that drug abuse has become widespread enough to be considered a national <u>crisis</u>.
3. <u>Potent</u> forms of drugs are often instantly addictive; overdoses can be <u>fatal</u>.
4. Students <u>rally</u> to attend lectures and meetings that are part of a nationwide <u>campaign</u> against drug abuse.

abuse	crisis	potent
fatal	rally	campaign

Developing Background and Skills
Context Clues

You know that **context clues** can help you to figure out the meaning of an unfamiliar word or term. Semantic context clues can be synonyms or direct definitions. They can also be familiar words, phrases, and sentences that describe or give examples.

Another important kind of context clue is a syntactic context clue. A syntactic context clue can be found in word order. Studying the position of a word in a sentence and the words around it can help you to figure out what part of speech a word is.

Let's review the main parts of speech.

NOUN: word that names a person, place, thing, or idea
often comes after *the, a, an,* or an adjective

VERB: word that tells what a noun does, feels, or is
often follows a noun

ADJECTIVE: word that describes a noun
often comes before a noun or follows a verb
such as *is* or *was*

ADVERB: word that describes an adjective or verb
often tells how or how much and comes before
an adjective and before or after a verb

The sentence below includes each of these parts of speech.

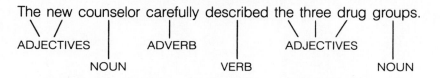

The new counselor carefully described the three drug groups.

ADJECTIVES   ADVERB   ADJECTIVES

NOUN   VERB   NOUN

Knowing what part of speech a word is can help you to figure out its meaning. Read the following example and choices.

Drug abuse can have <u>lethal</u> results. Many people die each year from the improper use of drugs.

a. unexpected: not expected
b. seriously: in a serious way
c. deadly: causing death
d. damage: destruction

Look at the position of the word *lethal.* It comes right before the noun *results.* What kind of word often comes before a noun? You know that adjectives usually come before the nouns they describe.

Reread the choices above. Which choice is a noun? Which is an adverb? You should have chosen **d** as a noun and **c** as an adverb.

Both **a,** *unexpected,* and **c,** *deadly,* are adjectives. Which word best fits into the meaning of the sentence? The second sentence provides semantic context clues that point to *deadly*

By using both syntactic and semantic context clues, you can figure out the meaning of an unfamiliar word. Try this strategy as you read the next selection.

Marilyn Z. Wilkes

Listen to the news. Read the headlines.

- Drug Overdose: Young Athlete's Career Over Before It Begins
- Drug Testing in Schools and on the Job
- Mayors Declare War on Drugs
- Students Rally to Say "No" to Drugs
- Stevie Wonder Honored for Fight against Drunk Driving and Drug Abuse

No matter where we look today—the news, the streets, our schools and neighborhoods—drugs seem to be everywhere.

A drug is any chemical substance that produces physical, mental, emotional, or behavioral changes in the user. All drugs have a powerful effect on the body and on the mind.

Taking a drug for any purpose other than health is drug abuse. When a person uses drugs in this way over a long period of time, chemical dependence results. *Physical* dependence means that the body has become so used to the drug that it needs it to avoid feeling sick. *Psychological* dependence means that the user must have the drug to feel good, to feel normal, or just to want to go on living. People who have these feelings are addicts. They are in the grip of a habit they cannot control.

Most abused drugs fall into one of three categories. *Depressants* are drugs that depress the central nervous system. Also known as "downers," they slow the heartbeat, breathing, and reflexes. They cause drowsiness and loss of coordination. Alcohol, the most abused drug in America, is a depressant. So are heroin, morphine, and barbiturates (tranquilizers or "sedatives"). These drugs may give users a feeling of relaxation and happiness at first. After a while,

however, a general depression sets in. Body functions slow down. With alcohol, sleepiness and then unconsciousness occur. In heroin users, it's called "nodding off." A heroin or barbiturate overdose can be fatal. Combining alcohol with tranquilizers is also deadly. So is driving while "under the influence." Of the 56,000 fatal automobile accidents in 1985, 21,000 were alcohol-related. Recent efforts to discourage drinking and

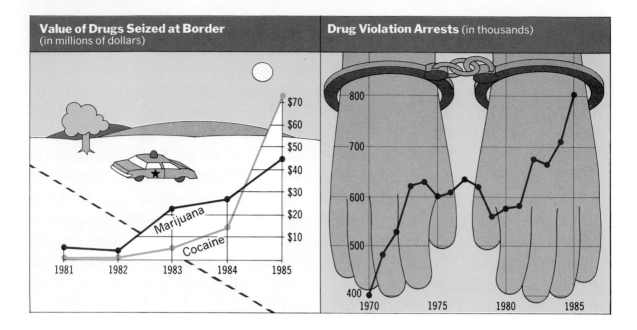

Value of Drugs Seized at Border (in millions of dollars)

Drug Violation Arrests (in thousands)

driving have helped a little, but there are still enough lives wasted each year to populate a small city.

Stimulants are the opposite of depressants. They include amphetamines, also called "uppers" or "speed." Nicotine, caffeine, and cocaine also belong to this category. When a person "snorts," smokes, or injects cocaine, there is an instant "rush," a high that makes him or her feel energized. This is deceiving. Cocaine, like all stimulants, is powerfully addictive psychologically. The more a person takes, the more he or she wants. Unfortunately, the higher the high, the lower the low. After a few minutes, emotions take a nosedive. The high is replaced by feelings of anger and depression.

The newest, most potent form of cocaine is called crack. Crack is smoked in a pipe. It takes its name from the crackling sound it makes while burning. Crack has attracted more and younger users because it is cheap, plentiful, and gives an intense high. But it is also almost instantly addictive. Many report being "hooked" after just one use. The possibility of overdose is tremendous.

The most popular of the so-called "recreational" drugs, after alcohol, is marijuana. Also called pot, grass, and many other things, it is a *hallucinogen* (hə lü′ si nə jen). Hallucinogens are mind-altering drugs. There is no way to predict how these drugs will affect an individual. LSD and PCP, or angel dust, are also hallucinogens.

WHAT ARE PEOPLE DOING ABOUT DRUGS?

The nation has finally awakened to the seriousness of the drug problem. More and more people are admitting that we are in a drug crisis. Nancy Reagan has focused people's attention on her longtime anti-drug campaign with the slogan "Just Say No." Just Say No clubs have been started in elementary schools around the country.

In towns and cities, students and parents run Safe Ride programs, offering a ride home with no questions asked to anyone who needs it. Also, busy teen centers are offering junior and senior high school students an alternative to hanging out and getting high.

Nationally known because of the television shows "Toma" and "Baretta" based on his life, David Toma travels around the country speaking, shouting, begging kids to stay away from drugs. He has visited schools—over 14,000 at last count—to deliver his message: Drugs, alcohol, and cigarettes will kill you. You don't need them. Get high on life!

Artist Keith Haring used his unique style to paint this anti-drug mural in New York City.

In an effort to keep drug dealers from using abandoned buildings in their neighborhood, members of a community lined the windows with stuffed animals. Their message—stay away.

Toma's thoughts are echoed by a high school counselor. "You can take charge of your own life," she tells the students who come to her. "There are places to find help and you can help other people to help you. You are not helpless, and you are not alone." Once students accept that, she says, it can be a source of strength to them for the rest of their lives.

Questions

1. Explain the differences between the drugs known as depressants and stimulants.
2. Why do you think the effects of hallucinogens are difficult to predict?
3. Why do you think people abuse drugs?
4. What advertisements or programs about drug abuse have you seen? Which in your opinion was the most effective?

Applying Reading Skills

Read each incomplete sentence below. Use syntactic context clues to choose a word that fits into the blank. Use semantic context clues to choose the word whose meaning fits the sentence.

1. The proper drugs in the proper amounts can have ___ results such as reducing pain and lowering fever.
   a. health: state of well-being
   b. unpredictable: impossible to predict
   c. beneficial: helpful
   d. survive: to live through
2. Taking stimulants over a long period of time can ___ the body of its needed rest and relaxation.
   a. stimulating: causing excitement
   b. consume: to use up
   c. effectively: in a way that brings about a desired effect
   d. deprive: to take away from
3. Hallucinogens have been known to cause a person to act so ___ that even friends and family cannot understand what the person is imagining.
   a. imaginary: unreal; existing only in the mind
   b. bizarrely: strangely
   c. reaction: response
   d. routinely: in a routine, or usual, way

PREPARING FOR READING

Learning Vocabulary

1. The <u>properties</u> of the metal filling in William's tooth allowed it to act as a radio receiver.
2. Broadcasts from outer space informed William that spacemen from the planet Spiegel were <u>assembling</u> for an <u>invasion</u> of Earth.
3. <u>Panic</u> broke out as the spacemen began to land along the eastern coast of the United States.
4. The <u>hostile</u> intentions of the invaders were obvious as they began breaking into grocery stores and stealing every sort of junk food.

properties   assembling   invasion
panic   hostile

Developing Background and Skills
Facts and Opinions: Persuasive Devices

As you read, you will come across statements that express facts and those that express opinions. A **fact** is a true statement. It is something everyone agrees on. Facts can be tested by experience or by observation. Many facts can also be checked in reference books.

An **opinion** is a statement that expresses a personal belief or judgment. Opinions cannot be proved to be either true or false.

Some materials are written to persuade, or convince, readers. The writers of these materials often use specific techniques to present their opinions. A technique is a method or way of doing something. Propaganda is an effort to spread opinions or beliefs in order to persuade others. Read the following descriptions and examples of propaganda techniques.

- **Glittering generalities** are broad statements that are not supported by facts. They are "glittering" because they try to give readers a very favorable impression.

  UFO Alert, the latest Steven Steelbig film, is his best yet. It has something for everyone—mystery, romance, adventure, and awesome special effects.

- A **testimonial** is a favorable statement that someone, often a famous person, makes about something.

  Academy Award-winning actress Karen Kelly says *UFO Alert* is the most exciting film of the year.

- In **name-calling,** the writer says something bad about someone or something in hopes of turning the reader against that person or thing.

  No intelligent viewer would ever pay money to see another one of Steelbig's predictable sci-fi cartoons.

- Writers who use the **bandwagon** technique try to convince their readers to do something by saying that many other people are doing it.

  Everyone is buying tickets for tonight's panel discussion at the YMCA. Don't be left out! Join the crowds who will hear Professor Backtrack discuss time travel.

Sometimes writers use a combination of these techniques. At other times, they may express their opinions or message in less obvious ways. As you read the next selection, think about the author's message. How does he present his opinion?

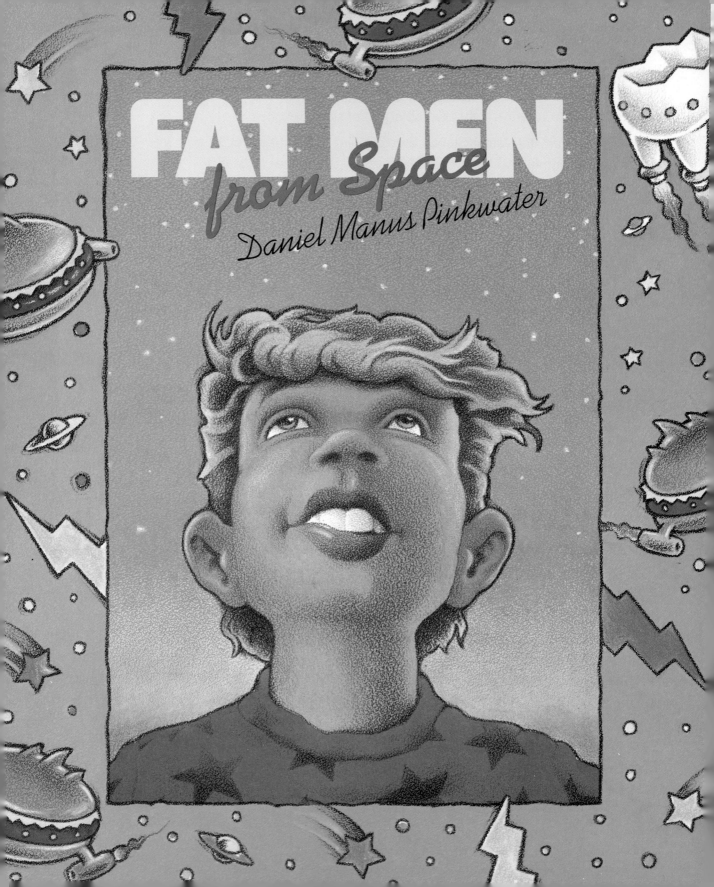

William's trip to the dentist wasn't really so bad—just a filling. There was a funny sour taste in his mouth that made him think of electricity, but he was able to eat his supper without any trouble, and after watching television with his mother and father, he went to bed.

One of the things William liked to do in bed was listen to the radio. This particular night, he was lying in bed listening to the Barry Garble talk show on the radio. A man who said he had taken a ride in a flying saucer was telling how the people from outer space were crazy about potato pancakes, and had come to Earth in search of millions of them, which they planned to freeze and take back to their own galaxy.

It was a good show, and William was enjoying it, when he realized that he had never turned the radio on. He checked this. He clicked on the radio next to his bed. It was tuned to a music station. He could still hear the man talking about the flying saucers, over the music.

William turned off the radio. The flying-saucer man was still talking! William lay quietly, trying to figure out where the radio program was coming from. It worried him. He rubbed the tip of his tongue against the new filling. The volume dropped very low. Wait a second! He did it again, and the volume dropped again. He pressed his tongue against the tooth. No radio program at all! It was the tooth! The one with the new filling was receiving radio programs! William clenched his teeth. The volume got louder. This was wonderful. William lay awake for a long time planning ways to use his radio tooth. Finally, though, he got bored listening to the man talking about flying saucers and potato pancakes. He put his tongue over his tooth and went to sleep.

The next day he called his dentist, Dr. Horwitz.

"This is William Pedwee," William said. "And what I'd like to know is, why is my tooth receiving radio programs?"

"Your tooth is receiving radio programs?" Dr. Horwitz sounded interested.

"Yes, it is," William said. "Did you put a little radio in my tooth?"

"I may have," Dr. Horwitz said, "but it wasn't on purpose. Sometimes when we put a metal filling in a tooth, it reacts with a different kind of metal in another filling. It makes an electric current. It is just possible that a filling could have the properties of a radio receiver, or an old-fashioned crystal set. This isn't a joke, is it, William?"

For an answer William gritted his teeth, and Dr. Horwitz heard, *"Tonight at the civic wrestling arena . . . the Human Ape versus Doctor Death! Be sure to see this great match."*

"Was that the tooth?" Dr. Horwitz asked.

"That was it," William said.

"Well, well," Dr. Horwitz said, "I've heard of this happening—once in a million fillings—but it has never happened to me. Tell you what. If you get tired of it, come see me, and we'll put a coating over that filling. Until then, enjoy your tooth, William."

William was happier than ever about his radio tooth. He felt that he was a special person to have such a special tooth. That night he had a bright idea.

All around the backyard was a metal chain-link fence. William could wrap one end of a piece of wire around a fence post, put the other end in his mouth, and the whole thing would act as one immense antenna.

He did it. Then he had a very unusual experience. He felt thumping—like a bass drum—and he heard a sort of rushing, buzzing noise. And he saw amazing colors, purple and red and blue. He noticed that he was lying in the grass and having a hard time catching his breath. Nothing hurt him, but he had a very funny taste in his mouth.

Then William noticed that his tooth was not receiving. He was able to hear some faint static, but there was no program. William clenched his teeth, and the static got louder. It was kind of rhythmical, like music. William thought it was almost like a language.

The static was starting to make sense to William. He could tell that the noises were spacemen talking to one another. Somehow his tooth had been converted to receive the signals between spacemen! Probably the charge of the fence's stored static electricity had done it.

William was listening to twenty or thirty conversations at once! Some of the conversations were about potato pancakes that some spacemen were assembling in huge piles in remote places on Earth! Other conversations were about navigation, and spaceships keeping in touch with one another. Some of the conversations were about a boy, an Earth-boy, who was listening in. The spacemen knew that he was listening! It made him shiver.

One of the spaceships seemed to be getting closer! As it got closer, the static got louder and clearer. It seemed to William that the spaceship was getting bigger and bigger. It was zooming toward him. William decided to get up and go inside the house. He discovered that he couldn't move. He couldn't even twitch a finger.

The next thing William knew, he was spinning and floating up, as though something were drawing him up toward the spaceship. It was a weird feeling. William didn't like it.

Inside the spaceship the first thing William saw, all around him, were cardboard cartons. They were ordinary cartons, the kind that pile up behind the supermarket. They were full of potato pancakes, fresh and frozen.

"You have been captured by a spaceburger from the planet Spiegel," said a little round thing with bumps, a sort of loudspeaker. It was making the same sort of static noise that William had been receiving on his tooth. He understood it perfectly. "In a few seconds a door will open, and you may go up the ladder," the speaker said.

William was a little scared at the thought of meeting the spacemen. He had seen a lot of science-fiction movies. Maybe they were green and scaly, like lizards. Maybe they had heads like flies, with big weird fly-eyes. Maybe they were like green weeds, and talked in whispers.

William climbed the ladder and walked along a corridor. A door appeared, and William stepped into a room. William could tell it was the control room, because it looked like all the ones he had seen in movies and on TV.

But the spacemen weren't at all what William had expected. They looked like ordinary Earth-people, except that they were fatter than most. William guessed that they weighed at least 350 pounds apiece. And they didn't have the sort of uniforms that William had always seen spacemen wearing in movies. All the spacemen were wearing plaid sport jackets and Dacron slacks. They had knitted neckties and black-and-white shoes with thick rubber soles. They all had crewcuts, and they all wore eyeglasses made of heavy black plastic. The only thing about their clothing that was sort of nifty and spaceman-like was their belts. Their belts had silver buckles in the shape of a cheeseburger with a bolt of lightning going through it.

"I am Hanam, the captain of this spaceburger," one of the spacemen said. "We apologize for having to capture you, but we had a bad experience not long ago. It seems one of our spaceburgers picked up an Earth-person, and as soon as he was released, he went on a radio program and blabbed about everything he had seen. We can't take the chance that you'll do the same thing—especially now, so close to the invasion."

"Invasion?" William said. "Are you going to invade Earth?"

"Of course we are," Hanam said. "Don't you ever go to the movies? Spacemen always invade places."

"But why?" William asked. "We never did anything to hurt you."

"Because we are pirates," Hanam said, "space pirates. When we invade a planet, we walk around and have a snack, and we don't pay for it either. After a while we use up all the things we came to get, and then we enslave the local population and get them to produce more of the things we like."

"In other words, you steal things," William said.

"Plunder," Hanam said, "plunder's the word. It's traditional. Now I have to get to work. You may look out the porthole if you like."

William walked over and looked out. What he saw was amazing. Everything was sort of shimmering and glowing and reflecting the light of the moon. There were clouds like strings of yarn near the earth, and the oceans and big lakes shimmered beautifully. William felt that Earth was a wonderful place, too wonderful to be invaded.

Standing next to the porthole, William realized that his tooth was starting to work again. He thought that maybe the metal spaceburger stopped the radio waves, but they could pass through the glass porthole. William had to clench his teeth so hard to hear the faint signals, it gave him a headache.

"Flash—the millions of round objects falling slowly through space are not meteorites as previously thought, but have now been identified as fat men, wearing plaid sport jackets."

The invasion had started. William hoped his mother and father weren't too scared.

"Reports from our affiliated stations seem to indicate that the fat men have started to land. It is estimated that there are hundreds of millions of them still in the sky. There is panic all over Earth, as the hordes of fat men from space continue to land. So far there have been no reports of hostile acts. People are asked to remain calm, and to stay in their houses."

William could see lots of other spaceburgers now, as hundreds of fat spacemen tumbled by his porthole.

"Crowds of fat men have surrounded hamburger stands throughout the civilized world. . . . They are also consuming great quantities of pizza . . . and cupcakes wrapped in cellophane . . . and hot dogs . . . and ice cream bars . . . and jelly doughnuts . . . chocolate-covered marshmallows. . . . It seems that the invaders from space are after every sort of junk food. . . . "

William was beginning to understand what sort of space pirates these were.

"Conditions of panic exist in many parts of the United States. Residents of most areas cannot get anything to eat but lean meat, fish, fruit, and vegetables. . . . "

What worried William now was what Hanam had told him about enslaving the people of Earth to make more junk food for them. William wondered if he could overpower Hanam and get to Earth to warn everybody about what was going to happen next. But he didn't know how to operate the spaceburger, and besides, Hanam was much bigger than he was.

"Late-breaking bulletin—In Coney Island, New York, hot dog men made a brave attempt to defend their hot dog stands against large gangs of fat spacemen. After a fierce battle,

lasting several hours, the hot dog men were overcome and tied up. They were forced to watch while the fat men devoured all the steamed corn and French-fried potatoes. This is one of the most heartbreaking and tragic stories of the current emergency. Citizens of Brooklyn have already stated their intention to erect a monument to these brave hot dog men."

William thought this was getting serious. "You spacemen had better leave, before war is declared," he said to Hanam.

"That doesn't worry us," Hanam said. "You don't have any weapons that we can't eat."

It looked extremely bad for Earth. It looked hopeless. It looked dismal. William looked at Hanam, who was licking his fingers, having just finished an ice-cream pop and a bottle of root beer. Hanam was idly working the levers and buttons that controlled the spaceburger. An orange light was flashing on the instrument panel, and a high-pitched beeper was beeping. It seemed to be a signal of some sort. Hanam shot a nervous look at William and went back to minding the controls.

William looked out the porthole and saw a tremendous stirring in the space above Earth. The fat men were falling upward! Then there was a thumping on the outside of the spaceburger. A door appeared and first one, then another of the crew tumbled in.

"What's happening?" William asked.

"We're leaving," Hanam said. "As soon as the rest of the crew comes aboard, we'll be off for another solar system. You see, a message just came through from Spiegel that there is a giant potato pancake launched in space in the vicinity of the planet Ziegler. A pancake like this only turns up once in fifty years or so. We're going after it."

"What about me?" William asked. "I want to go home."

"Well, the only thing I can suggest is that you float down in a spacejacket," Hanam said. He reached into a locker and pulled out a plaid sport jacket.

William tried the jacket on. It was about fifty sizes too large. It came right down to his feet.

Hanam pushed him out the door.

William floated down and landed on the sidewalk in front of the house! He gave a little push with his feet and floated over the house into the backyard. He took off the spacejacket, folded it neatly, and went into the house.

William put the spacejacket carefully away in his closet. He didn't have much time to enjoy it. The people on Earth devoted themselves to a massive effort to clean up the litter. William and his parents were out every day with rakes and shovels, and came home tired every night to their green salad and whole-grain bread, milk, and sometimes meat. William and his parents even got to enjoy the experience of living without cheeseburgers and pizza. After the clean-up was finished, the government said that it would be at least a year before soda pop, taco chips, and a lot of other things were once again in general supply. There was almost no sugar any-where on Earth, which turned out to be much less of a hardship than people expected.

William's radio tooth still worked, although not as well as it had before. When William went to the dentist a year later, the tooth hadn't played for almost a month, and Dr. Horwitz thought it would probably stop playing altogether after a while. He also told William that he had no new cavities—a common occurrence since sugar was still scarce.

But on some nights the tooth would play quite well, and on special nights—ones that were clear and cold—William could hear, behind the Barry Garble show, a kind of rhythmic static that was almost like a language.

Questions

1. How did William's trip to the dentist result in his receiving radio programs from outer space?
2. Was William upset about receiving the radio broadcasts? How do you know?
3. Although "Fat Men From Space" is intended primarily to entertain, it does have a message. In your own words, explain what the message is.
4. What do you think the planet Spiegel is like? What kinds of buildings are there? How do the people get around? What kinds of jobs do they have? Describe the planet as you imagine it to be.

Applying Reading Skills

Review the propaganda techniques described on page 75. Then use the techniques or what you know about them to write the answers to the following questions.

1. How might the spacemen have used the bandwagon technique to get other people from the planet Spiegel to join them in their invasion of Earth?
2. What glittering generality could William have used to persuade the spacemen that the people of Earth would never allow their planet to be invaded?
3. What testimonials might government officials have used to persuade people on Earth to help out in the clean-up campaign?
4. How is the term *junk food* an example of name-calling?
5. Imagine that you are a writer for a company that prepares ads for movies. What kind of ad would you write about a movie based on "Fat Men From Space"? What persuasive devices would you include?

WRITE A COMIC STRIP

Prewrite

William's adventure with the fat men from space could be made into a funny yet exciting comic strip or comic book. Suppose the comic strip is one of a series of stories about William who has enlisted in the Space Patrol as a space cop. William's adventures take him far into deepest space where he tries to stop the fat men from plundering helpless planets and civilizations. William becomes a SUPERHERO!

You are going to write a comic strip story for the series WILLIAM, SUPER SPACE COP. Think about how a comic strip looks. The pictures show most of the action in the story. The dialogue, or conversation, of the characters tells the rest. Each box or frame in the strip is carefully planned to present the sequence of events in the story in picture and print.

To create your comic strip, you must first make a story plan and then develop a story board that shows what will go in each frame of the strip.

Here are some ideas to help you make your story plan.

1. **Characters:** William, maybe Hanam. Who else?
2. **Setting:** Time and place. Remember, the setting changes as the story moves along.
3. **Main Problem:** William discovers that the fat men plan to. . . .
4. **Plot:** What happens first, next, then? List your events.
5. **Climax:** The most exciting part of the story is. . . .
6. **Resolution of the Problem:** William saves the day when. . . .
7. **Conclusion:** What happens to the fat men, William, the other characters?

Write

1. Use your story plan to lay out your comic book on a story board. Plan what art and print will go in each frame of the strip.

2. You have learned about persuasive devices. Look back at pages 74 and 75. Can you use any of those devices in your comic strip?
3. Use your Glossary or dictionary for spelling help.

Revise

Read your comic strip. Do your pictures and dialogue work together to tell the story? Does the sequence of the frames make sense? Read the dialogue with a friend. Does the characters' conversation make sense? Rewrite or redraw any frames now.

1. Proofread your dialogue for the correct use of punctuation and capitalization.
2. Color your drawings and neatly print the words on your final copy of the comic strip. Then prepare your work to share with other students.

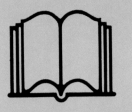

PREPARING FOR READING

Learning Vocabulary

1. Both diet and exercise are <u>essential</u> to good health.
2. It is important to <u>consult</u> a doctor before beginning a diet to lose or gain weight.
3. Once you have lost <u>excess</u> pounds, you still have to work at <u>maintaining</u> your new weight.
4. <u>Strenuous</u> exercise such as running, swimming, and weightlifting can use up many calories.

essential   consult   excess
maintaining   strenuous

Developing Background and Skills
Main Idea

A writer usually has a point to make in a paragraph. This point, the most important information given in the paragraph, is called the **main idea**. Find the main idea in the paragraph below.

Equal quantities of different foods vary greatly in their calorie content. A cup of milk, for example, has about 150 calories. A cup of ice cream has nearly twice as many calories (270), while a cup of salted roasted peanuts has about five and a half times as many. The calorie value of the same quantity of many vegetables (including carrots and broccoli) is about one third that of milk.

In this paragraph, the main idea is directly stated in the first sentence. The other sentences provide the **supporting details** for the main idea. These details help to explain the main idea by giving examples.

The main idea is not always found in a single sentence. Sometimes the main idea is implied, or not directly stated. All of the information given provides only supporting details.

Finding the main idea of a paragraph, even when it is implied, or unstated, is not too difficult. Ask, "What is the main point here?" to find the main idea. Ask, "What information explains the main idea?" to find the supporting details.

Read the paragraph below. List the details. How would you state the main idea?

   How many calories are used during exercise? A 100-pound person burns up about 34 calories in ten minutes of biking at 5.5 mph. Slightly more than twice as many calories are used by the same person during the same period while running at the same speed. Ten minutes of swimming by our "subject" uses about the same number of calories as biking.

The following selection is an informational article. As you read it, try to find the main ideas and ask yourself what details support these ideas.

DIET, EXERCISE,

Caroline Arnold

Unlike body height, body weight can change constantly. In fact, slight daily changes in body weight are normal. Most people, for instance, weigh a little less in the morning than at night. Seasonal changes may also be normal. Some people weigh more in the winter and less in the summer.

Although many factors affect body weight, daily eating and exercise habits are the most directly involved.

DIET

Millions of people go on diets every year. To most people the word *diet* means "weight-loss" diet. However, there are also individuals who diet to gain weight. In the United States alone over ten billion dollars a year are spent on weight control. Whether someone wants to gain or lose weight, an essential

& GOOD HEALTH

part of the diet's success is calorie counting.

One calorie is the amount of energy needed to raise one kilogram of water one degree centigrade. In order to find out how many calories a particular food contains, that food is placed inside a metal chamber surrounded by water. This mechanism is called a calorimeter (kal′ ə rim′ ə tər). After being ignited by an electric spark, the food is burned and the heat produced is absorbed by the water. By measuring the change in the water temperature before and after burning and knowing how much food was in the chamber, the calories per gram can easily be calculated.

Calorie charts, like the one on the following page, show the calorie count of common foods. If you want to find out how many calories you ate in a day, you can use this chart to find the number of calories in each item.

CALORIE AND NUTRITIONAL CONTENT
OF COMMON FOODS

	QUANTITY	CALORIES	PROTEINS (grams)	FAT (grams)	CARBOHYDRATES (grams)
MILK AND MILK PRODUCTS					
cheese, cheddar	1 oz.	115	7	9	trace
cheese, cottage (creamed)	1 cup	235	28	10	6
ice cream	1 cup	270	5	14	32
milk, skim	1 cup	85	8	trace	12
milk, whole	1 cup	150	8	8	11
yogurt, plain	8 oz.	145	12	4	16
MEAT AND RELATED FOODS					
bacon (fried crisp)	2 slices	85	4	8	trace
beef, lean only (roast)	1.8 oz.	125	14	7	0
chicken, drumstick (fried)	2 oz.	90	12	4	trace
egg, boiled	1	80	6	6	1
frankfurter (2 oz.)	1	170	7	15	1
hamburger, lean (broiled)	2.9 oz.	235	20	17	0
peanut butter	1 tbsp.	95	4	8	3
peanuts (roasted and salted)	1 cup	840	37	72	27
sausage, pork link (cooked)	1 link	60	2	6	trace
steak, lean only (broiled)	2 oz.	115	18	4	0
tuna (canned in oil, drained)	3 oz.	170	24	7	0
BREADS AND CEREALS					
bread, white (22 slice/loaf)	1 slice	55	2	1	10
bread, whole wheat (18 slice/loaf)	1 slice	60	3	1	12
cake, white; chocolate icing	1 piece	250	3	8	45
corn flakes (plain)	1 cup	95	2	trace	21
macaroni (cooked)	1 cup	155	5	1	32
pie, apple	1 slice	345	3	15	51
spaghetti, cooked	1 cup	155	5	1	32
VEGETABLES AND FRUITS					
apple	1	80	trace	1	20
banana	1	100	1	trace	26
beans, green (cooked)	1 cup	30	2	trace	7
broccoli (cooked)	1 cup	40	5	trace	7
corn	1 ear	70	2	1	16
cucumber	6 slices	5	trace	trace	1
grapefruit	½	45	1	trace	12
mushrooms (raw)	1 cup	20	2	trace	3
orange juice	1 cup	120	2	trace	29
pear	1	100	1	1	25
potato (boiled and peeled)	1	105	3	trace	23
potatoes, french fried	10 strips	135	2	7	18
tomato	1	25	1	trace	6
OTHER FOODS					
butter or margarine	1 tbsp.	100	trace	12	trace
cola	12 fl. oz.	145	0	0	37
mayonnaise	1 tbsp.	100	trace	11	trace
oil, corn	1 tbsp.	120	0	14	0
pickle, dill	1	5	trace	trace	1
potato chips	10	115	1	8	10
sugar, granulated	1 tbsp.	45	0	0	12

Calorie needs vary greatly from one person to another and depend on age, sex, height, weight, activity levels, and the climate in which the person lives. Look at the information on the chart called "Daily Nutritional Needs for Maintaining Good Health." As shown, a twelve-year-old boy who weighs 97 pounds and is 63 inches tall should eat about 2,800 calories a day, on the average. Yet a girl of the same age and weight who is only an inch shorter needs only an average of 2,400 calories a day. After the age of fifteen, when growth is nearly complete, a girl's calorie needs are reduced to an average of 2,100 calories a day. For a boy, who is still growing, calorie needs between the ages of fifteen and twenty-two can be 3,000 calories a day or more. In general, calorie needs go down after the age of fifty. They go up with strenuous activity. Because each person's body is unique in its requirements, the best way to determine your own calorie needs is to consult your doctor.

If you want to gain or lose weight you can decide where to add or subtract calories in your diet by comparing the number of calories in various foods. What you eat is just as important as how much you eat. For instance, whole milk has nearly twice the calories of skim milk. Skim milk has almost no fat. Fat makes the critical difference between a fried and a boiled egg as well, adding 33 calories. Everybody needs to eat some fat for good health. However, most people eat far more fats than they need. If you want to lose weight by eating fewer calories, a good start would be to reduce fat in your diet. However, it would be unwise to eat extra fats to gain weight, because too many fats promote heart disease.

Sweet foods such as candy bars and soft drinks can be a source of quick energy because they are super-loaded with sugar calories. But eating too much of them can quickly lead to excess pounds. Foods such as pies, cakes, and candy are concentrated calorie sources with little nutritional benefit. A piece of apple pie contains 345 calories, and cake with frosting has 250 calories. When compared to 80 calories in a fresh apple or 65 calories in an orange, the fresh

	AGE (years)	AVERAGE WEIGHT (pounds)	AVERAGE HEIGHT (inches)	CALORIES	PROTEIN (grams)
CHILDREN	1–3	28	34	1,300	23
	4–6	44	44	1,800	30
	7–10	66	54	2,400	36
MALES	11–14	97	63	2,800	44
	15–18	134	69	3,000	54
	19–22	147	69	3,000	54
	23–50	154	69	2,700	56
	51 on	154	69	2,400	56
FEMALES	11–14	97	62	2,400	44
	15–18	119	65	2,100	48
	19–22	128	65	2,100	46
	23–50	128	65	2,000	46
	51 on	128	65	1,800	46

*Note: The calorie and protein requirements on this chart are only a general guide to body needs. Since your weight, height, and energy needs may vary greatly from the average, you should always consult your doctor when trying to estimate your own body requirements.

The figures in this chart are based on studies done by the U.S. Food and Nutrition Board.

fruit is the clear choice for a lower calorie dessert.

It is important to follow the practices of good nutrition at all times, but particularly if you are on a weight-loss or weight-gain diet. In the search for a magic formula for weight control, millions of people look to new and often unsound diets which are constantly and readily supplied by authors in magazines and diet books. Some of these are crash diets promising that the reader will lose many pounds in a few days or weeks. Others severely restrict or overemphasize certain types of food. Diets like these can not only be dangerously unbalanced nutritionally, but misleading as well. The weight you lose at first is chiefly due to the loss of water in the body. As the glycogen* in the liver is used up during the first stage of dieting, the water necessary to store the glycogen is

_____

*glycogen (glī′ kə jən): a white substance that is one of the forms in which sugar is stored in the body.

used as well. As soon as the diet is stopped, the liver will again build up its store of glycogen and the water and pounds will return.

The most successful weight-loss diets are those with nutritionally balanced foods and a reduced calorie count. These may not give dramatic results at first. However, by causing the body to use its supplies of stored fat, they will provide longer-lasting weight loss as long as the dieter sticks to them. A permanent change in eating patterns may be the most important step toward a better weight for both an overeater and an undereater. However, no diet should be undertaken without a doctor's supervision.

EXERCISE

Both the athletes competing on a playing field and the spectators on the sidelines are using energy. The human body needs energy to perform every function, even during sleep. However, when we do physical exercise and use our muscles, more energy is used and therefore more calories are needed. The calories that are being "burned" by the body are those which were consumed earlier in the form of food. One of the most common recommendations given to people who are overweight is that they should exercise more.

Heavy work or sports can use many times the number of calories needed for seated work or sleeping. Even walking at 4 mph rather than 2 mph can nearly double the number of calories used. Increasing or decreasing the amounts of exercise can directly affect the amounts of body fat if food intake is kept the same. Look at the chart "Calories Used During Ten-Minute Periods of Exercise." It shows the number of calories used during various activities.

Exercise by itself does not cause big changes in body weight. One reason is that one pound of body fat equals approximately 3,500 calories. Spending those 3,500 calories in exercise can be a difficult task. For a 100-pound person, that means 12 1/2 hours of basketball, about 14 hours of walking at 4 mph, or about 6 hours of running at 7 mph. Larger individuals use more calories in exercise because it takes more energy to move their larger weight. A regular exercise program can help an overweight person lose about one-third of a pound a week.

A good exercise program is one that is done on a regular, daily basis. It can involve any kind of exercise you like and which fits into your schedule. Some people like to participate in team sports such as basketball or soccer. You may prefer individual exercise such as jogging or calisthenics. Even walking to school or to the bus stop can be good exercise if it is done at a brisk pace. Continuous exercise such as swimming, jogging, bicycling, or weight lifting are generally preferable for physical fitness to stop-

CALORIES USED DURING TEN-MINUTE PERIODS OF EXERCISE

ACTIVITY	BODY WEIGHT (pounds)			
	100	125	150	175
badminton or volleyball	34	43	52	65
baseball (except pitcher)	31	39	47	54
basketball	46	58	70	82
cycling—5.5 mph	34	42	50	58
dancing	28	35	42	48
football	56	69	83	96
horseback riding	45	56	67	78
mowing grass (power)	27	34	41	47
Ping-Pong	26	32	38	45
preparing a meal	25	32	39	46
racquetball or squash	60	75	90	104
running—5.5 mph	72	90	108	125
shoveling snow	52	65	78	89
sitting	8	10	12	14
skiing (Alpine)	74	80	96	112
skiing (cross country)	79	98	117	138
sleeping	8	10	12	14
standing	10	12	14	16
swimming	32	40	48	56
tennis	45	56	67	80
walking downstairs	46	56	67	78
walking upstairs	117	146	175	202
walking—2 mph	23	29	35	40

The figures in this chart are adapted from *The LEARN Program for Weight Control* by Dr. Kelly D. Brownell of the University of Pennsylvania School of Medicine, 1987.

start sports such as baseball or tennis. Whatever your physical activity, in order to benefit the body it must be vigorous enough to raise the body temperature, increase heart rate, and bring about heavy breathing and perspiration. Such exercise will cause a reduction in body weight. It will also firm flabby muscles, strengthen the heart, improve circulation and breathing, improve posture, increase flexibility of the joints, and promote general physical efficiency. In other words, exercise is an essential component of good health.

Questions
1. What two factors most directly affect body weight?
2. Why should people with weight problems consult a doctor before undertaking a diet?
3. Do you think that the charts are a useful and helpful addition to the article? Explain your answer.
4. Use the first two charts to draw up a well-balanced weekly diet that is appropriate for a person your age, height, and weight.

Applying Reading Skills
A. Find the paragraph from which each of the sentences below was taken. Read each paragraph to decide whether the sentence is a main idea or a supporting detail. Write your answers.

1. Some people weigh more in the winter and less in the summer.
2. Calorie needs vary greatly from one person to another and depend on age, sex, height, weight, activity levels, and the climate in which the person lives.
3. In other words, exercise, like nutrition, is an essential component of good health.
4. As soon as the diet is stopped, the liver will again build up its store of glycogen, and the water and pounds will return.
5. The human body needs energy to perform every function, even during sleep.

B. Read the paragraph below and state the main idea in your own words.

Exercise can result in a reduction of body weight. To do so, the activities must be vigorous. Such exercise will do more, however. It will result in general improvement of body condition. The heart will be strengthened, flabby muscles will be firmed, and circulation, breathing, and posture will be improved.

Spaghetti! Spaghetti!

■ *Jack Prelutsky* ■

Spaghetti! spaghetti!
you're wonderful stuff,
I love you, spaghetti,
I can't get enough.
You're covered with sauce
and you're sprinkled with cheese,
spaghetti! spaghetti!
oh, give me some please.

Spaghetti! spaghetti!
piled high in a mound,
you wiggle, you wriggle,
you squiggle around.
There's slurpy spaghetti
all over my plate,
spaghetti! spaghetti!
I think you are great.

Spaghetti! spaghetti!
I love you a lot,
you're slishy, you're sloshy,
delicious and hot.
I gobble you down
oh, I can't get enough,
spaghetti! spaghetti!
you're wonderful stuff.

Apple-Pie

■ *Ivy O. Eastwick* ■

I simply do not know why I
should be so fond of apple-pie.

And when I'm offered it with cheese
or cream, I always say: "Yes, please."

And no one has to ask me twice
I'll ALWAYS take a second slice.

The Perfect Turkey Sandwich

■ Steven Kroll ■

Is my craving so outlandish
For the perfect turkey sandwich?
All white meat sliced sweet and thin
Mayonnaise to soak it in
Crispy lettuce for the flavor
Well spread butter for its savor
Salt and pepper now, to taste
There won't be a crumb to waste
Sometimes in my sleep I sigh
Turkey sandwich please on rye.

Artichoke

■ Maxine W. Kumin ■

An artichoke
is a sort of joke
with layers of petals to peel,
like a box inside
of a box this wide
in a box in a box with a seal.

It's kind of a game
without any name
to nibble your way to the center.
Each petal you pull
tastes wonderful
till you get to the feathery splinter.

Well, you don't eat that,
you can bet your hat,
but under its thistly cloak
is the sweetest bite
for your appetite:
the heart of the artichoke.

PREPARING FOR READING

Learning Vocabulary

1. The doctor told Dinah, "Your body knows how much you've lost and <u>conveys</u> that information to you."
2. She was <u>relieved</u> when her weekly check-up, including the weighing, was done.
3. Dinah became annoyed with her brother's remarks and answered him <u>sarcastically</u>.
4. She was tired of listening to people who <u>preferred</u> thin friends.
5. Jack was <u>astounded</u> to discover that his sister had so much <u>vitality</u> and spirit.

conveys	relieved	sarcastically
preferred	astounded	vitality

Developing Background and Skills
Facts and Opinions: Persuasive Devices

You have learned about **persuasive devices** and **propaganda techniques,** such as name-calling, glittering generalities, bandwagon, and testimonial. Writers or speakers sometimes make use of these techniques when they try to convince others. At other times, however, they may use less obvious ways to persuade. They may use some techniques that you have used yourself.

Think about the last time you tried to persuade someone. What facts or information did you use? How did you organize your argument? Did you include any of the following techniques?

- List benefits

  If you lose weight, you'll feel better, look better, and your general health will improve.

- Identify others who support your idea, including authorities and experts

  Ms. Wyman, the track coach at the state university, has often spoken out in support of a dieting program carried out under a doctor's care.

Lawyers and members of debate teams often organize the points in their arguments in the following way.

- They use their most persuasive point last, because their listeners will remember it best.
- They use their second-strongest point first.
- They use their least persuasive point next.

Although authors are not usually lawyers or debaters, they, too, sometimes have an argument to present. Often their arguments are presented by one or more characters in a story. In the selection you will read next, you will meet a character named Dinah. Throughout the story, you will learn about the opinions other people express concerning Dinah's weight. You will also find out how others try to persuade her to agree with their opinions. Ask yourself how the opinions of others influence Dinah's own opinions.

DINAH

What is it like to be fat? Dinah Randall knows very well. She has to deal with the stares and the hurtful comments at school. She has to deal with the pressure from her family at home. As if that weren't enough, she also has to put up with her "perfect" cousin, Brenda. Brenda's mother died and her father's job keeps him away for long periods of time, so she has come to stay with the Randalls. But Brenda not only took over half of Dinah's room, she also seemed to take more than half of Dinah's mother's love and attention. It seemed that the only understanding Dinah could count on was from Francis, a homeless pup she can only keep as long as she meets her mother's demands about no sweets.

Isabelle Holland

Guess what?" Dr. Brand said when I visited him on Monday. "You've lost five pounds."

"That's funny," I said.

"What?" Dr. Brand asked. I didn't like him, because the moment I looked at him I felt as though I weighed five hundred pounds.

"I told a friend of mine that I'd lost five pounds."

"So what's wrong with that? You have."

"But I hadn't weighed myself when I said that. Do you think I can tell the future?"

"It's more likely that your body knows how much you've lost and conveys that information to you. Are you finding it hard to lose weight?"

Truthfully, I wasn't, most of the time. What with Francis and cleaning up after him, I'd been too busy. On the other hand, there'd been that time when the chocolate bars, which I had still not removed from my laundry bag, had been floating around in my head like giant blimps with chocolate peanuts.

"Sort of," I said.

"That brings us down to one fifty seven. Only twenty-seven more to go. But it should be a breeze now. Once you've started, it gets a lot easier." He patted me on the shoulder. "With that red hair and those green eyes, you're a very pretty girl."

Warmth started all over me. Then he spoiled it.

Dr. Brand smiled. "Or you will be—when you've lost that flab."

The warmth turned to anger. It was hard not to cry. I felt desperate. He didn't seem to care about anything concerning me except my weight. "I have a dog named Francis, and I'm trying to housebreak him," I said.

"Really? Watch those calories now. No desserts. No candy. And try to do as much exercise as you can."

I looked at him for a minute. I wanted to cry so much my throat ached. To him I wasn't even a person. I was just a body entirely surrounded by fat. Nothing else mattered. I watched him as he scribbled in his records. He wasn't even listening. I decided to try an experiment.

"I also have a large bull elephant," I said slowly. "Purple. The trouble is, he dirties Mother's carpet."

"That could be a problem," Dr. Brand said absently, still writing in his records. "How many calories a day did we put you on?"

"Twenty-five thousand, four hundred sixty nine and a half," I said.

"Ummmm. Well, be extra careful about staying within them now, won't you?"

"Right," I said. "I'll stay within them. No problem."

As soon as I walked into the kitchen and saw Mother I shouted, "Mom, guess what! I lost—"

"Dinah," she said, interrupting me, "something's come up that I want to talk to you about."

"Okay, Mom. But listen—"

"Later, Dinah. I want you to be particularly nice to Brenda this evening." She stopped. "Brenda got a letter from her father saying he wouldn't be coming back home this summer. Brenda is terribly upset. So I want you to go out of your way to be friendly to her. Okay?"

I pushed my anger down. I would be nice to Brenda, then maybe everyone would be pleased when I told them about the five pounds I had lost.

"Okay," I said.

"And go up and put on a dress for dinner. I'm trying to make it a special occasion."

Ironing the dress must have taken longer than I realized, because I had barely turned off the iron when I heard Mother's voice. "Dinah, dinner's ready! Come on down."

"Coming!" I yelled, and slipped the dress over my head.

After a few minutes of tugging at the zipper, first from the bottom and then from the top, I finally got it closed.

"Hi," I said as I walked into the dining room. I really felt terrific.

I sat down and glanced across at Brenda. And then, before I knew I was going to say anything, the words popped out of my mouth.

"I've lost five pounds," I said.

"Maybe you should have waited until you lost another five—or ten," my brother Tony said, grinning sarcastically. "You're putting a powerful strain on those seams."

"Why don't you shut up?" I yelled at him. All of a sudden I didn't feel thin anymore. And I saw something that made me even madder. For a second, or maybe even less, Brenda's eyes widened, and there was an odd, satisfied look on her face. Then she looked down.

"Brenda, would you like a roll?" Daddy asked.

"No thank you," Brenda said in a small voice. "I'm not hungry."

"Dinah?" Daddy was holding the plate in front of me.

I hesitated for a second. Then I reached out my hand just as Daddy, thinking, I guess, that I wasn't going to take a roll, swung the plate over toward Jack. Instead of my fingers closing over the roll, I knocked it off the plate and then tried to catch it, hitting the gravy dish. I saw it all in slow motion—the gravy dish toppling over, a brown stream flowing across the white tablecloth.

"Oh, Dinah!" Mother wailed. She shoved back her chair and left the room. In about two seconds she had returned with a dish towel in her hand. "The least you could do, Dinah, since you started the disaster, is to help. Go to the kitchen and bring back some paper towels."

I went into the kitchen and took a towel off the rack above the sink. Brenda was already in the kitchen pulling sheets off the roll of paper towels. Without looking at me, she trotted back to the dining room.

Mother was mopping up the gravy with the green paper toweling Brenda had brought when I arrived with the dish towel. "Here," I said, and held it out to her.

"I don't need it. I used the paper towels. You can take this back to the kitchen, though." And she handed me a slimy brown ball of gravy-soaked green paper. "Be careful how you carry it. This is the first time you've worn that dress since it was cleaned."

"I lost five pounds," I said. "That's why I put it on."

Mother glanced at me. As her gaze flickered over my stomach, I could feel my bulges go out like so many balloons. "Tony was right," Mother said. "You should lose five or ten more before you try to wear that dress. It's far too tight."

"You see?" Tony said. He was sitting tilted back in his chair and grinning at me. Something went off BOOM inside me. Gripping the brown greasy ball of paper towels, I went over to him and pushed it in his face and rubbed it all over his hair before he knew what I was doing.

He was pushing at the paper towels and trying to stand up. Tony is athletic and a lot stronger than I am, but the paper towels were slick and he couldn't get a grip on them or on my hand. Before he managed to stand up, I'd not only smeared his face and hair, I'd gotten a lot of gravy on his shirt and trousers.

"Dinah!" Daddy said. "I will not put up with physical violence. Apologize to Tony."

"I will not," I said. "You always talk about family togetherness, but nobody's on my side. You bug me and bug me and bug me to lose weight like it was the most important thing in the world, and then when I try to tell you that I've lost five pounds, you don't even listen. All you think about is that I'm fat. Nothing else matters."

"Dinah, will you stop yelling!" Mother said. "I told you that Brenda—"

"And I'm sick of you always sticking up for Brenda! I'm sorry she's not your daughter and I am, because you like her a lot better."

Tears had been coming down my cheeks and I had been half crying, half shouting, but I really started to cry now. And I knew I had to get away. So I ran to the back of the house, snatching my jacket off the hook in the hall as I went. I was on my way to the street leading into the fields, when I became aware of scampering feet behind me and heard a short bark. Francis flung himself at me.

"You'd better go home," I said, not really meaning it. And Francis knew I didn't mean it, delighted that we were going to have this unexpected walk in the fields.

I don't know how long Francis and I walked. I went over and over the whole dinner scene, and each time I got angrier than ever and cried harder than before. A dreary truth had become obvious to me in the long dark walk: Mother not only preferred Brenda to me, she would never like Francis, and, no matter what she'd promised, she would probably use the first excuse to send him off to the pound.

Later—I don't know how much later—I finally slowed and came to a stop. It was raining and had been for some time. The energy had steamed out of me. Now I just felt drained and miserable. Along with everything else, I had blisters.

"Oh, Francis," I said.

He whimpered and shivered a little. I put my hand on his coat. He was wet. "Come on, Francis," I said. "We're going to dry you off."

It was a long, damp climb up to the Van Hocht house, and my blisters hurt every step of the way. I went up and knocked on the door, feeling Francis shivering as I clutched him tightly.

The door opened, and Miss Amelia Van Hocht came out. "Dinah, what are you doing?" I opened my mouth but nothing came out, so I closed it again.

"Does your family know where you are?"

I shook my head. "No."

"Do you know what time it is?"

I cleared my throat. "Around ten."

"It is ten-thirty. How did you get here?"

I took a breath. "I got mad and ran away and have been walking with Francis around the field."

"And how long ago did you run away?"

"I guess—it was during dinner."

"And you've been walking around in the field in the dark ever since?"

"Yes."

"All right. You better come in." Her eyes wandered to my foot. "What did you do to your foot?"

I glanced down. "I took off my sandals for a bit and I stepped on something sharp. I guess that's blood."

"You'd better let me look at it. Sit down on the chair there. But before I do anything else, I'm going to call your parents." As she moved toward the phone on the wall, the robe she was wearing sort of billowed out behind her. It was funny, I thought. She was enormous, and yet she looked nice.

"I'm afraid Mother's going to be furious," I blurted out.

"I wouldn't be surprised. I'd be furious too. Worry often has that effect. What's your number?"

Grumpily, I told her. She lifted the receiver and dialed. After a minute I heard her say, "Mr. Randall? This is Amelia Van Hocht. Dinah is here." There was a pause. "Yes, apart from a cut on her foot, she seems all right. Very well, then, we'll see you in a few minutes." She hung up the receiver. "Your father is coming to get you."

"Did he sound mad?"

"He sounded relieved, which often takes the form of being mad."

"Miss Van Hocht," I burst out, "why are people so horrible to other people about being fat? It's so unfair."

"Well," Miss Van Hocht said, "I've been thin and I've been fat, and there's no question, thin is better. But sometimes staying thin has been more than I can manage, like now. And when that happens, you have to refuse to allow people to get to you and run your life."

"How?"

The doorbell rang. Before she left to answer it, Miss Van Hocht said to me, "I guess the best answer I can give you is to remember to respect yourself, no matter what size or shape you are. No matter who says what. And that's easy to say, but it takes a lot of doing."

Miss Van Hocht let Daddy in. He and I stared at each other.

"Dinah," my father said, "where have you been?"

"In . . . in the fields. I took a walk."

"You were in the fields, by yourself, in the dark, for three hours?"

"It wasn't dark all the time." I paused. "Are you mad at me?"

He came over and put his hands on my shoulders. "If you ever do that again—scare me, us, like that— I . . . I don't know what I'll do." He hugged me. Then he turned to Miss Van Hocht. "Thank you for calling me. My wife and I certainly do appreciate it."

As we were about to leave, I stood up. "Goodby," I said to Miss Van Hocht. "And thank you." Then I turned to Daddy. "I'm bringing Francis home with me."

"Of course," Daddy said as we left. "Why not?"

"I thought Mother would make me send him away. And I knew Miss Van Hocht would take good care of him. But then she said I shouldn't just run away. I should put up a fight."

"That's right. If you have a problem and feel that you're not being treated fairly, then you should talk it out." He squeezed my hand as we started for home. "I realize that hasn't always been made easy for you."

"I tried. People don't listen."

He hesitated and then went on. "I thought a lot about what you said at dinner and your problem with your weight, which is what brought all this on. Look, Dinah, you can diet and lose weight, if that is what you decide to do—and I believe that making your own decision is the only way you'll ever do it. Or you

can choose to stay fat and accept and like yourself as you are. Then what people say can't get to you."

We were walking more slowly now. I was crying and looking for a tissue, and as we came closer to our house Daddy handed me his handkerchief. "And you're at the beginning of adolescence. From now on, it's your show. The most your mother and I can do is to give you love and support."

Somehow I wasn't prepared to see Mother's tearstained face when we got home. I was even more surprised when she bear hugged me so tightly that I almost couldn't breathe.

"I'm sorry, Mom. Truly I am," I said, astounded to realize it was quite true.

"Oh, Dinah," Mother said. "I didn't mean to be such a beast."

"Mom," I said, "you aren't going to send Francis away, are you? I mean, I know I promised about not eating sweets, but I just don't want to have to think that if I eat a candy bar he's going to be exterminated or given away."

"No, darling, of course not. I shouldn't have ever made that a condition. It was terribly stupid and wrong."

"Bed," Daddy said. "I'm taking Dinah up right now."

"Yes, all right. Your father's right. We'll talk tomorrow."

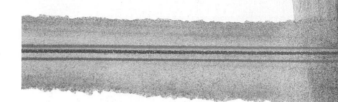

"D inah."

I opened my eyes. Mother was sitting on my bed holding a glass of orange juice. "Good morning," she said.

I sat up and took the orange juice and drank all of it. It tasted wonderful. "Thanks," I said. "What time is it?"

"Ten-thirty."

"Ten-*thirty*! What about school?"

"I called and said you wouldn't be in till later. I thought we might have a talk."

"Okay."

"Dinah, you remind me of some-body standing in front of a firing squad with her eyes closed saying, 'Okay, shoot!'" Mother sighed. "But I guess I have myself to thank for that." She took the glass from my hand and put it on the floor beside the bed. Then she sat up and took both of my hands in hers. "Let's begin at the beginning. I'm sorrier than I can tell you that I made you feel that the only thing about you that I thought about or noticed was your weight."

"Why did you act that way?"

"I don't really know, Dinah. My own father did that to me. So I should know better."

"About being fat?"

"No. Although I was when I was a teenager."

"You *were*? Why didn't you say so? You've always been thin since I can remember."

"I guess I never talked about it because I hated it so much. I finally got the weight off when I was about sixteen, and I was determined that nobody would ever know I'd been fat." She paused. "Last night, after you'd been gone a while, and I didn't know where you were, I remembered it."

"How did you get thin?"

"I decided I wanted to be thin, and so I went on a diet. And I guess that's really the secret—that *I* de-cided it. Nobody decided it for me." She looked at me. "I wanted you to be thin, I guess, partly because of my own history in that area, and also because it's healthier to be thin, and I knew you'd feel happier that way. I know it sounds crazy, but I think at some point I acted as though I thought you were a computer that would automatically come up with

the right answer if I fed it the right information."

She paused. When I didn't say anything because I couldn't think of anything to say, she went on. "About Brenda, I think the accusation that I loved her more than I did you was the worst of all. I lay awake most of the night and thought about it and tried to see how it looked from your point of view. And I realized then that you couldn't know why I was acting the way I was. You see, I've always felt sorry for her. I've never thought she had one-tenth of your brains or vitality or attractiveness. But I've been so busy harping on your weight, I forgot to tell you that I've always thought you were pretty outstanding. Brenda is a mouse. The trouble is, she's a jealous mouse—eaten up with envy of you."

"Of *me*!"

"Yes. Of you. Can you imagine your father deciding to stay away for two years and not see you? He'd tell all the oil and mineral and mining companies in the world to go fly a kite first. You must know that."

The moment she said it, I did.

Suddenly Brenda didn't seem such a creep. I rested my chin on my knees. "I'll try to get on better with her," I said. "Maybe she's not as awful as I thought."

Mother sighed. "She probably is. But she might blossom a bit if you'd give her a little approval. I must say, yesterday was not her day. To cap that letter from her father and that awful dinner, Jack short-sheeted her bed."

I giggled. "Why?"

"I think to avenge your honor."

"I got cross at him, too."

"He understood. He adores you. You're just about his favorite person."

"Even if I'm fat." The words were out before I knew it.

"Oh, darling, being fat doesn't have anything to do with people loving you."

I swung my legs over the side of the bed. "Yes, it does. When people tease you and make fun of you, they're not loving you. At least not what I think about as loving. If you're fat they treat you different." Suddenly I looked around. "Where's Francis?"

"I took him out for a little walk earlier, and gave him some breakfast." She got up and opened the attic door. A small, plump, lion-colored dog with a mashed-in nose flew in and onto the bed.

"Francis!" I said joyfully, and gave him a hug.

"I'll get you some breakfast," Mother said from the door.

"Fine. Mom—"

"Yes?" Mother said. She was still at the door.

"I'm sorry, well, half sorry I said all those things and ran away. But maybe if I hadn't, we wouldn't have talked."

It was odd. I'd always thought of Mother as powerful. But now, standing at the door there, she looked rather small and uncertain. I put Francis to one side and went over and put my arms around her.

Questions

1. What did Dinah "prove" by the experiment she tried with Dr. Brand?
2. Why do you think that Francis became so important to Dinah?
3. How did Mrs. Randall's past experiences influence the way she treated Dinah?
4. If you were Dinah's friend, what advice would you have given her?

Applying Reading Skills

A. Dinah has two key conversations during the story. One conversation is with Miss Van Hocht; the other is with her mother. Reread the sections that describe these conversations. Then copy and complete the chart below.

	MISS VAN HOCHT	MRS. RANDALL
MAIN ARGUMENT PRESENTED	You have to respect yourself.	I wanted you to be thin, but I care about you more than I care about your weight.
POINTS MADE		

B. Imagine that you have a friend who is underweight. How might you try to persuade him or her to gain weight? What argument would you present? How would you organize it? What persuasive devices would you use?

120

UNIT TWO

LEVEL 13

AGAINST ALL ODDS

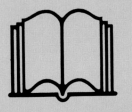

PREPARING FOR READING

Learning Vocabulary

1. Billy was <u>outraged</u> when the boy pulled his puppy's ear.
2. Billy took a fighting <u>stance</u>, and the battle began.
3. It was <u>sheer</u> luck for Billy that the marshal came by just then and broke up the fight.
4. Billy realized he had <u>undertaken</u> a big job carrying two puppies 30 miles, especially when he and the pups were threatened by a <u>vicious</u> mountain lion.
5. One of the pups was small and timid; the other was large and <u>aggressive</u>.

outraged	stance	sheer
undertaken	vicious	aggressive

Developing Background and Skills
Plot, Setting, Mood, Theme, Narrative Point of View

What makes up an enjoyable or interesting story? You might say excitement or adventure, interesting characters, or unusual places.

Authors plan their stories to make them enjoyable or interesting. In their planning, they think about five important story parts. Each part is explained below.

PLOT: the series of events that make up the action of the story

Whatever characters do and whatever happens to them is part of the plot.

SETTING: when and where the story takes place

The setting may be in the past, the present, or the future. It may be a real place or an imaginary one.

MOOD:	the feeling a story creates for a reader
	A story may cause readers to laugh or cry. It may keep them in suspense, or it may frighten them.
THEME:	the idea on which the story is based
	The theme is not usually directly stated in a story. Sometimes the title is a clue. Often, however, the theme is presented through what a character learns or does.
NARRATIVE POINT OF VIEW:	the person through whose eyes the story is narrated, or told
	Stories can be told in the first person or the third person. First-person stories are told by someone called "I" who tells only what he or she sees and feels. Third-person stories usually have an "all-knowing" narrator who knows what all the characters see and feel.

First Person: As I started up the next hill, I felt how hard my long journey was going to be.

Third Person: As Billy started up the next hill, he realized how difficult his journey would be. Meanwhile, his mother was thinking about him and hoping he would make it.

Authors weave these story parts together as they write. Think about how the author of the next selection used these story parts to create his story.

TWO DOGS AND A BOY

WILSON RAWLS

On arriving at the depot, my nerve failed me. I was afraid to go in. I didn't know what I was scared of, but I was scared.

Before going around to the front, I peeked in a window. The stationmaster was in his office looking at some papers. He glanced at me and turned back to the papers. I walked clear around the depot and again walked slowly past the office. Glancing from the corner of my eye, I saw the stationmaster looking at me and smiling. He opened the door and came out on the platform.

"You know," he said, "I have some puppies in there for a boy named Billy Colman. I know his dad, but never have seen the boy. I figured he would be in after them today."

On hearing this remark, my heart jumped clear up in my throat. I thought surely it was going to hop right out on the depot platform. I looked up and tried to tell him who I was, but something went wrong. When the words finally came out they sounded like the squeaky old pulley on our well when Mama drew up a bucket of water.

I could see a twinkle in the stationmaster's eyes. He came over and laid his hand on my shoulder. In a friendly voice he said, "So you're Billy Colman. How is your dad?"

I told him Papa was fine and handed him the slip my grandpa had given me.

"They sure are fine-looking pups," he said. "You'll have to go around to the freight door."

I'm sure my feet never touched the ground as I flew around the building. He unlocked the door, and I stepped in, looking for my dogs. I couldn't see anything but boxes, barrels, old trunks, and some rolls of barbed wire.

The kindly stationmaster walked over to one of the boxes.

"Do you want box and all?" he asked.

I told him all I wanted was the dogs.

"How are you going to carry them?" he asked. "I think they're a little too young to follow."

I held out my gunny sack.[1]

He looked at me and looked at the sack. Chuckling, he said, "Well, I guess dogs can be carried that way same as anything else, but we'll have to cut a couple of holes to stick their heads through so that they won't smother."

Getting a claw hammer, he started tearing the top of the box. As nails gave way and boards splintered, I heard several puppy whimpers. I didn't walk over. I just stood and waited.

After what seemed like hours, the box was open. He reached in, lifted the pups out, and set them down on the floor.

"Well, there they are," he said. "What do you think of them?"

I knelt down and gathered them in my arms. I buried my face between their wiggling bodies and cried. The stationmaster, sensing something more than just two dogs and a boy, waited in silence.

Rising with the two pups held close to my chest, I asked if I owed anything.

He said, "There is a small feed bill but I'll take care of it. It's not much anyway."

Taking his knife he cut two slits in the sack. He put the pups in it and worked their heads through the holes. As he handed the sack to me, he said, "Well, there you are. Good-bye and good hunting!"

Walking down the street toward town, I thought, "Now, maybe the people won't stare at me when they see what I've got. After all, not every boy owns two good hounds."

---

1. **gunny sack:** a sack made of burlap or gunny, a coarse fabric.

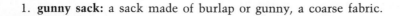

I hadn't gone far before I realized that the reception I
got wasn't what I thought it would be. People began to stop
and stare, some even snickered. I couldn't understand why
they were staring. Surely it couldn't be at the two beautiful
hound pups sticking out of the gunny sack.

I hurried on.

I don't know where they came from, but like chickens
coming home to roost, they flocked around me. Most of
them were about my age. Some were a little bigger, some
smaller. They ganged around me, screaming and yelling.

They started clapping their hands and chanting, "The dog boy has come to town. The dog boy has come to town."

My heart burst. Tears came rolling. The day I had waited for so long had turned black and ugly.

The leader of the gang was about my size. He had a dirty freckled face and his two front teeth were missing. He stomped on my right foot. It hurt like the dickens but I gritted my teeth and walked on. Then Freckle-face pulled the ear of my little girl pup. I heard her painful cry. That was too much. I hadn't worked two long hard years for my pups to have some freckle-face punk pull their ears.

Swinging the sack from my shoulder, I walked over and set it down in a doorway. As I turned around to face the mob, I doubled up my fist, and took a Jack Dempsey[2] stance.

Freckle-face said, "So you want to fight." He came in swinging.

I reached way back in Arkansas somewhere. By the time my fist had traveled all the way down to the Cherokee Strip,[3] there was a lot of power behind it.

Smack on the end of Freck's nose it exploded. With a loud grunt he sat down in the dusty street. Grabbing his nose in both hands, he started rocking and moaning.

But there were too many of them. By sheer weight and numbers, they pulled me down. I managed to twist over on my stomach and buried my face in my arms. I could feel them beating and kicking my body.

All at once the beating stopped. I heard loud cries from the gang. Turning over on my back, I was just in time to see the big marshal plant a number twelve boot in the seat of the last kid. I just knew I was next.

---

2. **Jack Dempsey:** heavyweight boxing champion of the world from 1919 to 1926.
3. **Cherokee Strip:** a strip of land in northern Oklahoma.

I lay where I was. He started toward me. I closed my eyes. I felt a hand as big as an anvil clamp on my shoulder. I thought, "He's going to stand me up, and then knock me down."

He raised me to a sitting position. His deep friendly voice said, "Are you all right, son?"

I opened my eyes. There was a smile on his wide rugged face. In a choking voice, I said, "Yes, sir. I'm all right."

He helped me to my feet. His big hands started brushing the dust from my clothes.

"Those kids are pretty tough, son," he said, "but they're not really bad. They'll grow up some day."

"Marshal," I said, "I wouldn't have fought them, but they pulled my pup's ears."

He looked over to my sack. One pup had worked its way almost out through the hole. The other one's head and two little paws were sticking out. A smile spread all over the big marshal's face. "So that's what started the fight," he said.

Walking over, he knelt down and started petting the pups. "They're fine-looking dogs," he said. "Where did you get them?"

I told him I had ordered them from Kentucky.

"What did they cost you?" he asked.

"Forty dollars," I said. "I bought them myself."

He asked me where I got the money.

"I worked and saved it," I said.

"It takes a long time to save forty dollars," he said.

"Yes," I said. "It took me two years."

"Two years!" he exclaimed.

I saw an outraged look come over the marshal's face. Reaching up, he pushed his hat back. He glanced up and down the street. I heard him mutter, "There's not one in that bunch with that kind of grit."

Picking up my sack, I said, "Thanks for helping me out. I guess I'd better be heading for home."

He asked where I lived.

I said, "Up the river a way. If you're ever up in my part of the country, come over and see me. You can find our place by asking at my grandfather's store."

"Store?" he asked. "Why, the only store upriver is about thirty miles from here."

"Yes," I said, "that's my grandpa's place."

He asked if I was afoot.

"Yes," I said.

"You won't make it tonight," he said. "Will you?"

"No," I said. "I intend to camp out somewhere."

I saw he was bothered.

"I'll be all right," I said. "I'm not scared of the mountains."

He looked at me and at my pups. Taking off his hat, he scratched his head. Chuckling deep down in his barrel-like chest, he said, "Yes, I guess you will be all right. Well, good-bye and good luck!"

I hadn't gone far before I realized that I had undertaken a tough job. The sack became heavier and heavier.

For a while my pups cried and whimpered. They had long since pulled their heads back in the sack. I would peek in at them every once in a while. They were doing all right. Curled up into two little round balls on my bundles, they were fast asleep.

Deep in the heart of the Sparrow Hawk Mountains, night overtook me. There in a cave with a stream close by, I put up for the night.

Taking my pups and bundles from the gunny sack, I used it to gather leaves to make us a bed. My pups followed me on every trip, whimpering and crying, tumbling and falling over sticks and rocks.

After the bed was made I built a fire. In a can of water from the mountain stream, I boiled three eggs. Next, I boiled some salt pork and fed it to my pups.

While they were busy playing, I dragged up several large timbers and built a fire which would last for hours. In a short time the cave grew warm and comfortable from the heat. The leaves were soft and felt good to my tired body and sore feet. As I lay stretched out, my pups crawled all over me. I played with them.

I noticed the boy dog was much larger than the girl dog. He was a deeper red in color. His chest was broad and solid. His puppy muscles knotted and rippled under the velvety skin. He was different in every way. He would go closer to the fire. I saw right away he was bold and aggressive.

The girl pup was small and timid. Her legs and body were short. Her head was small and delicate. She must have been a runt in the litter. I didn't have to look twice to see that what she lacked in power, she made up in brains. She was a much smarter dog than the boy dog, more sure of herself, more cautious.

I knew I had a wonderful combination. In my dogs, I had not only the power, but the brains along with it.

I was a tired boy. My legs were stiff, and my feet sore and throbbing. My shoulders were red and raw from the weight of the sack. I covered my pups up in the leaves and moved my body as close to them as I could. I knew as night wore on, and the fire died down, the chill would come. Tired but happy, I fell asleep.

Along in the silent hours of night, I was awakened. I opened my eyes, but didn't move. I lay and listened, trying to figure out what it was that had aroused me. At first I thought one of my pups had awakened me by moving and whimpering. I discarded this thought for I could see that they were both fast asleep. I decided it was my imagination working.

My fire had burned down, leaving only a glowing red body of coals. The cave was dark and silent. Chill from the night had crept in. I was on the point of getting up to rebuild my fire, when I heard what had awakened me. At first I thought it was a woman screaming. I listened. My heart began to pound. I could feel the strain all over my body as nerves grew tighter and tighter.

It came again, closer this time. The high pitch of the scream shattered the silence of the quiet night. The sound seemed to be all around us. It screamed its way into the cave and rang like a blacksmith's anvil against the rock walls. The blood froze in my veins. I was terrified. Although I had never heard one, I knew what it was. It was the scream of a mountain lion.

The big cat screamed again. Leaves boiled and stirred where my pups were. In the reflection of the glowing coals, I could see that one was sitting up. It was the boy dog. A

leaf had become entangled in the fuzzy hair of a floppy ear. The ear flicked. The leaf dropped.

Again the scream rang out over the mountains. Leaves flew as my pup left the bed. I jumped up and tried to call him back.

Reaching the mouth of the cave, he stopped. Raising his small red head high in the air, he bawled his challenge to the devil cat. The bawl must have scared him as much as it had startled me. He came tearing back. The tiny hairs on his back were standing on end.

My father had told me lions were scared of fire. I started throwing on more wood.

Hearing a noise from the bed, I looked back. The girl pup, hearing the commotion, had gotten up and joined the boy dog. They were sitting side by side with their bodies stiff and rigid. Their beady little eyes bored into the darkness beyond the cave. The moist tips of their little black noses wiggled and twisted as if trying to catch a scent.

What I saw in my pups gave me courage. My knees quit shaking and my heart stopped pounding.

I figured the lion had scented my pups. The more I thought about anything harming them, the madder I got. I was ready to die for my dogs.

Every time the big cat screamed, the boy dog would run to the mouth of the cave and bawl back at him. I started whooping and throwing rocks down the mountainside, hoping to scare the lion away. Through the long hours of the night, I kept this up.

The lion prowled around us, screaming and growling; first on the right, and then on the left, and above and below. In the wee hours of the morning, he gave up and left to stalk other parts of the mountains. I'm sure he thought he didn't stand a chance against two vicious hounds and a big hunter.

Questions

1. How did Billy plan to take the dogs to his home?
2. Why were the dogs so special to Billy?
3. How did the pups teach Billy a lesson in courage?
4. Have you ever worked or planned to do something for a long time? What was your goal? Did you succeed?

Applying Reading Skills

Read the following questions about "Two Dogs and a Boy." Write the answers you choose. Then label each to show what story part it describes.

1. How would you summarize the plot of the story?
   a. A boy learns that getting his new pups home is not easy as he faces first a gang of rude boys and then a mountain lion.
   b. A stationmaster and a marshal rescue a boy who is far from home.
   c. A boy struggles to save money to buy two hounds.
2. What is the probable setting of the story?
   a. the present in Kentucky
   b. the past in a city area
   c. the past in a country area
3. What is the mood?
   a. joyful   b. suspenseful   c. both a and b
4. What is the theme?
   a. The weak are not always powerless.
   b. Sometimes animals can cause problems.
   c. Only the strong survive.
5. What is the narrative point of view?
   a. first person, author's point of view
   b. first person, Billy's point of view
   c. third person, Billy's point of view

THE WOODMAN'S DOG

Shaggy, and lean, and shrewd, with pointed ears
And tail cropped short, half lurcher and half cur—
His dog attends him. Close behind his heel
Now creeps he slow; and now with many a frisk
Wide-scampering, snatches up the drifted snow
With ivory teeth, or plows it with his snout;
Then shakes his powdered coat and barks for joy.

William Cowper

PREPARING FOR READING

Learning Vocabulary

1. If we <u>analyze</u> information carefully, we can often predict the <u>outcome</u> of events.
2. In many cases, two possible events happen with equal <u>frequency</u>; for example, thoroughbred mares giving birth to male and female foals.
3. Drawing an <u>abstract</u> diagram may help you to figure out all possibilities in a given situation.
4. One way of expressing <u>probability</u> is to give the odds.
5. <u>Converting</u> probability to odds can be done by a simple formula.

| analyze | outcome | frequency |
| abstract | probability | converting |

Developing Background and Skills
Make Judgments

A **judgment** is a decision. Even simple decisions involve some steps.

1. Think about what you already know.
2. Gather information.
3. Evaluate, or figure out the value or importance of, what you know and what you found out.

Your math skills can help you to evaluate some kinds of information. Read the following paragraph to see how.

Jake wanted a bike for delivering newspapers. His parents agreed that he could buy one. Jake didn't have enough money to buy the bike outright. But by using his earnings, he thought he might be able to buy one on the installment plan. Two shops would allow him to buy the bike he wanted on time. At Wheels and Thrills, he would have to pay in monthly installments of $47.50 for four months. The Spoke Shop told Jake he could make weekly payments of $10 for 20 weeks. Jake would be making $18 a week for his work. He decided to get the bike at Wheels and Thrills.

To make the judgment he did, Jake did two important things. First, he gathered information from more than one place. Second, he evaluated the information by using his math skills. He wanted to know the total cost of the bike at each store.

Wheels and Thrills	$ 47.50	(monthly installment)
	x 4	(number of months)
	$190.00	(total cost)
Spoke Shop	$ 10.00	(weekly installment)
	x 20	(number of weeks)
	$200.00	(total cost)

Then he had to figure out if he could afford the monthly installment.

	$ 18.00	(earnings each week)
	x 4	(weeks in a month)
	$72.00	(monthly earnings)

With his earnings, Jake realized he could buy the bike at either shop and still have some money left. However, the total cost at Wheels and Thrills was less than the total cost at the Spoke Shop. Jake based his judgment on the information he evaluated. How much money did he save?

As you read the next selection, notice how the characters use mathematics to evaluate information and to make judgments.

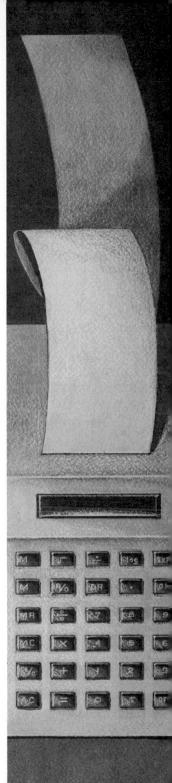

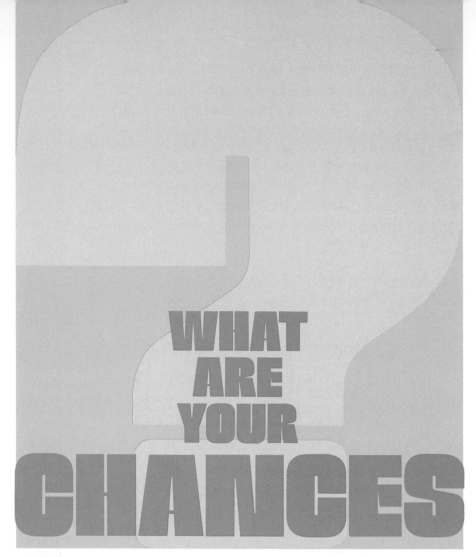

WHAT ARE YOUR CHANCES?

Have you ever noticed how often you use the words *probable*, *likely*, or *incredible*? And how often have you said "I'll bet . . . " or "I'll take a chance . . . "—not really meaning that you were a gambler?

We all take chances. Figuring your chances is what you are doing when you wonder how many tickets you might sell to the next school play, or how much longer your bike is going to last.

Taking chances is an important part of our life. We can take chances blindly and, by sheer luck, make the right decisions. Or the wrong decisions. Learning to analyze chances can help you make decisions more intelligently.

MANFRED G. RIEDEL

WHAT'S POSSIBLE?

Countdown on the Farm

Roberto and Alice lived on a thoroughbred horse farm. They knew that thoroughbreds have male foals (colts) and female foals (fillies) with equal frequency.

"If your mare has two foals in the next two years," said Roberto, "I hope they're both colts, because they'd be worth more."

"But I'll bet she'll have one filly and one colt," said Alice confidently.

"Why?" asked Roberto. "After all, there are three possibilities. She could have two colts, two fillies, or one of each. Your bet seems to have only one chance in three."

"Wrong," said Alice. "Before you start guessing at what's probable, you'd better get all your possibilities straight. And that means you have to count *all* the different things that could happen. You're right that she could have two colts or two fillies. But she could also have first a colt and then a filly, or first a filly and then a colt. So that makes four possibilities, not three, and gives me two chances in four."

"Pretty tricky!" said Roberto, smiling. "I left out a whole possibility."

The Telling Tree

"Next time you try to figure out what can happen in a given situation, draw a *tree diagram*," said Alice. "It shows *every* possibility."

"Weird name—what is it?" asked Roberto.

"Nothing funny about the name, and nothing wrong with the technique," said Alice. "It's called a tree diagram because it has branches that lead to each possible outcome.

141

The diagram helps you to *see* the possibilities. "There is the mare. Her first foal can be either a filly or a colt."

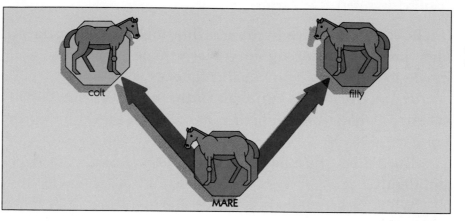

first foal

two possibilities

"You use the same branch system for the second foal. No matter what the first foal was, the second foal can, again, be either a filly or a colt."

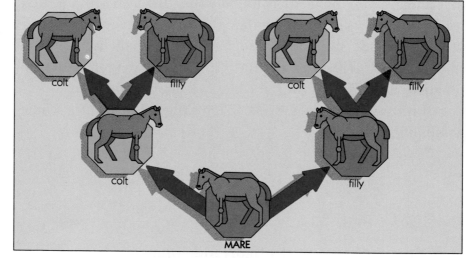

second foal

four possibilities

first foal

two possibilities

"I see—all we've got to do is count the branches," said Roberto. "That way I get the score for all the possibilities—four."

"Not only that," said Alice. "But the tree diagram also lets you easily figure out the combinations and make sure you don't overlook one:

a filly and another filly,
a filly and then a colt,
a colt and then a filly,
a colt and another colt."

"Neat trick," agreed Roberto. "But everyone's going to think I'm a nut if they see me drawing trees all the time."

"I don't see why," Alice said. "Scientists use them all the time. Often they will draw an abstract tree and turn it on its side. Even in that position, they call the abstract chart a tree diagram."

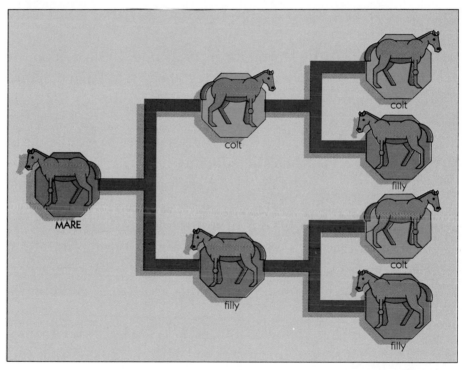

first foal   second foal

WHAT ARE THE ODDS?

"I'm getting to be such a good mountain climber, I bet I'll scale Mount Smoky by the end of summer," said Joan. "I'd say the probability of my reaching the summit is .25 right now. That's only a 25% chance, but I'm improving."

"Then your *odds* are only 1 to 3," said Hilary. "I wouldn't try it yet."

"What are odds?" asked Joan.

"Just another way of expressing probability," said Hilary. "Originally *odds* meant 'inequalities.' Gamblers used the term to describe in numbers how they would favor one side over the other in games and, therefore, how they would bet."

"*Odds*, then, is just another term for *chances*?" asked Joan.

"Yes and no," Hilary tried to explain. "The meaning is the same, but the counting is different. You said that the probability of your reaching the mountaintop is .25 or that you have a 25% chance. But you can't say that your odds would be 0.25."

"Why not, if the words mean the same?" asked Joan.

"Don't forget that gamblers like to bet," said Hilary. "How would they bet on 0.25? They have to establish odds for each side."

"I see," Joan interrupted. "0.25 is equal to ¼, so the odds are 1 to 4 that I'll reach the summit?"

"No, no," cried Hilary. "Your odds are 1 to 3. You think your chance is 25% that you can reach the mountaintop. You're saying that in 25 out of 100 times you might *make* it. Somebody else could say it the other way around. In 75 out of 100 cases you would *not* make it. Since the ratio between 25 and 75 is 1 to 3, you say your odds are 1 to 3 you'll reach the top."

"Converting probability into odds is tricky!" said Joan.

"There's a simple formula," said Hilary. "It says that the odds *for* an event are the probability to 1 minus the probability: p to 1 - p. In your case it is 0.25 to 1.00 - 0.25, or 0.25 to 0.75, or 1 to 3."

"So the odds *against* me would be 1 - p to p, or 1.00 - 0.25 or 0.75 to 0.25, or 3 to 1," laughed Joan as she put her knapsack back on. "Even I can see I'm not worth betting on at this stage. I need more practice."

Questions

1. What does a tree diagram show?
2. What does the letter *p* represent in the following formula?

   odds for something = p to 1 − p
3. What is the ratio between 20 and 100?
4. If the probability for your winning a race is .40, what are the odds that you will win? What are the odds that you will lose?

Applying Reading Skills

Use complete sentences to answer the following questions.

1. Jane is looking for a new computer software graphics program. She already has a computer, monitor, and printer. Why should Jane consider each of the items listed below before she makes a judgment?
   a. cost
   b. ease of use
   c. ability to be used with the hardware Jane already has
   d. location of store where software is sold
   e. guarantee offered
2. A class has saved $100 from the profits of a paper drive and bake sale. They want to use the money to buy a new tape recorder. What steps should they take before making a judgment?
3. In your judgment, which of the following is a better deal? What information supports your judgment?

   2 notebooks with 50 sheets, each costing $1.20

   1 notebook with 120 sheets, costing $2.15

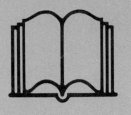

PREPARING FOR READING

Learning Vocabulary

1. To claim the land they <u>inherited</u> in Oregon, Holly and Jason made a <u>treacherous</u> trip across the Rocky Mountains.
2. In the blinding snow, even the guide Zach found it difficult to get his <u>bearings</u>.
3. The horses disappeared, but fortunately Jason had the <u>foresight</u> to take the gun from the saddle holster.
4. Zach felt a great <u>surge</u> of pride in the children, who, near <u>exhaustion</u>, struggled onward.
5. Zach urged the children to continue, but he thought it was <u>ironic</u> that he felt like giving up himself.

inherited	treacherous	bearings	foresight
surge	exhaustion	ironic	

Developing Background and Skills
Plot, Setting, Mood, Theme, Narrative Point of View

Thinking about the main parts of a story and how the author has used them can help you to appreciate what you read. Let's review these story parts.

PLOT:	events and actions
SETTING:	time and place
MOOD:	general feeling created by the story
THEME:	message or lesson
NARRATIVE POINT OF VIEW:	person through whose eyes the story is told

Authors use these story parts to plan their stories. They decide on a series of events to make up a plot. The setting they choose may influence the events that take place. For example, a story set during a blizzard will affect what the characters do.

Authors also must choose the narrator, or teller of the story. As a result of their choice, readers will learn about the setting and the events in the plot from a certain point of view.

The mood created by the story depends on the plot, setting, and narrative point of view. This is also true of the theme. It is difficult to describe a story's theme without referring to other story parts. Often the story's title reveals something about its mood and theme.

A story map is a visual way to show an author's plan for a story. The map shows how events in a plot are organized.

As you read the next selection, think about the author's plan. Notice how one story part relates to another. Also think about how you would map the events in the plot. After reading, you will have a chance to complete a story map.

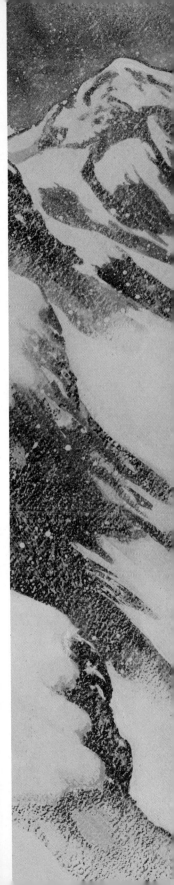

ACROSS THE
GREAT DIVIDE

SIMON JAMES

Holly and her younger brother, Jason, are bound for Oregon. They have inherited land there and must claim it before the end of the month—but their luck has run out. Grandpa died, their guide has robbed and left them, the wagon's broken down, and before them loom the jagged, snow-packed Rockies. Then Zach Coop shows up. He's a gambler and a fugitive, but he's the only person who can lead them over the two-mile-high mountains. Together, the three *may* have a chance. . . .

The blanket seemed oddly heavy. Holly opened her eyes in horrified amazement.

All around was a vast, thick covering of snow. Jason and Coop were no more than small, white humps. Their blankets were completely covered. Holly peered down to discover that her blanket, too, was invisible beneath inches of snow. It covered everything. There was an endless snowfield stretching as far as the eye could see. What was worse, more was falling—thick, heavy flakes driven by a whistling wind. The landscape was blank and frozen.

"Mr. Coop! Mr. Coop!" Holly struggled out from beneath her wet blanket and stumbled toward him.

"What is it?" Jason came awake, sensing, before his eyes opened properly, the change in temperature.

"What is it?" Coop repeated, hearing the alarm in Holly's voice. Then he saw what it was. "Why, it's just snow," he said.

Jason looked around, wonderingly. "It's all piled up," was all he could think of to say.

Coop took his bearings. Then he realized something was missing. Their remaining mount and the foal were nowhere to be seen. He tried to recall what had happened the night before.

"Well," he demanded, "where are the horses?" That had been Jason's responsibility.

Jason pointed to an empty space. "They were over there."

"Where?" asked Coop.

"Over there." Holly indicated the same deserted area. It bore no trace, not a hoofprint in the snow.

"They're gone now," remarked Coop, stating the obvious. "The snow musta spooked 'em."

Whatever the reason for the horses running off, Coop knew that they were in trouble if they continued on up the mountain. On foot, with no provisions, a blizzard blowing up. . . . He knew, too, how determined the kids were to get to Oregon. He began to weigh their chances. They were not good. Jason noticed Coop's serious expression. A boy with an active imagination, he knew the snow was an immediate worry, but he had some others to match it.

"I heard some wolves last night," he said nervously. He wasn't really sure whether it had been a dream or not.

Coop reassured him. "There's no wolves up this high, Jason." The boy relaxed a little, then realized what had been said. *Up this high*. It was too high, too cold for wolves. And they had to go higher—much higher!

Holly's fears were more immediate. "Now what're we gonna do?"

Coop had already decided. The way back was about as long and treacherous as the way forward. And with the kids' determination to go forward, they'd probably get off the snow faster by taking their chosen route. Either way, it was a big risk. But to go back was to lose; and Coop took only one kind of risk. If you gambled, you gambled to win!

He looked at the kids, knowing it was their gamble, too. Like him, they wanted to win. Well, they'd all freeze to death if they didn't make a start soon. It was time to move on—toward their inheritance in Oregon.

Coop forced a grin. "Well, we're gonna get off this mountain as fast as we can." He decided it was best to level with the children. "We can't spend another night up here. Wear your blankets."

He bent down and retrieved the blankets from the snow, shaking them, and folding one to go around Jason's shoulders. Then he picked up the rifle. Jason's one piece of foresight had been to remove it from the saddle-holster and keep it by him. With his own blanket drawn tightly around him and the rifle cradled in the crook of his arm, Coop led the way across the wilderness of snow.

They set out as briskly as they could. Coop and the kids kept their heads bowed against the freezing wind and driving snow. Already, their feet were wet through and icy cold. Only Coop looked up from time to time, checking their direction. Otherwise, they kept their eyes down, glumly watching their own feet plowing through the deep, powdery snow.

It seemed like hours. No, Holly corrected herself, it seemed like *days*. She had no real idea of how long they'd been walking. She only knew that it was endless. She hadn't been able to feel her feet for some time; but that was almost a relief. The cold seemed to eat into her, chilling her very bones. Automatically, she put one foot before the other, dragging herself on, trying to ignore the pain. Her face felt frozen, and tiny particles of ice clogged her eyelashes. Her cheeks were pinched and white, her lips blue. Her teeth chattered incessantly.

She prayed to be allowed to stop— just one rest, just *one*, so that she could regain some strength. That was all she needed. With difficulty, she raised her head and looked up the slope to where Coop and Jason walked ahead of her. Coop had been able to give the boy some assistance—steering, half-carrying him at times. But he could only do so much. Side by side, they muscled into the swirling snow. Jason's blanket was trailing behind him, but his hat was wedged firmly on his head. The boy wasn't doing badly. It was Holly that Coop was most concerned for.

It was clear that she was close to total exhaustion. Over the last couple of miles, she had begun to fall back. Coop knew that if she stopped she was dead. That went for all of them. Their only chance was to keep moving. It couldn't, he reasoned, be much further. They were really high now, well onto the shoulder of the peak, as far as he could judge. Surely they'd be out of the snow soon.

He wasn't convinced. The endless, featureless snowfield they were crossing made it almost impossible to find bearings. He could only hope he had led them in the right direction. If he hadn't . . . well, that scarcely bore thinking about.

Coop himself was tiring quickly. He could feel his strength draining. The cold was like something alive, attacking him, sapping his energy. And if he felt that way, how must the kids feel? He looked down at Jason, battling on at his side, and a surge of pride and admiration ran through him. The boy hadn't complained once, though he must have been suffering. He wondered briefly about the children's parents. Whoever they might have been, they'd produced kids anyone could be proud of.

Holly knew that her steps were shortening, but there was nothing she could do about it. The way seemed to be straight up now; it was like climbing a wall. Two more faltering steps and then she fell, going first onto her knees, then rocking forward, panting. It felt so good to rest. She was desperately tired. Perhaps just a moment's sleep and she'd have the strength to continue. Just a moment's sleep . . .

Get up, you fool, she said to herself. *Get up*. It was willpower, nothing else, that forced her to her feet. She swayed slightly, gathered the blanket about her, leaned into the wind, and forced herself on.

Coop had seen her go down. He'd been half-expecting it. Despite the fact that she'd gotten to her feet again, she couldn't possibly travel much further. Even as he thought it, she stumbled and fell once more—not going full-length, but simply kneeling in the snow.

Coop halted, then started back down the slope toward the girl. Jason plumped down on the snow too.

Holly looked up just as Coop reached her.

"Holly?"

She lowered her head, sobbing, her face drawn and streaked with tears. Coop sat down before her and, reach-

ing out, lifted her chin. He tried a weak smile. "You all right?" They both knew what the question meant. Gently, Coop wiped her face with his fingers, pushing back some stray wisps of hair from her cheeks. Her shoulders shook with great racking sobs.

"You're gonna make it," he said softly.

Holly nodded mutely and allowed Coop to help her back to her feet. Coop watched her carefully, trying to judge how much longer sheer will-power could keep her going.

"Okay!" he said, finally. Together they began to move slowly up to where Jason sat waiting.

Holly glanced up toward the small figure huddled on the skyline and realized how tired her brother must be. "How's Jason doing?" she asked Coop. It was like her, Zach thought, to worry about the boy when she was near dead from exhaustion herself.

"Jason's doing fine!" he assured her. "He's tough. He's like his sister."

Somehow—almost miraculously —they managed to stay upright and keep walking until late afternoon. Coop had carried Jason astride his shoulders for as far as he could. Jason had sat up there with his blanket drawn around his face and his hat brim tugged down. Eventually, though, Coop had to set him down. The weight on his aching shoulders and legs was more than he could take. Now the boy trudged beside him again, silent, but glancing up at Coop now and then with an unspoken question.

It was a question Coop had been asking himself for some time. There was no end to the snow, no sign of vegetation, nothing to indicate that they might be nearing safety. It was wrong, he thought. There should have been some break in the snow-field by now. He'd brought them the wrong way. Or they'd been doing no more than walking in circles. Time was running out. There could be little more than two hours before nightfall. He knew that another night on the mountain would be their last.

To make things worse, Holly was beginning to give up the struggle completely. She had fallen behind again and was moving like someone in a daze, staggering, stumbling with almost every step. Her courage had all but given out—sapped by the cold and the sheer difficulty of continuing onward and upward. Each step took a little more out of her. Her brain—her entire body—screamed at her to give up. When she next fell, going down heavily into a drift, she just sat there, showing no sign of getting up.

"Holly?" Coop yelled to her. "Don't stop now, Holly." He waited, hoping against hope to see her rise. She didn't move—just gasped for breath. Finally, she managed, "Go on! I'll catch up with you later."

Coop knew what that meant. "If you stop now," he shouted, "you're gonna die out here."

Holly lowered her head. She'd had enough. "I don't care," she groaned.

"What?" Coop could guess what she'd said.

Holly looked up through streaming eyes. In a voice filled with anger, desperation, and fear, she bellowed at him, "I don't *care*!"

Coop looked down at the girl as she sat sobbing in the snow. She meant it. He knew she meant it. And he couldn't blame her.

It was ironic, he thought. If it hadn't been for the kids, he might well have lain down and given up himself. It was a new feeling, this fondness, this sense of responsibility. Through his weariness, Coop realized with a small shock of surprise that it was a feeling he liked. It wasn't all going to end out here in the snow if he could help it. There was one more chance, one more gamble left to take. He knew that they should have come out of the snowfield by this time. They were over the mountain. Unless they really *had* been walking in circles, they must be close to the edge of the snowline.

They had been trekking up toward the sharp ridge when Holly had fallen. Now they were some sixty feet below. It was possible that on the other side lay a sight of grass and trees. It should be there! On the other hand, they could top that rise to find nothing but more snow and another hard climb ahead of them.

If there was ever a time to play an ace in the hole, thought Coop, this was it. He flung his arm out toward the ridge above and shouted, "It's just over the top, Holly."

She looked up to where he was pointing, then shook her head. Good try, she thought wearily. Then she yelled, "You don't know that, Coop."

"I do!" Coop put everything into the bluff. His voice took on a ring of complete confidence. "I'm tellin' you. It's just over this ridge! We've made it! Come on!"

Jason joined in, almost believing Coop because he wanted to. "Come on, Holly!" he shouted.

Holly smiled. Well, they were both of them certainly trying. Not knowing quite how she did it, she struggled up on to her knees, then paused indecisively.

Coop's voice floated down to her. "Come on, Holly! We *made* it, Holly! Come on! Come *on!*"

She didn't believe it for a minute. But she was grateful, despite her exhaustion, to be given a chance to believe. They'd get to the top, there'd be more snow, then she'd give up with a clear conscience. As she rose to her feet she smiled wearily and muttered to herself.

"You're trickin', Coop. You're trickin' like you're always trickin'." But she took a step, then another.

They watched her slow progress up the slope for a while. Maybe, Coop thought, he'd be able to keep her going further if his guess had been wrong. Still watching her, he reached out and took Jason's hand. Then he turned with the boy and began to walk toward the ridge.

155

Jason looked up at him. Coop had been so convincing that he wasn't sure what to believe. "Is it really up there?" he asked hopefully.

Coop's tone was level. "I don't know, Jason."

Coop and Jason stood atop the ridge waiting for Holly to catch up to them. They were smiling. Around them, in the distance, were vast, snow-capped mountains. Below them, leading off from the ridge, was more snow. And beyond that, clearly visible, was a valley with sheltering pines and green, peaceful grass. It was beautiful. More than that, it was impossible! They had made it, just like Coop said. They were across the divide!

No one spoke for a full minute. Then, without taking her eyes off the trees and the grass and the rocks, Holly asked, "How did you know?"

"It's my profession," Coop replied easily. "I'm a gambler."

And what a gamble, he thought. *Calling Nature's bluff. Crazy! But it had come off. Well, when you're lucky....* And he started to move down toward the valley. The kids found renewed strength to follow him.

As they got closer, they broke into a run, spurred on, now, by the welcoming sight of shelter and dry ground. Coop flung out his hands to steady them. Hand in hand, they ran until they felt firm ground beneath their feet and the warmer air of the valley on their faces. They kept running until they could hear the sound of songbirds and the sighing of wind through the pines.

Questions
1. Why was Zach Coop so worried when he discovered that the horses were gone?
2. Holly didn't believe Coop when he said they had made it, yet she struggled on. Why?
3. What do you think might have happened if there had only been more snow beyond the ridge?
4. Do you think Coop will stay with Holly and Jason once they reach their land? Why or why not?

Applying Reading Skills
Complete the story map for "Across the Great Divide" shown below by writing an important event from the plot for each number. Two events have been listed for you.

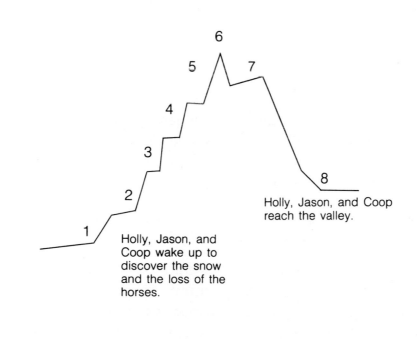

Holly, Jason, and Coop wake up to discover the snow and the loss of the horses.

Holly, Jason, and Coop reach the valley.

PREPARING FOR READING

Learning Vocabulary

1. Hoa's hope for a new life of freedom was <u>vindicated</u> when the Peckhams helped bring him and his family to the United States.
2. Joy was <u>recuperating</u> nicely from the chicken pox when she suddenly took a turn for the worse.
3. <u>Statistics</u> were scant on Joy's disease, but the odds were strongly against recovery.
4. Joy's <u>ordeal</u> in the hospital was long and painful, but she successfully <u>defied</u> death through each operation.
5. Dan Koko <u>excelled</u> at stunt work and went on to make it his career.

vindicated	recuperating	statistics
ordeal	defied	excelled

Developing Background and Skills
Make Judgments

You know that a **judgment** is a decision based on information that you have examined and evaluated. Some information may be in the form of statistics, or numerical facts. In most cases, you can rely on information, including statistics, to help you make a judgment. Sometimes, however, even a very careful evaluation of information can lead to an incorrect judgment.

You have probably seen newspaper headlines like the following.

UNDERDOG CANDIDATE WINS ELECTION TO DISPROVE POLLS

MIRACLE PATIENT DEFIES DOCTORS' PREDICTIONS

SENDER FINDS OWN BOTTLE MESSAGE 15 YEARS LATER

STUNTMAN PUSHES 1 TO 1 ODDS IN SUCCESSFUL LEAP

These headlines tell about outcomes that most people would not have judged to be possible. They show that "chance" and "luck" sometimes play a role in what happens.

The first headline says that an underdog candidate won. An underdog is a person who is not expected to win. A poll is a survey of public opinion. Pollsters ask many people to tell who they plan to vote for. Based on their answers, the pollsters predict who will win. Why might the results of a poll not match what actually happened? Perhaps some people changed their minds between the time the poll was taken and the time they voted. What other reasons can you give?

What might cause a patient to get better when doctors judge that such an outcome is unlikely?

Would you have predicted the outcome in the third headline? Why or why not?

What were the stuntsman's odds to fail in his attempt? What were his odds to win?

The selection that follows includes three true-life stories about people who "beat the odds." As you read, think about what part chance and luck had in the outcomes. Think about what part courage, daring, and "taking chances" play in the way things turned out.

PEOPLE WHO BEAT THE ODDS

EXCERPTS FROM PEOPLE MAGAZINE

WHEN DAN KOKO WAS OFFERED A COOL MILLION TO SET A WORLD STUNT RECORD, HE REALLY FELL FOR IT

"T he man's got to be a nut," said one bystander in a crowd outside the Vegas World Hotel. "I wouldn't do it for love or money," said another.

Suddenly the noise hushed. Twenty-five stories up, Dan Koko, a thirty-year-old, part-Cherokee stuntman, appeared on the roof. He climbed higher, up a 90-foot scaffolding to a tiny platform 326 feet above the ground. Then Koko crouched, muttered an Indian blessing his grandfather had taught him, and threw himself spread-eagled into space. "My last thought," he said later, "was 'it sure looks a long way down.'"

Four seconds later, after plummeting at a speed of 98 miles per hour, Koko landed unhurt on his back on a 22-foot-high, 2,000-pound custom-made air bag. With his leap, he became the new holder of the world "high fall" record. He had bettered the 311-foot dive set by fellow stuntman Dar Robinson, who jumped from a helicopter in 1978.

After the fall, Koko smiled and gulped down a glass of water. Then he was whisked into a Rolls-Royce for a ride around the building to the lavish hotel's entrance. Inside, one million dollars in cash awaited him—the highest prize ever paid for a high fall. That was the amount guaranteed by the hotel's owner, Bob Stupak. "Koko walked in here, offered me the deal, and I took it," he says.

Koko had previously gained attention for himself and Stupak's hotel on May 19. He set the world "fire fall" record by leaping off the roof (only 250 feet that time) in a blazing, flame-resistant suit. "All the preparations are done carefully," Koko said. "I never like to gamble."

For the "high fall" jump, the veteran stuntman again took every precaution. His air bag, which cost

$45,000, was designed by John Scurlock, a former engineering professor. It came equipped with two giant fans. "With those fans blowing air in there at 300 miles per hour, it's going to hold its shape no matter how big a tear it may get," Koko said. Nonetheless, he tested it by jumping out of the hotel from the eleventh and eighteenth floors.

Koko sort of fell into stuntwork accidentally. The son of an Italian father and a Cherokee mother, he grew up in Cherokee, North Carolina. His father, a construction worker, taught the Indians how to build their own houses. When his dad moved the family to California, Dan took up track. He set a state record in the 120-yard high hurdles while in high school. He also won thirty-two medals in track meets throughout the United States between 1972 and 1974.

After high school, Koko got a job designing glass bottles while attending night school. One day during those years of struggle, a friend offered him a job in a low-budget film. All he had to do was crash a car. "I was working all week to make $500 and there I made it in one day," he recalls. "I went straight to the Screen Actors Guild and got my union card." Koko excelled and went on to work in a variety of TV shows.

He plans to donate part of his one million dollars to the Motion Picture Association for American Indians. He founded the group last year with his girlfriend, actress Terri Crane, who is part Choctaw. Koko took a year off to raise money for the Indian community in 1983.

Jumping remains his work, but doesn't he ever get scared? "If I don't have more than a 50-50 chance, I don't want to do it," Koko says, as though those were enviable odds. □

JOHN AND DOTTIE PECKHAM'S MESSAGE IN A BOTTLE LED A VIETNAMESE FAMILY TO FREEDOM

Three days after Christmas, 1979, John Peckham, a Los Angeles trial lawyer, and his wife, Dottie, put a message in a bottle and tossed it from a cruise ship carrying them from Acapulco to Hawaii. They listed their names and a postbox number, enclosed a dollar for return postage, and promised a reward to the finder.

More than three years later and across 9,000 miles of ocean, Nguyen Van Hoa (ən gī′ ən van hō′ ə) spotted the bottle floating past his boat. He was ten miles off the coast of Thailand (tī′ land) in the South China Sea. Hoa was a former lieutenant with the South Vietnamese army. He had escaped the "re-education camp" where he had been imprisoned following the fall of South Vietnam in 1975. He had fled aboard a fishing boat with more than thirty other refugees,

163

including his brother. Now they had no drinking water. But Hoa's disappointment at finding nothing to drink in the bottle changed when he read and understood the message. "It gave me hope," he says.

That hope was vindicated for Hoa; his wife, Kim Hoang; their 16-month-old son, Thai; and Hoa's brother when they landed at Los Angeles International Airport on April 26, 1985, to begin a new life. On hand to greet them were their American sponsors, none other than John and Dottie Peckham. Five years after pitching their bottle into the ocean, the Peckhams were united with the Hoas in a tearful embrace. "I didn't think I would get emotional," says John, "but when I picked up their baby, I couldn't stop crying."

Hoa's efforts to reach America began almost as soon as his boat reached Thailand and he, his future wife, and his brother got to a United Nations refugee camp. There he composed a note to the Peckhams. "We tried to find freedom according to [your] letter," he wrote. "Now we send a message to the boss and we wish you will answer us soon." The letter arrived on March 4, 1983, John's seventieth birthday. During the next two years the Peckhams corresponded with Hoa. They sent him and his new wife money when their first child, Thai, was born. Finally, Hoa asked them to sponsor his family so that they could emigrate to the United States. "We decided to do so," says Dottie, 67, "because this was fate. We felt the bottle ended up as it did for a reason."

The Peckhams' generosity gave Hoa "the first freedom I have had in ten years," he says. During his internment in Vietnam, he cut timber and dug irrigation ditches. His meals consisted of only a little rice or corn. After more than four years, he managed to escape. He lived underground in Ho Chi Minh (hō chē min) City until he was able to work passage on a fishing boat illegally transporting Vietnamese refugees to Thailand.

Hoa and his family now live in an apartment that the Peckhams found and partly furnished for them in Los Angeles. Hoa wants to work as an auto mechanic. Kim Hoang, who is pregnant again, says she knows that "America will offer great opportunity for my children." Indeed, for Hoa and his family the promise carried by the message in the bottle has been fulfilled. The reward was freedom. □

A MYSTERIOUS DISEASE COST JOY SPERING HER LEGS, BUT SHE BOUNCED BACK AND BECAME A CHAMP

She was always so healthy, a natural athlete who was swimming at two, skiing at five, and dreaming of becoming a gymnastics champ. In May 1982, when Joy Spering was six, no one could have foreseen the trial of pain—and courage—awaiting her. Because she "just felt sick," Joy was sent home from her first-grade class at South Valley School in Moorestown, New Jersey. Dr. William Kane diagnosed her ailment as a mild case of chicken pox. For the next several days Joy lolled around the house recuperating.

Then Joy's complaints took on an urgent tone. Her legs hurt, she kept repeating. "That wasn't like her, she's not a whiner," says her dad, Ken. On inspecting Joy's legs, her mom, Karen, found marks like a "strange, fine webbing— very, very faint—on her thighs." By the next morning, the marks had turned into black-and-blue splotches. Now thoroughly alarmed, the Sperings rushed Joy to the local hospital. After blood tests, doctors advised them to drive her at once to the Children's Hospital of Philadelphia, about 40 minutes away.

There, the little girl, screaming in pain, was wheeled into intensive care. Soon, Dr. Mortimer Poncz came to the family with the horrifying report. "By our calculations," Karen Spering recalls him saying, "Joy has twelve hours to live."

She had purpura fulminans (pėr′ pyǝ rǝ fŭl′ mǝ nǝnz). It is a deadly disease so freakish that modern medicine still knows little about it. Essentially, it is an extremely rare blood disorder that can occur after infections such as scarlet fever or chicken pox. Statistics are scant, but doctors estimate the odds against an extreme case of purpura fulminans are about five million to one.

Stunned though they were, Joy's parents refused to fall apart. With Joy's older sister, Tina, the Sperings vowed to make every moment that they had left with their dying child count. As it turned out, their constant vigil would continue for a four-month hospital stay.

In that time, Ken and Karen could see Joy's medical costs soaring past one million dollars. "But nobody at the hospital ever mentioned a penny," Ken says gratefully.

Joy's schoolmates raised more than $700. Dr. Kane led a committee that solicited $50,000. Ultimately, Joy's condition officially qualified as a disaster case. What medical insurance didn't pick up, the doctors and the hospital absorbed.

"Everyone was so incredible," says Karen, no one more so than Joy herself. In the first days, though medication could not control her pain, she never lost consciousness. "She was crying, 'Mommy, help! Mommy, do something!' and this went on every minute of every hour," Karen remembers, "but Joy somehow never gave up."

"I had to fight to live," Joy says now with a wisdom beyond her years. And how she fought! Through her hospital ordeal, Joy endured forty operations, sometimes two in a single day. Mercifully the disease did not cripple her upper body. However, when Dr. John M. Templeton, Jr., assistant surgeon, told her that her legs could not be saved, Joy admits, "I just felt terrible, but it wasn't my whole life I was losing."

She lost her right leg to midcalf and her left foot below the ankle. Still, her battle was not over. There were 106-degree fevers and complications, such as pneumonia. Most of all, there was the desperate struggle against massive infection. She came to be known around the hospital as "The Miracle Girl." "Over and over again," says Templeton, "she defied death."

Joy finally left the hospital in September in a wheelchair. Doctors doubted she would walk again for at least a year. To everyone's astonishment, she began getting about on her stump protectors. By November she got her artificial legs and walked out of the doctor's office without practice or crutches. In January she was cheerfully back in school. "What is extraordinary," says her teacher, "is that Joy has absolutely no self-pity."

Almost nine, Joy thinks that she may one day study medicine. "I know what pain feels like," she says, "and I want to help others like my doctors helped me." For now, she is interested mainly in rock stars and sports. A year ago she joined an amputee ski group in Pennsylvania and took the slalom championship in her double-amputee class. Two weeks ago, she was back defending her title. Did she win again? Of course, but why would anyone need to ask? □

Questions

1. List the events that led to Hoa and his family coming to the United States.
2. Why was it so unusual for Joy Spering to develop the disease called purpura fulminans?
3. Give examples to support Dan Koko's statement that he never likes to gamble.
4. Describe a time when you or someone you know or read about "beat the odds."

Applying Reading Skills

Reread each story in "People Who Beat the Odds." In the chart below, the actual outcome of each story is listed. Imagine that you do not know the actual outcome. Copy the chart and list the outcome you would have expected on the basis of the information in the story. Then give reasons supporting your judgment.

	actual story outcome	expected outcome	reasons for expected outcome
1	John and Dottie Peckham's message led a Vietnamese family to freedom.		
2	A mysterious disease cost Joy Spering her legs, but she bounced back a champ.		
3	Dan Koko jumped 326 feet to set a world record.		

BRAVADO

Have I not walked without an upward look
Of caution under stars that very well
Might not have missed me when they shot and fell?
It was a risk I had to take—and took.

Robert Frost

WRITING ACTIVITY

WRITE A SPEECH

Prewrite

The people described in "People Who Beat the Odds" share some character traits. A character trait can be a positive quality such as bravery, honesty, or kindness. A character trait can also be a negative quality such as selfishness or greed.

Many people look for a person to admire, to serve as an example of positive character traits. Joy Spering, for example, demonstrates the kinds of positive character traits that make her a great example for young people.

You have been asked to speak to a group of fifth grade students. Your purpose is to persuade those students to choose people with positive character traits to serve as examples for their own lives. Before you write your speech, you must do some thinking about what you believe. You can't persuade anyone if you don't believe what you are saying.

1. First reread the selection and make a list of the positive traits the people had. Then think of a person whom you admire and try to be like. Add the traits of that person to your list.
2. Review your list. Choose at least three positive character traits. Why are these traits meaningful to you?
3. Now think about what is the *most* important idea you want your audience to remember from your speech. In writing, this kind of statement is called a thesis statement.
4. Think of some anecdotes or examples that will help your audience remember the positive character traits you have chosen.

Write

Try this form of organization for your speech.

1. **Paragraph 1**

   Begin or end this paragraph with your thesis statement. Try to use an anecdote, or brief story, about a familiar person who demonstrates the character traits you are going to discuss in your speech.

2. **Paragraph 2**

   Describe the character traits you have chosen and give your reasons. Try to include an anecdote about a real person who demonstrates each character trait in his or her life.

3. **Paragraph 3**

   Review your character traits and reasons briefly. Try rewording your thesis statement as a slogan so students can remember your main idea more easily.

4. Use your Glossary or dictionary for spelling help.

Revise

Read your speech. Will your opening anecdote catch the attention of your listeners? Did you clearly state the positive character traits you chose? Are your reasons and examples ones that fifth grade students can relate to?

1. Proofread your speech for the correct use of commas and end punctuation in sentences. This punctuation will help you know when to pause, raise or lower your voice, or show excitement when you give your speech aloud.

2. Practice your speech before a mirror. Then try it with a friend. Are there any parts you could change to make a more interesting presentation?

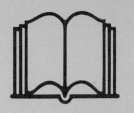

PREPARING FOR READING

Learning Vocabulary

1. Everything in nature seemed to be <u>conspiring</u> against Spinner as she attempted to land the fish.
2. Remembering her father's advice to keep the line <u>taut</u>, Spinner reeled it in to keep the tension.
3. <u>Grudgingly</u>, only to keep it from breaking, Spinner gave back the line.
4. Spinner felt the <u>contempt</u> of her family for her lack of skill and enthusiasm.
5. The fish twisted and <u>catapulted</u> into the air, landing near the river bank.

conspiring	taut	grudgingly
contempt	catapulted	

Developing Background and Skills
Character's Motives or Feelings

Story characters, like people in real life, have **feelings.** Authors can show how a character feels in several ways.

Some clues authors use are listed in the chart on the next page along with examples. Notice the five kinds of clues authors can use to help their readers understand what a character feels.

CLUES TO CHARACTER'S FEELINGS	EXAMPLE	FEELING
What author directly tells us	Spinner was dreading the day ahead.	uneasiness
What character says or thinks	"It looks like I really can do it," thought Spinner.	hope
How character speaks	"I did it!" exclaimed Spinner.	pride
What character does	Spinner threw the fishing line down.	anger
How character looks	Spinner's face was streaked with tears.	sorrow

Characters also have **motives**, or reasons for doing things. In looking for motives, it is helpful to ask yourself, "Why did the character act or speak as he or she did? What was the reason or purpose?" Read the passage below and see if you can find Spinner's motive.

It was hopeless, Spinner decided. She would never catch a fish. Suddenly the line tightened and spun out through the water. Spinner jumped to her feet and began to reel it in with all her might.

You probably figured out that Spinner's motive was wanting to catch a fish.

As you read the next selection, see if you can figure out the motives and feelings of the characters—especially those of the main character, Spinner. Try to relate Spinner's feelings and motives to your own experiences.

Fish

Jean Craighead George

A skinny girl in mountain boots and bulky clothes stood on the bank of the river. In one hand she held a fishing rod. With the other she pushed the long black hair away from her face.

Suddenly the fishing rod bowed like a question mark, and the girl braced as a fish took her line. The stones of the gravel bar rolled under her feet, and she was pulled into the icy Snake River. She glanced around desperately. The entire valley of Jackson Hole, Wyoming—its sky and saw-blade mountains, its people and wild things—were conspiring against her. She, Spinner Shafter, age thirteen, a dancer in the Roundelay Dance Company, was about to be drowned by a fish.

"Get in here!" she screamed to the creature pulling her. She dug in her heels, gained a better footing, and yanked.

"Get in here—this minute—so that I never have to fish again . . . ever. . . ." The reel spun like a windmill in a hurricane, and the line darted into the sparkling water where Ditch Creek meets the thunderous Snake.

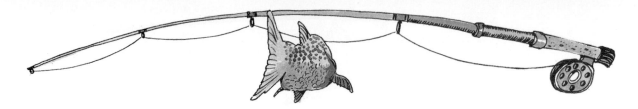

Awed by the strength of the fish, Spinner let it run out the line. Not until the reel screamed to a stop did she remember that she should be reeling in. With great effort she pulled on the line with her free hand.

"You're heavy," she said as she took a wider stance, leaned backward, and gained three feet of line. She reeled in the slack. The stones avalanched under her feet again and delivered her calf-deep into the river.

The fish surged away. Grudgingly she was forced to give back the line she had gained so the fish would not break it. Spinner threw herself backward on the gravel bar and reeled in.

She really wished she could be an excellent fisher for her father's sake; she knew he would like it. Years ago he had nicknamed her Spinner after a fish lure. And when he gave her a fly rod the night shc did her dance solo, it was clear that he wanted a fisher, not a dancer.

"Well, FISH," she said out loud. "He hasn't got one. He hasn't got a fisher to brag about."

She clutched the rod to keep the fish from pulling her into the river. The line trembled. She pulled. It trembled again. The fish was speaking to her.

"I hear you, FISH," she whispered. "You're fighting for your life out there in that terrible water." Spinner tugged. "I said, 'Hello,'" she called aloud. The fish tugged back. "Is that 'hello,' or are you frightened? I am. I've never caught a fish before." The fish tugged twice. "What are you saying? You're asking me to let you go? I will, I will, if you'll come in here and let me show you to my father."

The line went limp.

"What does that mean?" she whispered. "I forget what to do when the line goes limp. Pull in? Yes, yes, Daddy said, 'Keep the line taut.'"

Spinner dropped the rod and grabbed the line. She yanked it in hand over hand, pulling faster and faster to keep the tension on the charging fish. It swirled, not very far away. The water broke into a shower of bubbles, the line zagged, zigged—and went limp.

"I've lost it!—the big fish I was supposed to catch to beat the family record." She sat down and drooped her head.

Spinner recalled her father saying for the hundredth time, as they were fastening their seat belts on the plane in New York. "It's time to win the family fishing medal back. Your granddad took it from me; my brother Augustus

took it from him; and now it's your turn again. We'll give 'em some real competition." He laughed, but somehow Spinner knew it was not funny. Her father wanted that medal back.

She looked at the hopeless mess of nylon line at her feet. "Me from the city," she mused, "competing with two boys who fish from dawn to dusk. Some chance I've got against Paul, who's been fishing since he was born nineteen years ago.

" . . . Or for that matter," she said out loud to the fish, "some chance I've got against the kid my age, that boy, Al. Al for Alligator." She chuckled at her nickname for him. She called him Alligator because he grinned and grunted and never said more than "umph" or "hmmm."

"Umph," she mimicked. Alligator was probably landing a trophy right now. He knew all the good fishing holes and places where the big fish went at twilight. He had dashed past her this evening like a prong-horned antelope to get that spot where the Snake dug a dark den beneath a fallen cottonwood tree. What could she do against a boy like that—or against Paul, who had claimed the riverbank across from the old ferry, where the "big one" lay? By the time she had tied on her fly, there was no place to fish but the pool off the bar at Ditch Creek. The pool was the first river stop at the end of the fishing path, and it was, according to her fishing relatives, "all fished out."

Spinner kicked her tangled line and felt almost relieved that the fish was gone—almost. She had seen it, and it had been as big as a whale. She only hoped no one had seen her lose it.

She tried to unsnarl her line, gave up, and hauled the mess up on the bank. Suddenly the line tightened and cut

a Z in the rough water. Spinner grabbed it with both hands and was yanked to her feet like a water skier. Down to the river's edge she was pulled again.

Spinner turned, put the line over her shoulder, and hauled it up the bar. At the top she threw herself forward and jumped into the quieter waters of Ditch Creek. She struggled to a large log that was jammed against the bank, looped her line around a snag, pulled, and wrapped it once more. When the line was secure, she leaned out and hitched in another loop. This, too, she wrapped on the snag.

"You've got a log." It was her father's voice. "Broke my line on it."

"A log?" she cried. "I've got a trout! Help me!" He did not stir.

"By golly," he said. "You do have a fish. Pick up your rod. You can land it." He glanced around nervously. Spinner realized he was embarrassed. "You've got a nice whitefish; now land it correctly."

"I've got a trout! A cutthroat trout. I saw its big dorsal fin . . . like in the book."

"There're *no* cutthroats in this part of the Snake. Haven't been for years."

Spinner felt the strength seep out of her body. She stumbled and tried to haul in more line. Well, whatever the fish was, she would land it right in front of him and promptly announce she would never fish again.

"Wow! She's got a beaut!" Alligator was on the other side of Ditch Creek. He had spoken a complete sentence.

"Spinner!" her father shouted. "Get your rod. Land it right."

"Let her alone." Her grandfather was speaking. He was here too. Spinner stared at the river, feeling the eyes of the

three generations of fishermen upon her. They were
watching her as she fished, and she could sense their
contempt. But what could she do? She had to keep tension
on the fishline, and she had to keep out of the terrible river.
The fish dashed toward the wild water again, and she
lunged, wrapped the line around her hand three times, and
then tugged.

"Whitefish?" her grandfather asked.

"Yeah," said her father.

"It's a cutthroat!" she shrieked.

The fish turned and came toward her. She ran up the
bar and threw herself down on her stomach. She rolled
several times and took up the line with her body.

"For heaven's sake, Spinner!" her father shouted. "Get
up and fish."

"Wow!" Uncle Augustus had arrived. He whistled and
jumped to the gravel bar. His face was serious but kind.

"Nice going, Spinner," he said. She sat up. Alligator
leaped to her side, crouched silently, and studied the end of
her line.

"It's a whopper!" he said.

"It sure is." Paul had arrived.

"Those whitefish really put on a show," her father said. "And so does Spinner. Very dramatic kid."

Alligator grunted in her ear, "Help?"

"No!" she snapped. "I'll mess this up my own way." She pulled, the line cut into her hand, but she felt no pain; her fingers were too cold to be sensitive.

As the men watched, she inched the fish toward shore. Suddenly the surface exploded like a flame, and a huge head rose into view. Uncle Augustus gasped. Alligator whistled. Her father made no sound. The fish lunged toward the channel, turned, and shot back to the gravel bar. Its huge dorsal fin emerged above water.

"Cutthroat!" Alligator exclaimed.

"Cutthroat?" It was Paul. "Can't be."

"Oh, FISH," Spinner whispered. "You *are* a cutthroat. I know you are. Come in out of the water so Daddy will be proud of me. He'll throw you back, I promise. He always throws fish back."

181

Spinner wriggled up the bar, hauling on the line with all her strength. Alligator reached out to help. She shook her head furiously and clutched the line at the water's surface. She yanked it in. The fish splashed near her boot, rolled to its side, and lay still. It was almost as tired as she, but not quite; with a powerful twist it flipped out of the water. It fell into the pool and disappeared from sight.

"No!" Spinner stood up and hurled herself backward. The fish came with her, out of the water, up the stones, to the very top of the bar. It flopped, tore the hook from its mouth, and was free. With a twist it catapulted into the air and landed three inches from the river. One more flop and it would be gone. Spinner threw herself upon it. The great trout was caught.

"Bravo!" her father cheered.

Spinner rolled to her back exhausted and looked up as her father slowly lifted the great fish up against the sky. The speckles on its back and side glowed so brightly that it seemed to be lit from within. Its belly glowed orange, and the red marks under its jaw that gave it the name "cutthroat" gleamed like rubies. Its tail was an enormous fan, its body a torpedo. No one spoke for a long moment.

"I think she's got the record," Grandfather finally said.

Questions

1. How did Spinner get her nickname?
2. Why did Spinner end up fishing in Ditch Creek, a place that her relatives said was "all fished out"?
3. Would Spinner have won the competition if the fish had been a whitefish instead of a cutthroat? Explain your answer.
4. Do you think Spinner will throw the fish back into the river? Why or why not?

Applying Reading Skills

Choose the word or phrase that best completes each sentence below, based on "Fish." Write the complete sentence on your paper. Then write **F** if the sentence describes a feeling or **M** if it describes a motive.

1. As Spinner lost her footing and was pulled into the river, she felt ____ .
   a. relieved   b. angry   c. frightened   d. sad
2. When Spinner thought about her chances of winning the competition, she was ____ .
   a. confident   b. discouraged   c. upset   d. pleased
3. Spinner's father said, "We'll give 'em some real competition" because he wanted ____ .
   a. Spinner to be a fisher, not a dancer
   b. to encourage Spinner to win the medal back
   c. Spinner to live up to her name
4. Spinner was ____ as the three generations of fishermen watched.
   a. nervous   b. jealous   c. confused   d. hopeful
5. Spinner entered the contest and did her best to land a fish in order to ____ .
   a. show up Paul and Al
   b. prove that she was a good fisher
   c. please her father

PREPARING FOR READING

Learning Vocabulary

1. The tiny ketch *Tzu Hang* (tsü hang) was threatened by the <u>ominous</u> waves that reached higher than its masts.
2. It seemed that the raging storm would <u>overwhelm</u> the small boat.
3. <u>Undaunted</u> by their troubles, the crew of the *Tzu Hang* felt a spirit of <u>optimism</u> when the seas became calm and the sun shone.
4. Twice during the voyage, the *Tzu Hang* <u>encountered</u> the same weather conditions and suffered <u>identical</u> disasters.
5. Several months later, the terrible ordeal was <u>duplicated</u>.

ominous	overwhelm	undaunted	optimism
encountered	identical	duplicated	

Developing Background and Skills
Cause and Effect

When you read, you discover how things are related to one another. One way in which things are related to one another is called **cause and effect**. In a cause-and-effect relationship, one event or action—the cause—results or leads to another event or action—the effect. The sentence below is an example.

Because it could not stand the pressure of the waves, the mast broke.

In this sentence, the effect—the breaking of the mast—was caused by the pressure of the waves. The word *because* signals a cause-and-effect relationship. Sometimes—but not always—a writer uses signal or clue words such as *since, because, so that,* or *in order to* that help you recognize cause-and-effect relationships.

Often, however, there are no signal words to help you. In that case, you can ask "What happened?" The answer will be the effect. You can then ask "Why did it happen?" The answer will be the cause. Try the questions on the example below.

Water burst into the cabin. Miles had to fight his way to the deck.

The first sentence stated the cause; the second stated the effect.

Sometimes one event or action can be both a cause and an effect. Study the example below.

CAUSE ⟶ EFFECT

| The mast could not withstand the force of the wind. | The mast fell | The lifeboat was smashed. |

CAUSE ⟶ EFFECT

As you read the following selection, think about how different events and actions are related. Look for cause-and-effect relationships that are signaled by clue words and those that are not.

TZU HANG

Basil Heatter

Tzu Hang (tsü hang) may be the luckiest ship in the world—with the unluckiest crew. Or it may be the other way around. In any case, *Tzu Hang* survived an ordeal never before recorded in history. And she survived it not once, but twice.

Her owner was Miles Smeeton, a former British army officer. General Smeeton did not know very much about the water when he bought *Tzu Hang*. But he thought she looked seaworthy. *Tzu Hang* was a 46-foot teakwood ketch[1] built in Hong Kong. She looked as though she could go around the world, and that was what the Smeetons (Miles, his wife Beryl, their daughter Clio, and a pet cat) decided to do.

All went well on the merry ship *Tzu Hang*. The Smeetons sailed from England across the South Atlantic to Panama. Then they went through the canal and on up the west coast of the United States to Vancouver, British Columbia. From there they eventually made their way to Australia.

In Australia some new decisions were made. Clio would have to go back to school in England, and her parents would sail home without her. They decided to go back to England by way of Cape Horn, the dreaded no-man's-land of deep-water voyaging.

The voyage around Cape Horn is extremely dangerous. It has been done by small boats before, but not often. Old Josh Slocum, the first of the singlehanders, did it. But in the years that have followed, fewer than a dozen small yachts have duplicated his feat. Now Miles and Beryl and the cat would attempt it.

In the end there was another man on board. He was a young Englishman named John Guzzwell. John had sailed

---

1. **ketch:** a small sailing boat with two masts, which are the poles that support the sails.

187

halfway around the world alone on a small yacht he had built himself. He was a ship's carpenter of the highest order. This skill would prove very valuable to the crew of the *Tzu Hang*.

The first stage of the voyage, from Australia south and east to New Zealand across the Tasman Sea, went well enough. The real test, however—the ominous Roaring Forties—still lay ahead. These are the forty degrees of south latitude,[2] so called because of the fierce roaring of the wind in a boat's rigging.

As the *Tzu Hang* drove south, the weather got steadily worse, but they had been expecting that. At no point were they seriously worried. They had plenty of time and plenty of food.

The seas were mountainous. The Smeetons and Guzzwell had, of course, seen big seas before, but never anything like this. The wave tops reached higher than their masthead.[3]

---

2. **latitude:** the distance north or south of the equator, expressed as degrees measured from the equator.
3. **masthead:** the highest part of the mast.

At that time, shortly after daybreak, they were running under bare poles and dragging 360 feet of heavy rope in an effort to slow the yacht down. But even so, *Tzu Hang* continued to move too fast. It was decided to carry on until there was a lull in the storm.

At nine o'clock in the morning, Beryl took over the helm. For as long as Miles Smeeton lives, he will never forget what happened next. He was lying in his bunk reading. Suddenly he was thrown with terrific force. There was a tearing, cracking sound as if *Tzu Hang* were being ripped apart. Water burst into the cabin. Miles was buried in darkness under a great surge of water, bedding, and smashed pieces of wood. He fought his way to the surface and saw that the entire cabin top was gone. There was a great gaping hole in the deck.

His first thought was for Beryl. Obviously she had been washed overboard by the tremendous sea that had swept the decks. He fought his way out to the cockpit and saw Beryl in the water about thirty yards away. Swimming strongly, with her head above water, she appeared unafraid and smiling. "I'm all right, I'm all right," she shouted above the howling of the wind.

The yacht had been completely dismasted. Masts and rigging were strewn in the sea. Beryl managed to reach some of this wreckage and slowly pull herself closer to the boat. Once she was alongside, John and Miles dragged her up on deck. She was bleeding from a deep cut on her forehead, and she had a broken collarbone.

Tzu Hang was a wreck. The storm was still raging, and great seas threatened to overwhelm her at any moment. The situation looked hopeless. But the three sailors set to work at once with buckets to get the tons of water out of the hull.

The next problem was to prevent more water from getting in. John at once set to work with tools and canvas to cover the hole in the deck. Even when this was accomplished, their situation still appeared hopeless. They were a thousand miles from land in the stormiest seas in the world. They had no masts, no engine, no compass, and not too much food and water. Even so, the idea of giving up—of surrendering to the sea—never crossed their minds.

Their first job, of course, was to get the boat to land. They began rigging a jury[4] mast under which they might be able to carry some sort of sail.

John Guzzwell took over the job of building it. The new mast—only fifteen feet high—was up and *Tzu Hang* was sailing before the wind under a small square sail.

It was then that Miles found the rudder[5] gone—sheared right off. How could a yacht under jury rig travel a thousand miles without a rudder? Once again John rose to the occasion. He fashioned a steering oar out of bits of scrap.

All told, they did amazingly well under their rag of sail, sometimes logging close to a hundred miles a day. Then the

4. **jury:** intended or designed for emergency or temporary use.
5. **rudder:** a vertical piece of metal or wood, hinged to the stern, or rear, of a boat and used for steering.

mast broke again. John, undaunted, set to work and built a new one. After two days of work, they had the new mast up and now, at last, the weather began to improve. The sun shone, and the seas became calmer. The mood on board was one of optimism. They made bets on when they might reach land. Beryl said a hundred days, John said fifty, and Miles said forty. Miles was almost exactly right. In the fifth week, they picked up the coast of Chile and crept into port.

No sooner were they ashore than they began the monumental task of rebuilding the boat. For four months they worked on the boat. At the end of that time, *Tzu Hang* was almost ready for sea. John, long overdue on a cruise of his own, had to leave them.

On December 9, nine months after reaching Chile, Miles and Beryl put out to sea again in *Tzu Hang*. They were determined to round the Horn, to finish what they had started. They sailed south again to the region of the great storms and huge gray seas.

On Christmas Day they were in a violent storm. The Smeetons opened their Christmas presents, and tried to pretend that all was well. But all was far from well. The weather worsened and the boat trembled under the impact of the seas. They had the uneasy feeling that once again they were headed for disaster.

At four o'clock in the afternoon, *Tzu Hang* heeled over and buried herself under a raging blackness of water. The sea burst into the ship. Miles found himself struggling for air inside the flooded cabin. All he could think was, "Oh, no, not again! Not again!"

As in a nightmare, everything was repeated. The yacht turned upside down. They had come to the same place, encountered the same conditions, and suffered the same incredible but identical disaster.

Tzu Hang rolled over and righted herself. Once again the Smeetons began the backbreaking task of getting the water out and rigging a jury mast. Somehow they managed it. Somehow, four weeks later, they were once again within sight of the coast of Chile.

It would be nice to report that the Smeetons again fixed up their boat and that *this* time they did round the Horn. But even this pair was ready at last to admit that fate simply would not allow them to get around Cape Horn. *Tzu Hang* was shipped home to England to be repaired, and Miles and Beryl are sailing her once more. They are unquestionably the only two people in the long history of the sea to have survived such an experience—twice.

Questions

1. What experience did the *Tzu Hang* and her crew survive twice?
2. List in order the places along the route the Smeetons followed on their first voyage.
3. Why do you think the Smeetons might have decided to sail around the world by way of Cape Horn?
4. If you could travel around the world on a ship, what places would you choose to visit?

Applying Reading Skills

Copy and complete the chart below about cause-and-effect relationships in *"Tzu Hang."*

CAUSE	EFFECT
1. The forty degrees of south latitude are a region where the wind roars fiercely in a ship's rigging	
2.	*Tzu Hang* was running under bare poles and dragging 360 feet of rope.
3. The crew wanted to prevent more water from getting into the hull.	
4.	The crew began to rig a jury mast.
5. The sun shone and the seas became calmer.	
6.	John left the *Tzu Hang*.

Roadways

One road leads to London,
    One road runs to Wales,
My road leads me seawards
    To the white dipping sails.

One road leads to the river,
    As it goes singing slow;
My road leads to shipping
    Where the bronzed sailors go.

Leads me, lures me, calls me
    To salt green tossing sea;
A road without earth's road dust
    Is the right road for me.

A wet road heaving, shining
    And wild with seagull's cries,
A mad salt sea-wind blowing
    The salt spray in my eyes.

My road calls me, lures me
    West, east, south, and north;
Most roads lead men homewards,
    My road leads me forth.

John Masefield

PREPARING FOR READING

Learning Vocabulary

1. The water that rose around Elly's feet wasn't cold. Logically, she <u>deduced</u>, it should be.
2. As Elly progressed stroke by stroke through the water, the wreckage of the plane began to <u>recede</u>.
3. The <u>interval</u> between Elly's shouts and their echoes gradually shortened.
4. Elly realized that the great bowl created by the surrounding mountains was large enough for a plane to <u>maneuver</u> within it.
5. The task of forming the giant letters *H E L P* using logs was a <u>formidable</u> one.
6. Elly suddenly wondered if she was correct in her <u>assumption</u> that the bay was uninhabited.

deduced	recede	interval
maneuver	formidable	assumption

Developing Background and Skills
Character's Motives or Feelings

Recognizing and understanding a character's **motives** and **feelings** can make a story more interesting to you. You may realize that the character's feelings are ones that you have had. You may find that you have shared the character's motives in things that you have said or done yourself.

Writers reveal the feelings of characters in several ways. Sometimes authors explain them directly. At other times, they give you information that can help you figure out what a character is feeling. The list that follows describes some of the ways in which readers can learn about a character's feelings.

1. What the character or the author says directly
2. What the character thinks
3. What the character does, or how he or she acts
4. The way the character does or says something
5. How the character looks or appears

Motives, or reasons for doing something, are also sometimes explained directly. In such cases, the writer may use the word *because*. But many times you will have to use other information provided by the author to figure out motives for yourself. By asking "What reason or reasons did the character have for saying or doing what he or she did?" you can usually determine the character's motive.

Your own experience, too, can be helpful in figuring out characters' motives and feelings. You can ask yourself "How would I feel in this situation? What reasons might I have had for doing or saying that?"

There is only one character, Elly, in the following selection. You will notice that she says very little. Her feelings and motives are revealed in other ways. As you read, try to determine what her feelings and motives are. Think about the ways in which they *are* revealed. Put yourself in Elly's place and imagine what your feelings might be. Consider what you might have done in her place and see if you can understand her reasons for acting as she did.

OUT·OF·THE
WRECK

DAVID MATHIESON

Like a clock running backward, the altimeter unwound. The rate of descent gave them a little over two minutes before they hit the sea. Elena, on her way to join her father on an archaeological dig, was the lone passenger on this small plane in distress. She followed the pilot's instructions and worked her way into the flotation jacket. Suddenly they lost the radio signal. Without it, they could not call for help, and it was all Jim could do to steer the plane away from the mountain off the rugged coast of British Columbia, Canada. A bank of fog rolling in from the ocean hid them in its midst. The plane plummeted through it and crashed.

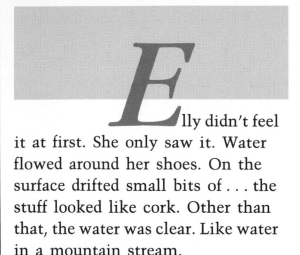

*E*lly didn't feel it at first. She only saw it. Water flowed around her shoes. On the surface drifted small bits of . . . the stuff looked like cork. Other than that, the water was clear. Like water in a mountain stream.

Except it wasn't cold.

Calmly, logically, she deduced that it *ought* to be cold. And only after reaching this conclusion did she actually feel how cold it was. She also became aware of the control yoke pressing against her ribs, and the constriction of the seat belt.

She was facing sideways, with her left shoulder against the control panel. The way she was turned, she could look out the side window and watch the plane's wingtip slowly, slowly descend until it touched the water—where it stopped.

The water around her legs kept rising.

Small creaking, groaning noises came from the structure of the aircraft, but other than this it was quiet.

She pushed herself upright, and the movement triggered a small avalanche to the left. The cabin was a wreck. The cargo in back had moved forward into the place where the pilot had been sitting. It was a wall of canvas-covered parcels, surveyor's equipment, and luggage—all entangled with the tie-down straps that should have held it in place.

The water had reached her hips now. She wasn't sure what to do.

"Jim?" Her voice sounded metallic, machinelike inside the enclosure. "Jim! Are you all right?"

She couldn't see anything of him. He was hidden behind the cargo. A sudden, horrifying insight came to her: if she couldn't get him out, he would drown.

It shocked her into action. Desperately, she worked to push away the wreckage. Lighter pieces she threw in back. The bigger ones wouldn't budge—they were held by a net of cords and straps, knotted together. She knew about knots and worked quickly. The first came undone. She went on to the next, praying for time.

But the plane went down with a rush. She barely had a chance to lift her face, to suck in one last breath, before going under.

Everything became green and blurred. Over the sound of escaping air, she heard a measured thudding. She listened to this—the beating of her heart—while struggling with the door. She decided the door was jammed and wouldn't open.

Then it did more than open. It detached completely, vanishing into the darkness below.

With new hope, she started to rise from the seat . . . and was unable to move. A dozen heartbeats went by, pounding even louder in her ears, but struggle though she might, she was still a captive.

Finally, she remembered—the seat belt.

Undoing the clasp, she swam from the cockpit, turned face up, and pulled herself to the front of the wing. The light called from above. But for the second time she was held back. The plane, she realized, was traveling forward as it sank. There would be no escaping past the leading edge of the wing, for she could never fight the current.

She let go. The light went away. In the dark, she could feel the wing sliding by her face. When it was gone, she allowed the gentle, friendly hand of the flotation jacket to take her up, and came at last to the air.

For companions, she had a metal pontoon[1] and a floating yellow pencil. Off in the mist, just barely visible at a distance of a hundred meters or so, was a rock.

The best solution to the problem, she thought, would be to climb aboard the pontoon and paddle it like a surfboard until she reached the rock. The pontoon, however, proved traitorous. It floated bottom-up, and when she tried to pull herself onto it, the structure rolled toward her, like a log, and she slipped. A saw-toothed edge of aluminum ripped open the palm of her left hand. The pontoon then sank, leaving her alone in the water with a bleeding hand.

Several minutes had already gone by. A person could survive the waters of the Northwest for a quarter hour or so. She thought she'd have more time than this herself, as the jacket was lined with plastic foam, a good insulation. She wasn't suffering from the cold as yet. Nevertheless, it would be foolish to waste time. There might be a current bearing her away from the rock.

---

1. **pontoon:** a float on a seaplane.

She began with a crawl stroke.

To her astonishment, she found she simply wasn't moving. At the end of a minute, the pencil was no farther away.

It was the jacket! Its flotation layer made the thing stiff and bulky. It was like a parachute below the water. The sleeves, when she lifted them to take a stroke, were like enormous, water-filled sausages.

The jacket couldn't be left behind, however. Once she got to the rock (*if* she got to the rock) she would die of hypothermia[2] in a matter of hours without the insulation it afforded.

And yet it was beginning to look as if she'd die anyway, before reaching the rock, *because* of the jacket. A classic double bind!

Grimly, she began experimenting. She tried every facedown stroke she knew. None was any better than the first.

She rolled face up, trying a backstroke. Now she made a small amount of progress. The pencil began to recede. Not rapidly, but at least it was receding.

The labor of swimming became uncomfortable, then painful, then agonizing. It was like an endless race. A sprint followed by another sprint. Doggedly, she kept at it, for she knew her life was in the balance. She had to ignore the pain of breathing and the incredible, burning cold at the back of her neck. She swam on, her mind strangely clear despite the pain. She thought of her father, and of the sailboat he had found for her; it would be at the dock, waiting for her. She thought of the house in Victoria. And in the end she found she didn't care about any of it. The only thing that mattered was to stay alive—this would be such a *foolish* way to die. The search planes would come in the morning, and they'd find nothing but a dummy, a stupid puppet floating lifeless in a big orange jacket. It would be a disgrace. And so she went on.

Another few meters and she wouldn't have made it. She lost all sense of direction, all sense of up or down, and fought blindly in her pain, and it was this that brought her feet into contact with the rock. She was able to stand and to walk beyond the water.

The enormous labor of swimming with the jacket had produced

---

2. **hypothermia** (hī′ pō thẽr′ mē ə): the condition of having a body temperature greatly below normal.

a carry-over effect. For a time she felt remarkably warm again, and the pain in her chest went away. Her cut hand had begun to hurt, but at least it no longer bled. She congratulated herself on being alive and reasonably alert. Her chances, as she saw them, were quite good. Thanks to the jacket, she could last until morning. Then the fog would clear, and the search planes would come.

She began a survey of her island. It was a flat slab of stone, tilted up at one end. Along its length, the rock was marked with fresh gouges—the track of the pontoons. Here and there lay chips and slivers of aluminum, while right at the crest, not far from where a small driftwood log was balanced, she found a curious metal cap, pressed tightly around a knob of rock. The scrap of metal from the plane had struck the knob so forcefully that the texture of the rock underneath could be seen through the aluminum. It had welded itself in place.

By now, the effect of the exercise had worn off and she was feeling chilled. More chilling still came the realization that the tide was on the rise.

"So *that's* why the log is at the

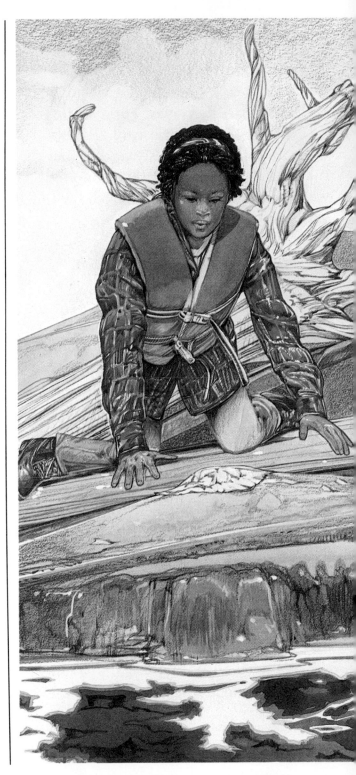

203

top of the rock," she said to herself. "Because the tide carried it
and then left it there."

Suddenly she felt like weeping,
and closed her eyes. For a while
she stood, with the tiny droplets
of fog brushing softly against her
face. They made minute pinpricks
of coldness as they traveled on the
breeze.

She must resign herself to yet
another effort, she decided. It was
the only way. If she stayed where
she was, she'd drown during the
night.

Somewhere, there was a mountain. They'd almost run into it
with the plane. She'd be safe there;
she'd be able to rest. And, just possibly, the mountain was but a
short distance away.

"And possibly it *isn't*!" jeered
the voice of Defeat. "Just *possibly*
you'll be heading in the wrong
direction!"

Ignoring this, she rolled the log
to the water. She found a piece of
driftwood and broke it in half. The
halves went alongside the log, one
to port, one to starboard. They'd
act as sponsons,[3] for stability. It
made a feeble excuse for a raft,

---

3. **sponson:** an air-filled part that sticks out
   from the body of a seaplane to keep the
   plane steady on the water.

but no other timber was available. She removed her wool shirt and used it as a rope to tie the three timbers together at the bow. Then she sat astride the log at the stern, the roots against her back, and clamped the after ends of the sponsons to the log with her knees.

Even with her legs submerged, the raft barely floated. It was also extremely unstable. One false move would cause her to tumble sideways into the water. The raft would then disintegrate, and in a few minutes she would be dead.

It took every scrap of her willpower to leave the rock behind. Paddling with her hands held inside the sleeves of the jacket, she headed to windward, steering by the slight riffle on the water. Not by accident had she chosen this course. The long scratches in the rock had pointed the way to the concealed mountain—the direction from which the plane had come. Upwind. In the silence and the fog.

After a time she began to shake with cold, and the shaking increased, threatening to overturn her. To make matters worse, the breeze died down. She was in the lee[4] of the mountain: near enough for the wind to be blanketed, but not so near as to make any of the mountain visible.

"It will happen to you, Elly, just as it happened to Jim," said Defeat.

"Not yet," she replied.

She shouted into the fog with all her might. Again and again. At first there was no reply, but then after laboriously turning the cranky little raft to face in the opposite direction, she began hearing a faint echo.

Evidently she had traveled half a circle since losing the wind.

Methodically, she hunted for the source of the echo. It led her on a frantic yet slow-motion chase through the fog, first a little to one side, then a little to the other side.

She began to understand now. There were two echoes. But gradually they were becoming louder. The interval between shout and reply shortened. A heaviness appeared in the fog. Under it ran a pale band. And under that, a strip that was quite dark.

A steep, dark beach. Made of stones.

Pale driftwood above.

And forest. A wall of forest.

---

4. **lee:** the side away from the direction from which the wind blows.

205

"Their last report put them here, two hundred kilometers south of us."

She could see the gesture her father would use, pointing with the stem of the pipe she'd given him at Christmas. He and Alex would be in the radio tent, with a chart spread before them.

"There's a chance they're alive. An excellent chance, don't you think? Engine trouble. That's what this Tate fellow thought, and he ought to know. They'd simply land in the water. The strait's calm. They'll be in fine shape. At least . . . they should be."

Alex, the practical one, is drawing a pencil line on the chart. The line runs northwest from the plane's last position, parallel with the coast. Somewhere along it is the spot where the plane is to be found.

Alex, perhaps, is less hopeful than her father. He is a flyer himself, and would have a better idea of what the fog the evening before might mean. He would also be thinking about the loss of radio contact. He'd keep it to himself, however. Alex would be more likely to draw attention to the number of planes available for the search. He would be looking up the time of sunrise, saying: "The light'll be strong enough for them to take to the air before long. Some of the planes'll be in the search area by breakfast."

For the tenth time since the crash she pushed the stud on her watch . . . to be reminded once again of what the salt had done. Instead of the warm glow of lighted numerals, she saw only the reflection of a gray dawn. The watch was dead.

Her shivering had eased enough by now for her to undo the clasp. Taking off the watch, she peered at the back of the case. It was still too dark for her to decipher the engraved words, but that didn't matter; she knew them by heart.

For my cherished Elena
on her 16th birthday
Father

She cried for a time, thinking of that birthday of a year and a half before. Then she slipped the watch back in place and began swinging

206

her arms and stamping her feet in the gravel of the beach.

The long night had been more hideous than anything she ever imagined. She had spent it huddled at the base of a tree. Part of the time her knees had been tucked under the jacket for warmth. Other times, she'd been forced to stand to regain circulation. Her face still ached from clenching her teeth against the cold, and sleep had been impossible. Even with her eyes open, the darkness had flamed with images. A waking nightmare endlessly repeated itself. Again and again the pontoon had reared above her, like a ship lifting its stern as it sank. The rudder would sidle downward, threatening to snag the jacket and drag her under, and when it was gone there was the blood from her hand, staining the water.

But that was now past. Such things could not survive the light of day; already she was feeling more herself. She began walking along the beach, keeping the water on her right. The exercise warmed her. After a time, she came to a place where the angle of the beach increased and the rounded stones clattered and yielded underfoot. In the gloom, it was hard to stay upright, so she turned and headed back.

The water was to her left now and noticeably brighter than before, reflecting the light of the sky without trace of a ripple. Not even the long, slow movement of a swell.

Interesting.

It meant she must be on the protected inner shore of a bay, or at the very least, a channel.

Abruptly, the beach came to an end, blocked by a great monolith.[5] The evening before, she had been unable to see the top of it clearly, due to the fog. Now the thing looked like a medieval fortress, rising vertically from the beach, the outer portion reaching into the water, the landward side linked to the mountain by a series of turrets and ledges. The resemblance to a castle didn't stop here. The beach around her was peopled with dark shapes. Over the centuries, blocks of stone had split away from the solid ramparts above and now stood watch below the wall. Like the soldiers of an army, assembled at a spear's length from one another.

As night became day, the stones took on a less forbidding aspect. The great monolith itself seemed less like a fortress. It was, after all, only a tall stone pinnacle.[6] Out in the water stood part of the same formation—the summit of another spire—this one hidden in the water and only showing its top as the tide receded.

She was shocked to realize that this was the very rock on which she had landed the night before. It looked so remarkably innocent, like the smooth rounded back of a whale. One had to look closely to see the glint of aluminum on it.

Beyond, the mist had begun to lift from the water. She saw that her deduction had been correct: she was on the shore of a bay. It was a long bay, with a narrow opening to the sea, a channel framed by tall headlands. The surrounding mountains were immense, rising straight from the water. It seemed incredible that trees could grow on a slope that steep, but grow they did. The somber embrace of the conifers was unbroken.

She was inside a well, a forested well.

---

5. **monolith:** a large single upright block of stone.

6. **pinnacle:** any tall, pointed formation.

Fortunately, though, the well had been created on such a titanic scale that an aircraft could manage to maneuver within it.

"They'll be low enough to catch sight of someone on the beach," she said to herself, "especially if that someone is waving an orange jacket."

There was something else she could do to attract attention. But it would be best for her to move away from the pinnacle first, so the view from the air would not be obstructed.

Going to the place where the beach was steepest, she dragged pieces of weathered timber down from the level of the driftwood, arranging them against the dark stones to form the letter H. She made the H fifteen paces high by nine paces wide, and it was nearly an hour before the thing was complete. Clearly, the task would be a formidable one, for each of the three remaining letters would have to be in proportion to the first.

She wiped the sweat from her eyes, took off the jacket, and went on working. She had to use great caution, extracting her building material from the timbers at the top of the beach. The enormous logs along the outer edge were

easily dislodged, and she remembered well the lesson of the night before, when the first log she touched had gone crunching down the incline and into the water like a quick-moving steamroller.

And so the work progressed. The H was followed by an E, which was followed by an L, which in turn was followed by the letter P.

She debated whether or not to add an exclamation mark, but decided enough effort had been invested. Low tide had arrived, which meant it was about six in the morning. From now on she would try to avoid noisy activities, such as dragging timbers over stone, and to keep an ear tilted toward the sky.

Perched comfortably in a natural seat of driftwood, she watched a flight of puffins skittering above the water. Puffins were such comical birds—with their great triangular beaks and drooping ear tufts below, they seemed to be dragging long pieces of seaweed about with them.

With surprise she realized that her various discomforts, both physical and emotional, had all but disappeared. She was watching the flight of birds with genuine pleasure. Despite the loss of sleep, she didn't feel tired. Her hand wasn't hurting much. Her clothing was nearly dry.

Her eye followed the uneven sequence of gravel beach and marl[7] bluff as it meandered off to the left. After a kilometer or two it ended in a small promontory.[8] This restricted her view of the rest of the bay, and she wondered what lay beyond.

All along, her assumption had been that the bay was uninhabited. But she couldn't be certain there were no people until she'd seen all of the shoreline. "I'd look awfully silly," she told herself, "having to be rescued within walking distance of a marina . . . or near a scientific outpost like my father's."

For the first time in many hours, she laughed. Tossing the orange jacket on her shoulder, she set off along the tide line, whistling as she went.

You can find out what happens to Elly by reading the book from which this excerpt was taken, Trial by Wilderness.

7. **marl:** clay containing chalk or limestone.
8. **promontory:** a high ridge of land or rock jutting out into a sea or other large body of water.

Questions

1. Where was Elly going before the plane crashed?
2. What happened to Jim? Why?
3. Why did Elly decide to leave the rock where she first landed?
4. If you were stranded on an island, what would you need to survive? Describe how you would find or make something you needed.

Applying Reading Skills

A. Read each sentence below. Then choose the word from the box that best describes how Elly felt at the time the event took place in "Out of the Wreck." Write the word on your paper.

frantic	surprised	shocked
hopeful	relieved	fearful

1. Elly followed the instructions to put on her flotation jacket, and then the plane crashed.
2. Elly looked back at the wall of parcels as the water reached her hips and called, "Jim?"
3. Although a person could hope to survive the water for 15 minutes, Elly thought she would have more time because of her insulated jacket.
4. From her makeshift raft, Elly saw a dark band that she knew was a beach.

B. Write a sentence describing Elly's motive for each action described below.
1. Elly worked to push away the wreckage of cargo that had moved forward into the cockpit.
2. Elly shouted into the fog with all her might.
3. Elly began walking along the beach at the first sign of light.
4. Elly formed the letters H E L P by placing pieces of driftwood on the beach.

WRITING ACTIVITY

WRITE A SURVIVAL STORY

Prewrite

"Out of the Wreck" is a survival story. In a survival story, a character such as Elly must overcome great mental and physical odds to survive an accident or other catastrophe.

Every story has a plan of organization. Such a plan is called a story map. Work with other students to complete this story map of "Out of the Wreck."

Characters:

Setting:

Problem: Elly must find a way to survive until rescued.

Opening Event: The plane with Jim and Elly crashes off the coast of British Columbia, Canada.

Events in the Story: (Make a list of important events in order.)

Solving the Problem: (What does Elly do to survive?)

Conclusion: (What does Elly plan to do next?)

You are going to write a continuation of Elly's story. It will continue from the point where "Out of the Wreck" ended. Use a story map to help you make a story plan.

Keep in mind that your story must begin where "Out of the Wreck" ends. Elly will be your main character, but you may introduce others if you like. "Out of the Wreck" is a real-life adventure, so your story must be a real-life adventure also. In other words, the events in your story could possibly happen in real life.

Write

1. Use your story map to write a continuation of "Out of the Wreck." Open your story with a description of the first event on your story map. Remember, you want to catch the attention of your readers, so try to make your writing exciting and lifelike.
2. You might want to try a flashback to explain how Elly ended up alone on the beach. A flashback is a writer's way of explaining what happened to a character at a previous time or place. Your flashback could be a summary of the most important events in "Out of the Wreck."
3. When you have finished, write a title for your story.
4. Use your Glossary or dictionary for spelling help.

Revise

Read your survival story. What was your original purpose for writing? Does your story make sense as a continuation of the original story? What sentences could you move around to make the order of events more clear to your readers?

1. Proofread to make sure you used complete sentences.
2. If you used conversation or dialogue, check your use of commas and quotation marks.
3. Rewrite your survival story to share.

THE CITADEL

JAMES RAMSEY ULLMAN

The Citadel was the last unconquered mountain in Switzerland. Rudi Matt's father, Josef Matt, one of the greatest of the Swiss guides, had lost his life trying to climb it. Now it was Rudi's dream to do what no one had ever done—to conquer the Citadel. Accompanying Captain John Winter, the foremost mountaineer of his day, and his guide, Saxo, he might have had a chance. But when the three make a start and then agree to go back for supplies—Winter and Saxo west to the village of Broli, Rudi east to Kurtal—something happens to Rudi. The great mass of rock and ice beckons, and Rudi begins to climb.

here was the sky. There was rock and ice. There was a mountain thrusting upward into blue emptiness—and at the foot of the mountain a tiny speck. This speck was the only thing that lived or moved in all that world of silent majesty.

Rudi climbed the white slope of the upper glacier. He did not hurry. He looked neither up at the peak nor down at the valley, but only at the ice flowing slowly past beneath his feet. In the ice were the marks of their boot-nails from the previous day, and it was easy to follow the route. When the slope steepened, there were the steps cut by Winter and Saxo with their axes. He had only to step up, balance briefly, step up again—and again.

With the step-cutting, it had required two hours to reach the *bergschrund*.[1] Today it took him perhaps a third of that time. Coming out on the rim of the great crevasse, he approached the snow-bridge, tested it, and crossed without mishap. Then, still following the trail of the day before, he threaded his way through the steep maze of the icefall.

The seracs[2] rose around him in frozen stillness. And Rudi's mind seemed frozen too. What he was doing was not a result of conscious choice or decision; it was simply what he *had* to do. He had not lost his senses. He knew that alone, and without food or a tent, there was no chance on earth of his reaching the top of the Citadel. And it was not hope for the top that pushed him on. It was simply—well, he wasn't sure—perhaps simply the hope to set foot on the mountain. Or more than the hope. The need. The need of his body,

---

1. **bergschrund** (bėrk′ shrunt): a crevasse (kri vas′), or deep open crack, at the head of a glacier which separates the moving ice from the ice that is attached to the walls of a valley.
2. **seracs** (sə raks′): large masses of ice broken off the main body of a glacier and remaining behind in a crevasse.

his mind, his heart, to come at last to the place of which he had dreamed so long; to stand on the southeast ridge; to follow where his father had led; to climb, perhaps, even as high as the Fortress, which was as high as any man had gone. That was what he wanted; what he *had to have*.

He climbed on. The seracs slid past like tall hooded ghosts. And then they dropped away behind him, and he came out at the base of the snowslope. Above him he could see a trail of zigzagging footprints, extending perhaps halfway to the ridge and disappearing into smooth drifts where the avalanche had erased them. The drifts were huge, billowing, dazzling in the sunlight; but he knew that they had frozen overnight, and that the sun was not yet strong enough to dislodge them. He shuffled his boots in the snow, and it was firm and dry. As Captain Winter had said, the slope was safe in the morning.

Even so, he was cautious as he climbed upward, testing every step before trusting his weight to it. And when he came to the avalanche area he detoured to the left and kept as close as possible to the bordering rock-wall, so that he would have something to cling to, just in case . . . But nothing happened. The snow stayed as motionless as the rock. In all that spreading wilderness there was no movement except that of his own two legs plodding slowly on and on through the billowing drifts.

Rudi moved on. Through the stillness. Up the white slope. Kick—step, he went. Kick—step. Kick—step. And though the going through the deep drifts was slow, it was neither steep nor slippery, and his progress was steady. He looked back—and the icefall was far below; ahead—and the ridge loomed nearer. . . . Nearer. . . . And then at last the great moment came, and the slope was beneath him. There was no longer snow under his feet, but solid rock. He took a step up—a second—a third . . . and stood on the southeast ridge of the Citadel.

Here he sat down and rested. He pressed his hands against the cold stone, as if to convince himself that he was really there. Not on its glaciers; not on its approaches; but on the mountain itself. He looked down along the way he had come, and there, beyond glacier and snowfield, forest and pasture, tiny and remote, lay the green valley of Kurtal. On the far side of the ridge he could now see all the way to the village of Broli. It was as if he were already on a mountaintop, with all the world below him . . . .Until he looked up. And then everything changed . . . .Then he was no longer on a mountain's summit, but at a mountain's base, and there was the whole great mass of the Citadel still towering above him into the sky.

His eyes moved slowly upward across the slanting wilderness of rock and ice. To the right was the east face, to the left the south: two monstrous, almost vertical precipices[3] soaring up out of the bounds of sight. Between them, and joining them, was the twisting spine of the southeast ridge; and while this, too, was steep, it was not so steep as the faces, and was broken up into a maze of towers, clefts,[4] and ledges that at least offered the possibility of being climbed. From where Rudi sat he could not see to the summit of the Citadel, nor even to its high shoulder. Some two thousand feet above him the ridge flared up into the bold broad promontory that was called the Fortress, and what lay beyond it was hidden from view. There remained, Rudi knew, fully two-thirds of the mountain—another four thousand feet of savage rock thrusting up and up to the final pyramid. But, in practical terms,

---

3. **precipices** (pres′ə pis′ əz): extremely steep masses of rock.
4. **clefts:** cracks; crevices.

it was still as remote from him as when he had stared up at it through the blue miles from the valley below. The Fortress was as far as he could see. And as far as he could go.

If he could go that far . . .

He looked at the sun and estimated it to be not quite noon. If he were to be down safely by dark, he could allow himself—what? Perhaps two hours for going up. That meant about another hour to get back where he was. Three o'clock. He figured the times down the snowslope, the icefall, the upper glacier. Yes—two hours up, and he could still be down to the hut by nightfall. Beyond the hut he did not figure. He could not force his mind to think of it.

He stood up. He grasped his ax.

Then he began the ascent of the ridge.

As he had judged from below, it was steep—but not too steep. Indeed, for the first few minutes the going was even easier than on the snowslope or glacier, and he was able to swing up from boulder to boulder with long easy strides.

This did not last long, however. Soon the gradient[5] sharpened, the boulders gave way to solid rock, and pausing, he slung his ax through his pack-straps to give himself the free use of both hands. From here on it would be real climbing. He worked up a series of slabs and gained fifty feet; along a shallow gully for another fifty. Then there was a bulge to be rounded and a wall to be scaled, but he chose his route carefully and negotiated both without trouble. Hand- and footholds were plentiful. The rock was sound and firm. At the rate he was going, he thought, he would reach the Fortress in nearer one hour than two.

But the rate, of course, did not continue. Presently he came to a pitch of almost smooth rock, on which he had to

---

5. **gradient** (grā′ dē ənt): the steepness of a slope.

search and grope for every stance. And above this, faced with two possible ways around a crag,[6] he chose the wrong one, came out at the base of an unclimbable wall, and was forced to backtrack and try again. The angle of the ridge itself remained fairly constant, but the two faces of the mountain, on either side of it, fell away with ever-increasing steepness, until his route was no more than a thin slanting line between two gulfs of space. Sheer height, as such, did not bother him, as it would have bothered a lowlander. He could look down without dizziness or panic. But, nevertheless, he looked down no more than he had to. He concentrated on what lay ahead and made absolutely certain of the soundness of his holds before each upward move.

There was an easy stretch. Then a harder one. For a distance of some thirty feet the ridge narrowed to knife-edged thinness, and he was forced to straddle it and push himself up with his hands. Then came a series of towers, or *gendarmes* (zhon′ därms′), blocking the ridge completely, so that he had to leave it and work his way out onto the south face. Here the going was by far the hardest he had yet encountered. Behind and below him was a thousand feet of emptiness, and often as much as a minute passed while he clung motionless, searching for holds in the smooth granite above.

Once or twice he came close to despair. "It is impossible," he thought. "I cannot do it." But no sooner had he thought it than he heard Winter's voice as he spoke to Saxo down in the hut. "It has been done before," Winter had said.

Rudi's lips tightened. His eyes narrowed. . . . Yes, he knew it had been done before. And he knew *who* had done it before. . . .

---

6. **crag:** a mass of rock that sticks out from a cliff.

the platform—and he carefully followed it around. He took four steps—five—six. And stopped. The ledge ended, petering out into the vertical walls of the Fortress. But from its farthest end he could see what he had hoped to see: the one break in the great cliff's defenses. No more than five yards beyond him, and starting at about the level at which he stood, a long cleft, or chimney, slanted upward through the otherwise unbroken rock.

This, he knew, was the way past the Fortress—the "key" to the upper mountain which his father had found fifteen years before. From where he stood he could not see the inside of the cleft, but its depth and angle were such that he was sure he could climb it. If—*if* he could reach its base. . . .

Moving to the very end of the ledge, he studied the gap beyond. There was no place to stand—he could see that at once; nor were there any cracks or knobs for handholds. But the wall, though vertical, was not altogether smooth. The rock between ledge and cleft protruded in a sort of wrinkled bulge, and if one could cling to the bulge for as much as a few seconds it would be possible to worm one's way across. For a long moment he remained where he was; gazing, measuring. Then suddenly he moved. Stepping out from the ledge, he inched out onto the bulge, using not only hands and feet, as in ordinary climbing, but all of his body that he could bring into play. He gripped the rock with arms and legs, pressed against it with chest and thighs, holding on not by any actual support but by the friction of his moving weight. Space wheeled beneath him. The remote glaciers glinted. But once committed, he could not stop, or even hesitate, for such a maneuver had to be made quickly and in perfect rhythm, or it could not be made at all. His clothing scraped against the granite; his knees and elbows churned; his fingers clawed and kneaded. Once he slipped—and once more—but both

He found his hold, pulled himself up, climbed on. And on.

Beyond the *gendarmes* the going was again easier. The ridge broadened, buckled, and slanted skyward like a vast ruined staircase. He moved up through absolute stillness. There was no wind. Now and then a cold tide of air seemed to flow down from the heights above, pressing against his clothing and fingering through to the flesh. But the air made no sound. Earth and sky, mountain and valley—the whole world that spread above and beneath him—was as transfixed as the world of a dream, and in all of it only he, Rudi, was awake and moving and alive.

He moved on. The stillness deepened. The cold, too, seemed to deepen, creeping through his clothing, through his flesh, into his blood and bones.

Suddenly he stopped and turned. He had felt a shadow behind him. But when he looked back there was only the empty ridge slanting down into gray distance. . . . Squinting, he turned his gaze upward. Was it the sun? . . . No, the sun seemed the same as ever: yellow and flaming in the dark blue of the sky.

And yet—

His eyes searched the cliffs on the far side of the snowfield. Perhaps he could find something—anything—that lived and moved. But there was only rock and ice, space and stillness. Only the shadow that still hovered about him, and the coldness that seemed to touch his very heart. Suddenly fear gripped him. Fear far worse than that of failing; fear such as he had never known before in his life. "I cannot go on," he thought wildly. "It is the warning of the mountain."

He waited, motionless. As motionless as the rocks around him. And slowly, blessedly, he felt the fear draining from his body and heart. When he stood up again, the coldness was

gone. The shadow was gone. He studied the ridge above him, hitched up his pack, and began to climb.

He stepped up, balanced himself. Stepped once more—and stopped. Before him the ridge flared out into a curving, almost level platform, and beyond the platform rose a sheer wall of granite. As Rudi stared up at it his heart was pounding. For he had reached the Fortress.

If he was tired, he did not know it. If it was growing late, he did not know it. All he knew, all that mattered, was that he had gained his goal; that he was standing now on the highest point of the Citadel that any man had reached before him. A wave of emotion filled him, different from any he had ever known. It brought no need to exult, to yodel, to shout in triumph, as had always happened on his other, lesser mountain victories. What he felt was too deep for that; too strong for that.

Slowly his eyes moved upward over the great battlement before him, and he saw that it was indeed like the wall of a fortress. With a fifty-foot ladder based on the platform, a person could have topped it, but without the ladder it might as well have been a wall of glass. He looked to the right, where it merged into the east face of the mountain; then to the left where it joined the south face. And from that moment on he looked nowhere else, for he had seen what he was looking for. . . . "To the left," Captain Winter had said, "—that was Josef Matt's way. . . ." And it would be his, Rudi Matt's, way as well.

He moved toward where the platform curved out of sight above the south face, and in a moment he was standing on the edge of an abyss.[7] The platform still continued—or, rather, a narrow sloping ledge that formed an extension of

---

7. **abyss** (ə bis′): an immeasurably deep or bottomless pit.

times the friction of his body held him, and a moment later, with a final twist and thrust, he swung off of the bulge into the base of the cleft.

His shirt and trousers were torn. His fingers were bleeding. But he scarcely noticed them. All he had eyes for was the long slanting shaft that now rose directly above him up the sheer wall of the Fortress. And yet, he thought suddenly with a great lift of the heart—he had been right; his father had been right. The cleft extended all the way to the top of the precipice. It was climbable. It was the way past the Fortress!

Instinctively he started up. . . . And in the next instant stopped. . . . For in that instant, for the first time since he had begun the ascent of the ridge, he thought of the hour. He glanced at the sun and saw that it was halfway between the zenith and the western horizon. Obviously he had been climbing more than two hours, but how much more he could not be sure. "It is time to go back," he thought. "You *have* to go back." But it was one thing to think it and another to do it. A hundred feet above him, within easy reach, were the upper slopes of the Citadel, which no one had ever trod—or even seen. He could not go on up and explore them: that he knew. There was no choice but soon to start down. But first he must have one glimpse, one moment's experience, of that high, hidden world above the Fortress.

He moved up again. Stopped again. . . . No, he thought—it was too late even for that. He must turn back here. He must start down. . . . But when he moved again it was still forward, still upward. The prudence that tried to hold him back was no match for the magic that drew him on.

The lower third of the cleft presented no difficulties. Then followed a stretch where it became a sort of narrow smooth-walled shaft, which at first appeared impassable;

He found his hold, pulled himself up, climbed on. And on.

Beyond the *gendarmes* the going was again easier. The ridge broadened, buckled, and slanted skyward like a vast ruined staircase. He moved up through absolute stillness. There was no wind. Now and then a cold tide of air seemed to flow down from the heights above, pressing against his clothing and fingering through to the flesh. But the air made no sound. Earth and sky, mountain and valley—the whole world that spread above and beneath him—was as transfixed as the world of a dream, and in all of it only he, Rudi, was awake and moving and alive.

He moved on. The stillness deepened. The cold, too, seemed to deepen, creeping through his clothing, through his flesh, into his blood and bones.

Suddenly he stopped and turned. He had felt a shadow behind him. But when he looked back there was only the empty ridge slanting down into gray distance. . . . Squinting, he turned his gaze upward. Was it the sun? . . . No, the sun seemed the same as ever: yellow and flaming in the dark blue of the sky.

And yet—

His eyes searched the cliffs on the far side of the snow-field. Perhaps he could find something—anything—that lived and moved. But there was only rock and ice, space and stillness. Only the shadow that still hovered about him, and the coldness that seemed to touch his very heart. Suddenly fear gripped him. Fear far worse than that of failing; fear such as he had never known before in his life. "I cannot go on," he thought wildly. "It is the warning of the mountain."

He waited, motionless. As motionless as the rocks around him. And slowly, blessedly, he felt the fear draining from his body and heart. When he stood up again, the coldness was gone. The shadow was gone. He studied the ridge above him, hitched up his pack, and began to climb.

He stepped up, balanced himself. Stepped once more— and stopped. Before him the ridge flared out into a curving, almost level platform, and beyond the platform rose a sheer wall of granite. As Rudi stared up at it his heart was pounding. For he had reached the Fortress.

If he was tired, he did not know it. If it was growing late, he did not know it. All he knew, all that mattered, was that he had gained his goal; that he was standing now on the highest point of the Citadel that any man had reached before him. A wave of emotion filled him, different from any he had ever known. It brought no need to exult, to yodel, to shout in triumph, as had always happened on his other, lesser mountain victories. What he felt was too deep for that; too strong for that.

Slowly his eyes moved upward over the great battlement before him, and he saw that it was indeed like the wall of a fortress. With a fifty-foot ladder based on the platform, a person could have topped it, but without the ladder it might as well have been a wall of glass. He looked to the right, where it merged into the east face of the mountain; then to the left where it joined the south face. And from that moment on he looked nowhere else, for he had seen what he was looking for. . . . "To the left," Captain Winter had said, "—that was Josef Matt's way. . . . " And it would be his, Rudi Matt's, way as well.

He moved toward where the platform curved out of sight above the south face, and in a moment he was standing on the edge of an abyss.[7] The platform still continued—or, rather, a narrow sloping ledge that formed an extension of

---

7. **abyss** (ə bis'): an immeasurably deep or bottomless pit.

the platform—and he carefully followed it around. He took four steps—five—six. And stopped. The ledge ended, petering out into the vertical walls of the Fortress. But from its farthest end he could see what he had hoped to see: the one break in the great cliff's defenses. No more than five yards beyond him, and starting at about the level at which he stood, a long cleft, or chimney, slanted upward through the otherwise unbroken rock.

This, he knew, was the way past the Fortress—the "key" to the upper mountain which his father had found fifteen years before. From where he stood he could not see the inside of the cleft, but its depth and angle were such that he was sure he could climb it. If—*if* he could reach its base. . . .

Moving to the very end of the ledge, he studied the gap beyond. There was no place to stand—he could see that at once; nor were there any cracks or knobs for handholds. But the wall, though vertical, was not altogether smooth. The rock between ledge and cleft protruded in a sort of wrinkled bulge, and if one could cling to the bulge for as much as a few seconds it would be possible to worm one's way across. For a long moment he remained where he was; gazing, measuring. Then suddenly he moved. Stepping out from the ledge, he inched out onto the bulge, using not only hands and feet, as in ordinary climbing, but all of his body that he could bring into play. He gripped the rock with arms and legs, pressed against it with chest and thighs, holding on not by any actual support but by the friction of his moving weight. Space wheeled beneath him. The remote glaciers glinted. But once committed, he could not stop, or even hesitate, for such a maneuver had to be made quickly and in perfect rhythm, or it could not be made at all. His clothing scraped against the granite; his knees and elbows churned; his fingers clawed and kneaded. Once he slipped—and once more—but both times the friction of his body held him, and a moment later, with a final twist and thrust, he swung off of the bulge into the base of the cleft.

His shirt and trousers were torn. His fingers were bleeding. But he scarcely noticed them. All he had eyes for was the long slanting shaft that now rose directly above him up the sheer wall of the Fortress. And yet, he thought suddenly with a great lift of the heart—he had been right; his father had been right. The cleft extended all the way to the top of the precipice. It was climbable. It was the way past the Fortress!

Instinctively he started up. . . . And in the next instant stopped. . . . For in that instant, for the first time since he had begun the ascent of the ridge, he thought of the hour. He glanced at the sun and saw that it was halfway between the zenith and the western horizon. Obviously he had been climbing more than two hours, but how much more he could not be sure. "It is time to go back," he thought. "You *have* to go back." But it was one thing to think it and another to do it. A hundred feet above him, within easy reach, were the upper slopes of the Citadel, which no one had ever trod—or even seen. He could not go on up and explore them: that he knew. There was no choice but soon to start down. But first he must have one glimpse, one moment's experience, of that high, hidden world above the Fortress.

He moved up again. Stopped again. . . . No, he thought—it was too late even for that. He must turn back here. He must start down. . . . But when he moved again it was still forward, still upward. The prudence that tried to hold him back was no match for the magic that drew him on.

The lower third of the cleft presented no difficulties. Then followed a stretch where it became a sort of narrow smooth-walled shaft, which at first appeared impassable;

THAT'S ENTERTAINMENT

PREPARING FOR READING

Learning Vocabulary

1. Alicia confided her plans for becoming a famous singer-songwriter to her mother.
2. Marshall Brickman, Woody Allen's collaborator, wrote some of the films Allen produced.
3. Alicia wrote old-fashioned ballads, but she also wrote contemporary music.
4. Steve spoke with conviction as he described Alicia's talents in his endorsement of her.
5. He felt his opinion would be considered objective if his friendship with Alicia were not known.
6. Alicia wished she could have been more eloquent in her conversation, and not just have mumbled.

confided	collaborator	contemporary	conviction
endorsement	objective	eloquent	

Developing Background and Skills
Draw Conclusions

Read the paragraph below.

The girl sat stiffly in the darkened room, tightly clutching her guitar case. The only light was focused on a young man singing on a makeshift stage. As soon as he had finished his song, the girl's name was called. She rose and advanced hesitantly toward the spotlight.

As you began to read, did you wonder where the girl was and what she was doing there? As you continued to read, you probably decided that she was at an audition.

When you decided that, you were **drawing conclusions**. A conclusion is a decision based on information and experience.

Drawing conclusions is an important reading skill. Writers do not always tell you everything about the characters, the setting, and the events in their stories. (You would probably be bored if they did!) But they do give you information that, along with your own experience, you can use to draw certain conclusions. When you are "forced to use your imagination," you may find that you become more involved in a story, and the story will probably be more interesting to you.

In order to draw conclusions, you must think carefully about the information a writer presents. You must also rely on your own experience: what you know from what you've done and seen or heard and read about. Read the sentences below. What conclusion can you draw?

> Steve told Alicia that she was good, really good, but that it was important to keep practicing. For the next three weeks, Alicia practiced three hours every day.

Were you able to conclude that Alicia valued Steve's opinion?

In the selection that follows, the author explains a great deal about the characters and the situation. As you read, think about what questions you have that the author leaves unanswered. Use the information provided and your own experience to draw conclusions that answer your questions about the characters, the setting, and the events.

THE AUDITION

MARISA GIOFFRE

How pathetic can you get? My first big break and I can't even tune my guitar, that's how badly my hands are shaking. If I'm this nervous while I'm alone in my room, how crazed will I be when I get to my audition at the Great Wave? I'm afraid I already know the answer. At best, I'll be a borderline basket case. At worst, they'll have to cart me off the stage in a straitjacket.

I wonder if Linda Ronstadt was a wreck before *her* first professional audition. I'll have to remember to ask her after we become chummy. Even if Linda and I never become fast friends, there'll be plenty of opportunities to compare notes on the subject; for instance, at the party following the Grammy Awards or backstage at Madison Square Garden on a night we're both appearing at a benefit concert. By then, I probably won't even remember what it feels like to have stage fright. Who knows? I might even laugh when I look back on today.

When Papa was alive, we would take walks through Central Park on days he wasn't working. I'd tell him how I planned to become a famous singer-songwriter when I grew up. He never made me feel like it was a crazy dream. With Mama, it's another story. One night I confided my plans to her as we were clearing away the dinner dishes. "If things go according to schedule, I should have a gold record by the time I'm twenty-one," I said. She raised her eyebrows. That should have been sufficient warning. But like a fool, I continued. "Maybe I'll have even won a Grammy by then."

"Why not, Alicia? And maybe tonight when we turn on the news, we'll find out the mayor has sold Manhattan back to the Indians," she answered.

Ordinarily Mama doesn't have much sense of humor. That's because she worries so much, especially since Papa died four years ago. The truck my father was driving crashed on a New Jersey highway one night. It's still hard for me to talk about it.

Anyway, Mama may never have joked all the time like her sister Yolanda, but some of her put-downs can be pretty funny.

The little clock on my bureau says ten to four. It's almost time to leave for the audition. Steve will murder me if I'm late. He's the reason I'm in this mess. He's the emcee at the Great Wave coffee house, and he arranged the tryout for me.

Steve and I have been buddies since our freshman year. After our last class today, he must have known I was having second thoughts about the audition. He said to me, "Just remember Marshall Brickman's famous line."

I was confused. "That nerdy guy who sits behind me in trigonometry?" I asked.

Steve looked appalled. "Not Marshall *Bromberg*, nitwit. Marshall *Brickman*. Woody Allen's lifelong collaborator. The genius who wrote all his best films with him before branching out on his own."

"Okay, so what did this Marshall Brickman say?"

"He said that eighty percent of life is showing up. Isn't it an absolutely brilliant insight?"

"I don't get it," I answered truthfully.

"He's saying you have to be willing to put yourself on the line . . . that you can't hit a home run, unless you get up to bat."

"Last time I got up to bat, I nearly got beaned by the pitcher's spit ball," I reminded him.

Steve sighed and his blue-gray eyes looked melancholy. I hate it when he acts hurt because we're not on the same wavelength, as if I'm misunderstanding him on purpose.

"Why don't we just drop it, Marin?" he retorted. Steve always calls me by my last name. I think he just prefers the way Marin sounds. Alicia is old-fashioned, but Marin is more contemporary.

With departure time approaching, I can see Brickman's point of view a lot more clearly. For starters, showing up takes courage. Particularly when your guitar has a flat C sharp and a hopeless G. Linda Ronstadt might have had knots in her stomach the first time she sang for strangers, but I'll bet anything her guitar was in tune. Get a grip on yourself, Marin, I tell myself. I zip my guitar case in one quick motion, no small accomplishment when you consider my hand tremor. Then I look in the mirror one last time. To be honest, I look flushed. I feel my forehead. It's warm. Maybe I'm developing a fever.

It's too late to cancel out, so just make the best of it, I tell myself. I hurry through the apartment, double lock the door, and rush down the stairs.

Right now, as the bus crawls along, I'm trying to decide what would be worse: If I botch up my song during the audition this afternoon, or if I open my mouth to sing and absolutely no sound comes out. It *could* happen. Mr. Aarons, our guidance counselor, says that extreme stress can trigger a hysterical paralysis. To tell the truth, I think developing a hysterical paralysis wouldn't be so bad. For one thing, everybody would feel sorry for me. And Jessica Flynn, who owns the Great Wave, might even let me audition again someday when I've got it more together.

The Great Wave is sort of funky and real classy at the same time, if that makes any sense. To hear Steve tell it, it's one of the best showcases in town for young performers. The pay isn't great, and you have to wait on tables between sets. But Steve swears record producers and talent agents cover the shows all the time. When I pinned him down, he admitted they showed up only occasionally. "But it still beats singing on your stoop, Marin," Steve pointed out. No argument there.

On the night I checked out the Great Wave, Jessica seemed pretty nice. If I bomb out today, I'm praying she will just let me slink away quietly. I'd die if she made a cutting remark in front of everybody. Something like, "Young lady, if I were you, I'd be grateful the composer isn't around to hear how you mangled that song." If she said that, I'd never have the guts to tell her the truth. Namely, that the song I'd mangled was one of my own.

Suddenly, I notice the street sign. I'm practically there, and I scramble to get off the bus. I'm late. Now that zero hour is here, I remember Steve's final advice: "The main thing, Marin, is to *act* confident—even if you're not."

Steve's right. So what if I feel like pure jelly? There's no reason to let Jessica Flynn in on that fact. I toss my head back defiantly. Then I march toward the Great Wave and swing open the door.

Me and my big ideas. I didn't have to wait to get on stage to make a fool of myself. I managed to do it the minute I walked in the door. I'd pushed it open so hard it banged back with a thud—smack in the middle of someone else's audition.

Steve, who is sitting beside Jessica, glares at me. My heart drops when I notice Jessica frowning as she sizes me up. Some great first impression. I mouth the words "I'm sorry." To my relief, she smiles, as if to say it's no big deal. Steve, however, still looks disapproving. So much for counting on him. He's assisting Jessica with the auditions. Now he gets up and walks around, looking very official, a clipboard in his hand, a pencil behind his ear. Sometimes he can be a real pain.

Meanwhile, the guy whose audition I disrupted is still pouring his heart out. He's tall and wiry and very intense. The ballad he's singing sounds pretty flowery, and a piano player is backing him up with some very fancy chords. Truthfully, I'm not impressed.

Steve ambles over to me in this very casual manner. He decided beforehand that it would be a good idea if we pretended to be just acquaintances rather than fast friends. That way Jessica would consider his endorsement of me an objective opinion. I don't know why he assumed she'd depend on his judgment, because she hardly seems the type of person who needs help making up her mind.

"Great entrance," Steve mutters to me under his breath as he checks my name off his list. I knew he wouldn't be able to resist rubbing it in.

"You told me to walk in like I own the place," I say in defense.

"Like you own it, not like you're out to demolish it."

"Am I late?" I ask. Anything to change the subject.

"You just made it. Calm down."

That's easy enough for him to say. Suddenly it's hit me hard. Eighty percent of life may be showing up, but it's the other twenty percent that really matters—what you do once you get there.

Steve realizes I'm a wreck and takes pity on me. "Just sing like you do when you're at home, Marin, and you can't miss." Not only does he say this with conviction, but he smiles at me. Steve is no Robert Redford, but he does have an excellent smile. To be fair about it, Steve has other nice qualities. He's one of the few people who takes my dream seriously. To be perfectly blunt, he's the *only* person who takes it seriously.

The guy who was singing a moment ago is already on his way out. "She'll let me know—I like that," I overhear him griping to his accompanist. From the sound of it, J.F. has given him the brush-off. She calls me forward.

"Jessica, this is—uh—Alicia Marin," Steve says, glancing down at the sheet before he tells her my name. That's how hard he's trying to pretend we hardly know each other. What a character. If he keeps up this routine, I swear I'll crack up.

"Hello, Alicia," Jessica says warmly. She has a very soothing voice. "What are you going to sing for us today?" she asks. She has a very calming effect on me, and I realize

that even if I'm lousy, she's too nice to say anything cruel.

"It's called *My City Song*."

"Well, anytime you're ready." I'm as ready as I'll ever be, so I plunge right in.

"The boys on the corner, talkin'
They whistle as I pass through,
But I don't look, I keep on walkin'
On my block, that's what nice girls do. . . ."

Surprisingly enough, my voice doesn't sound shaky. In fact, it fills the room. A look of relief crosses Steve's face, and Jessica Flynn leans forward. Not a lot, but enough to convey the impression I'm not boring her to death. I unwind a little.

"But in my heart, I know they're shy,
That's why they come on so strong,
And I sing
La la la le lo.
My city song."

Believe it or not, Jessica seems even more attentive. Steve is starting to look very pleased with himself. Best of all, I discover I am actually enjoying myself.

"Rumble of the subway, passin' by
Green banana man, you hear his cry,
Pigeons on the roof, too fat to fly
I can hear the music,
City, let me use it. . . ."

240

By the time I finish, I'm really cooking. I look up and see that Steve is grinning. Jessica's reaction is more reserved, but when she says, "Good song, Alicia," it's with real enthusiasm.

"Where did you find it?" she asks.

"I wrote it," I answer.

"Have you written many songs?"

"A few here and there," I mumble idiotically. Suddenly I feel excruciatingly shy.

It's funny how much more comfortable I felt when I was singing, than I do now answering questions. Fortunately, Steve comes to my rescue. "She's written dozens of them. Ballads, uptempo stuff, and all of it's special." I stand there staring at my feet. Compliments always make me squirm.

"You'll have a chance to try your songs out here," Jessica says in a matter-of-fact way.

Is this really happening to me?

"I have an opening for five nights a week," she continues. "That sound good to you?"

"Sounds great." *Why can't I be more eloquent?*

"Remember, you'll be singing only about one-tenth of the time. The rest you'll be waiting on tables. Have you ever waitressed before?"

I'd forgotten about that part of the deal. "No," I admit.

Jessica is silent. She must be having second thoughts about hiring me. I knew it was too good to be true.

To my relief, she says, "You'll learn. Talk to Larry Egans, our Assistant Manager. He'll brief you."

"Uh-huh," I reply brilliantly. I continue to stand there like a dummy until I notice Steve gesturing me to get off the stage. Apparently, Jessica's last sentence had been my exit cue. But in my shock at being hired I didn't pick up on it. I clear the stage with all the grace of a robot as Steve calls for the next auditionee.

When he meets me outside a few minutes later, I finally emerge from my daze. "Someone is actually going to pay me to sing my songs!"

"I knew Jessica would like you," Steve answers. His tone implies his confidence in me had never failed. He could have fooled me, but I decide to let it pass.

"You're on your way, Marin," he adds. "Today the Great Wave, tomorrow Madison Square Garden." Steve is as excited as I am. This makes me feel I've been a little hard on him. What's fair is fair. Not only did he set up the audition, he shamed me into not copping out.

"Play your cards right, and I'll dedicate my first album to you." That's as close as I can come to saying thank you.

"I'm really touched, Marin." I guess that's as close as he can come to saying you're welcome.

Questions

1. Why was Alicia embarrassed by the way she made her first entrance at the Great Wave?
2. Why do you think singers and musicians would want to perform at the Great Wave?
3. Alicia presented herself as nervous and worried before the audition. Do you think she was as uncertain about her abilities as she made herself out to be? Explain your answer.
4. Imagine that you were Alicia's friend. What advice would you have given her about preparing for and performing at the audition? Draw on your own experience.

Applying Reading Skills

Read the paragraph listed after each number below. Then write the conclusion that can be drawn from the information in the paragraph.

1. Page 233, first paragraph
   a. Linda Ronstadt was a successful performer whom Alicia admired.
   b. Linda Ronstadt and Alicia were friends.
   c. Linda Ronstadt and Alicia would someday appear together at a benefit.
2. Page 233, third paragraph
   a. Mrs. Marin had a sense of humor.
   b. Mrs. Marin worried a lot.
   c. Mrs. Marin thought it unlikely that Alicia would ever become a successful performer.
3. Page 238, eighth paragraph
   a. Jessica probably will not hire the singer.
   b. Jessica will probably hire the singer later.
   c. The singer thought he had not performed well.

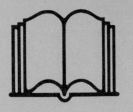

PREPARING FOR READING

Learning Vocabulary

1. The Apollo Theatre is <u>unique</u> among the theatres of New York City.
2. For years the Apollo held a regular <u>amateur</u> night, when hopeful performers could display their talents.
3. For more than a decade, big bands <u>dominated</u> evenings at the Apollo, but in the 1950s, they were replaced by small rock 'n' roll groups.
4. By the 1970s, the neighborhood around the theatre became rundown and had <u>deteriorated</u> so much that attendance had fallen.
5. Concerned businesspeople and city officials worked together to <u>renovate</u> the theatre as a neighborhood center.

unique   amateur   dominated
deteriorated   renovate

Developing Background and Skills
Main Idea

You know that in a well-written paragraph, the sentences are all related to one another. The most important point is called the **main idea**. The other information given in the paragraph makes up the **supporting details**.

Sometimes the main idea is stated in a single sentence that may come at the beginning, in the middle, or at the end of the paragraph. Read the paragraph below and see if you can find the main idea.

A theatre is a building or place where plays and other spectacles are performed. The word *theatre* comes from a Greek word meaning "a place for seeing." There are many different kinds of theatres. The first Greek theatres were marked-out circles at the foot of a hill. Later, rows of seats were built into the hillside. In medieval times, platforms or wagons were stages for plays presented in town squares or marketplaces. Many of today's theatres are shaped like rectangles and have a raised stage at one end. However, some modern theatres are built "in the round." The audience surrounds a central platform in a full circle.

Did you decide that the main idea is stated in the third sentence? What information given in the other sentences supports the main idea?

When writers do not directly state the main idea, you can use the details presented to state the main idea in your own words. Read the paragraph below.

Early Greek theatres were marked-out circles at the foot of a hill. Later, seats were built into the hillside. In the Middle Ages, platforms or wagons became stages for performers. Later the rectangular theatre developed; it is the style common today. Another modern type is the theatre in the round, in which the audience is seated in a full circle around a central stage.

You probably figured out that the main idea of this paragraph is the same as that of the first paragraph. But here the main idea is not stated at all. It is only implied, or suggested, by the details given.

As you read the next selection, look for the main idea of each paragraph. Find the details that support both stated and implied main ideas.

"It's SHOWTIME at the APOLLO!"

Through a silver curtain, multicolored lights outline a band playing a mellow blues with a dancing beat. As the audience begins to cheer, the curtain slowly rises. The music rises, too. Slowly the steady wah-wah of the saxophones is topped by the sharp high notes of the trumpets and the rat-a-tat-tat of the drums. A handsome man steps quickly to the front of the stage. He takes a microphone that grew like magic from the wooden floor.

"Ladies and gentlemen," he says with a wave of his hand and a big smile. "Welcome to the Apollo Theatre!"

For more than fifty years the red neon sign of the Apollo Theatre has been the brightest light on New York City's 125th Street, the Broadway of Harlem. Through the decades, however, the Apollo has been more than a theatre for Harlemites. It has been a center of their community and has become a symbol of a proud tradition. So many of the great artists of American popular music have appeared on its stage that the history of the Apollo is also the history of a half-century of music.

THE SWINGING THIRTIES

When the Apollo opened its doors in 1935, the swing sound of big bands was the most popular style of jazz. Big bands featured trumpets, trombones, and saxophones. They often had twenty or more musicians. Big bands played hot jazz for dancing and cool jazz for quiet listening.

The big bands of Duke Ellington and Count Basie (bā′ sē) were the top favorites of Apollo audiences during the theatre's first ten years. Fans called Ellington and Basie "The Royalty of Jazz." The Duke and the Count were both pianists. Both played swing, but the flavor of each man's music was very distinct.

Edward Kennedy Ellington first wanted to be a painter. Perhaps that is why his music sounded like shades of many colors delicately mixed. Ellington often gave his songs colorful titles like "Azure," "Black Butterfly," and "Mood Indigo." He knew exactly how to combine the tones of each instrument to create the sounds of any mood, from lively joy to regretful sorrow.

William Basie began playing music in Kansas City night-clubs, where the band's job was to make the audience dance. Then he played the piano for vaudeville shows that made audiences laugh. Not surprisingly, the Basie band had a friendly, good-humored sound and a powerful, toe-tapping rhythm. On a good night at the Apollo, when Count Basie's band was really swinging, the whole building seemed to shake. As one Apollo regular put it, "The music seemed to lift us out of our seats and up through the roof."

HOME SWEET HOME

In the 1940s and early 1950s, female vocalists started singing with the big bands. These women became some of the Apollo's biggest stars. Lena Horne went on from the Apollo to stardom in Hollywood and Broadway musicals. Sarah Vaughan (vän) became a jazz singer as well known in Europe as in the United States. The two women singers most fondly remembered at the Apollo, however, are Billie Holiday and Ella Fitzgerald.

"There's nothing like an audience at the Apollo," laughed Billie Holiday as she came offstage one night after a standing ovation. For the Apollo, there was no one like Billie. Lady Day, as her fans called her, had a unique way of turning a simple song into a dramatic emotional statement.

A tall woman, she stood straight and still while she sang. Much of her music was flavored with sadness. Even in her love songs, black audiences could hear the pain Billie felt from racial prejudice. They cheered her for expressing the emotions they also felt deeply.

Left to right: Billie Holiday and the Hot Lips Page Band, Duke Ellington with his band, Ella Fitzgerald

249

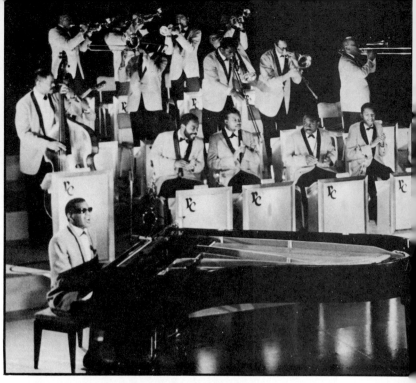

During the early 1960s, Apollo audiences rocked to the sound of James Brown (left) and Ray Charles (above).

Ella Fitzgerald sings with a natural grace and a bubbling sense of fun. She first sang at the Apollo on the regular Wednesday Amateur Night. She won the contest that week and every Wednesday afterwards, until owner Frank Schiffman gave her a paid booking. Ella soon felt so at home at the Apollo that she set up a picnic table in her dressing room for the other performers and the theatre crew.

The Apollo was home for many entertainers who often spent months on the road. Working at the Apollo meant a long day. There were four shows and a movie between each one. Performers arrived there in the morning and stayed until late at night. Waiting through the hours before going on, musicians, comedians, and dancers chatted together. Old-timers gave newcomers tips on how to perfect their acts. Performers working at other New York City theatres flocked to the Apollo to say hello to friends and hear the latest news. "The Apollo was known as the Big Top," said tap dancer Honi (hun′ ē) Coles. "It was the center of everything."

THE APOLLO ROCKS

Rock 'n' roll changed popular music in the middle of the 1950s. Small groups dominated by electric guitars replaced the big bands. The leaders of this change came to the Apollo from Chicago, Illinois. Muddy Waters was first with his electric blues. Then came Chuck Berry and Bo Didley with their uptempo rock.

When Elvis Presley arrived in New York from his home-town of Memphis, Tennessee, he went straight to the Apollo to see Bo Didley. After he became famous himself, Presley went back to the Apollo many times. He always got new ideas on how to excite an audience.

Ray Charles was another great artist in the rock move-ment. Teenagers who liked Fats Domino and Little Richard liked Charles's rock songs. Older listeners loved his ballads, which reminded them of Count Basie and Duke Ellington. Like the Count and the Duke, Ray Charles is also a pianist. But Apollo audiences gave him his title, Brother Ray, for his extraordinary singing voice. Charles could go from a growled whisper to a high shout on one breath. He could make talking, laughing, and even crying part of his songs.

James Brown was Ray Charles's chief rival at the Apollo in the early 1960s. Brown brought a whole show with him to the theatre. He called it the James Brown Revue. It included his own band, background singers, dancers, and comedians to warm up the audience. Brown called himself

Some of the brightest stars in show business have shone forth on the well-worn planks of the Apollo's stage. During the 1960s, four of the biggest show-stoppers were (left to right): Stevie Wonder, Smokey Robinson and the Miracles, Aretha Franklin, and Diana Ross and the Supremes.

"The Hardest Working Man in Show Business." Onstage he proved it, singing and dancing to the point of collapse.

It took a whole company to mount a show that could equal the James Brown Revue. That company was Motown. Motown was founded by businessman Berry Gordy and singer-songwriter William "Smokey" Robinson. Together they created the Motown Sound, a popular blues-rock music that appealed equally to black and white audiences. They also assembled a "family" of artists. That family included singers Diana Ross and Stevie Wonder, and groups like the Four Tops and the Temptations.

The Apollo became a second home for the Motown family. Wonder recalls that when he first played there, he was in the sixth grade. "I was called Little Stevie Wonder then," he has said. "Through high school, my dressing room was my schoolroom. Everybody helped me with my homework."

A LITTLE BIT OF SOUL

The "soul" music of the 1960s expressed the spirit of black pride that marked the decade. Soul music combined the beat of the blues, the horns of big band jazz, and the intense feeling of gospel music. Singers like Wilson Pickett and Otis Redding sometimes crooned, sometimes shouted their songs. What mattered to Apollo audiences was how much honest emotion, or soul, they poured into their music. Aretha Franklin was the Apollo's favorite among this new generation of performers.

Lady Soul, as some fans called her, brought a new personal intensity to popular music. "I've got the music in me," Aretha sang in one song; in another, "I'm young, gifted, and black, and that's a fact!" Aretha Franklin was one of the first women artists to create the musical arrangements for her own records. A strong-minded person, she spelled out in song what was important to her: "R-E-S-P-E-C-T."

A NEW BEGINNING

In the 1970s attendance at the Apollo began to decline. By then many blacks had moved from Harlem to neighborhoods all over New York City and the suburban towns of the area. Going to the Apollo became a long trip. Former Apollo stars like Ray Charles and Aretha Franklin became so popular that they performed in concert halls far larger than the twelve-hundred seat Apollo. The neighborhood around the theatre also deteriorated. Many stores were vacant and boarded up. Street violence kept couples and families home at night. The Apollo finally closed in 1976. For the next nine years, the stage and the red velvet seats gathered dust.

Harlem, however, never forgot the Apollo. Business people, bankers, and city officials worked together to renovate the theatre as the center of a neighborhood rebuilding program. In May, 1985, just in time for the Apollo's fiftieth anniversary, they were successful. The theatre's new owners had not only repainted and recarpeted the Apollo. They had also installed a fully-equipped video recording studio so that the stage could be used to produce shows for television. Motown brought in an all-star cast for the Apollo's gala re-opening celebration. That show was taped and became a three-hour special shown a few weeks later on network television.

Today the Apollo is still not open seven nights a week as it was in its heyday, but there are shows most weekends. Many shows feature Spanish music to attract the new Hispanic residents of the area. One thing has not changed at all, however. Amateur Night still fills the theatre every Wednesday.

Wilson Pickett (above) and an all-star
cast (below) celebrate the Apollo's gala
re-opening.

CATCH A RISING STAR

One recent Amateur Night, emcee Ralph Cooper danced out to the microphone, dapper in a lavender suit. "This is the place," he told the cheering crowd. "The Apollo is *us*!"

This Wednesday, Cooper said, was Top Dog Night. It featured the best amateurs selected from the previous three Wednesdays. Some of the young performers seemed nervous and unsure of themselves when they walked out. But once the music started and the audience shouted encouragement, they relaxed and worked like professional entertainers. Rod Wayne drew cheers for his pure high notes. The Electric Company got laughs and "wows" of amazement at their loose-jointed break dancing. Girls in the front row jumped up to catch a red rose that singer Chop Turner threw them.

After two hours and twenty-one performers, it was time for voting. All the amateurs crowded together under the bright lights. Cooper went from one to another, calling their names and asking for applause. Those that got a weak response, he asked to step back. They did, disappointed but still smiling. Then there were only nine in front, then seven, then four, two, and finally one—Alonzia (ə lôn′ zē ə).

This tall young man in a blue suit had electrified the crowd with his gospel rapping. He started to laugh when he knew he had won. But when he shook hands with Cooper and accepted a first prize of $2,000, there were tears in his eyes. The audience gave him a deafening standing ovation.

"Thank you for trying, for working, and for hoping," Cooper told all the amateurs. Then he turned to the audience. "For coming out tonight, and for your encouragement, support, and love through the years, I thank you. The performers thank you, and most of all, the Apollo thanks you. See you next Wednesday. Good night!"

Questions

1. Choose three of the performers mentioned in the selection and write two sentences about each.
2. Why did the Apollo close its doors for so many years?
3. Do you think it is important to preserve and maintain historic places such as the Apollo? Explain your answer.
4. Have you ever watched (live or on TV) or taken part in an amateur contest? Describe the event.

Applying Reading Skills

A. Find the paragraph in "The Legendary Apollo" from which each of the numbered sentences below is taken. Read the paragraph and decide whether the sentence is a main idea or a supporting detail. Write your answers.

1. For more than fifty years, the red neon sign of the Apollo has been the brightest light on New York City's 125th Street, the Broadway of Harlem.
2. Performers working at other New York City theatres flocked to the Apollo to say hello to friends and hear the latest news.
3. James Brown was Ray Charles's chief rival at the Apollo in the early 1960s.
4. In the 1970s attendance at the Apollo began to decline.

B. Read the paragraph listed after each number below. Then, in your own words, state the main idea.

1. The first paragraph under "Home Sweet Home"
2. The fifth paragraph under "The Apollo Rocks"
3. The first paragraph under "A Little Bit of Soul"

PREPARING FOR READING

Learning Vocabulary

1. Debbie Allen is a <u>multitalented</u> entertainer who acts, sings, directs, choreographs, and produces.
2. Debbie experienced <u>rejection</u> at several important points in her career, but she never gave up.
3. At eight, Debbie was rejected by the Houston Ballet, but at 14, she was accepted and given a full <u>scholarship</u>.
4. Debbie had a small part in the movie *Fame*, and later she went on to direct and produce <u>episodes</u> of the TV series based on the movie.
5. Debbie sums up her outlook with the <u>philosophy</u> that those who achieve and maintain fame have not only worked for it but also chosen it.

multitalented   rejection   scholarship
episodes   philosophy

Developing Background and Skills
Author's Purpose and Point of View

Authors write for many different reasons. The reason that an author has for writing is called the **author's purpose**. Read the chart below.

PURPOSE	EXAMPLE
1. to entertain	a joke
2. to persuade	an advertisement
3. to give factual information	an encyclopedia article
4. to describe	a "help-wanted" advertisement
5. to explain	directions for making something

If you think carefully about the purposes, you will probably realize that 3, 4, and 5 may overlap. For example, a poster may give you factual information about a coming event. It may also describe the event to take place and explain how to get to the place where it will be held. In fact, two or more purposes are often combined in written material.

Usually, however, one purpose is more important than the others. Read the paragraph below and see if you can decide what the author's main purpose is.

Don't miss the Ronnie Larson show on Channel 10 this Friday at 7:30. Ronnie will be his usual fun-filled self, and, in addition, he will be interviewing an Olympic champion, a newly elected governor, and a kooky inventor.

Would you agree that the author's main purpose is to persuade? Would another purpose be to describe?

Besides having a purpose, an author also has a point of view. The **author's point of view** refers to his or her attitude about something. Authors reveal their point of view by their choice of words. Which of the following passages was written by an author who probably thinks television is a waste of time? What words helped you to know?

● TV is the great wasteland of our time. The new shows look like the old ones. The rerun season is longer than the regular season.
● You never know what you'll discover as you change channels—musicals, movies, science reports, dance, and drama. TV has it all.

In the selection that follows, you will be presented with a great deal of information. As you read, try to figure out what the author's main purpose is for writing the article. Try to determine the author's point of view. How does the author feel about the people and events she describes?

FAME IS

DOROTHY SCHEUER

Most people are lucky if they can juggle two jobs successfully. Debbie Allen has managed to juggle at least nine. Debbie is probably best known for her role as Lydia Grant on the TV series "Fame." But this multitalented entertainer is much more than an actress. She is also a dancer, a choreographer, a singer, a director, and a producer. She has been in movies and on Broadway stages. She has performed at the Apollo Theatre and cut a record album. She's a wife, a mother, and a teacher.

What made Debbie decide to become a juggler? How did she become so successful at it?

Debbie was born in Houston, Texas, in the early 1950s. She was one of four children. Debbie's parents talked to their children about history and art. They gave them lessons in music and dancing. They encouraged them to find out what they

NOT ENOUGH

were best at, and then to "go for it." Debbie decided early what she wanted to "go for" first. "At five I knew I wanted to be a ballerina," she says. "I just knew I could do it."

When Debbie was eight, she auditioned for the Houston Ballet Foundation—and was turned down. The experience didn't shake her faith in herself. With her mother's encouragement, Debbie continued to take private ballet lessons. When she was fourteen, a teacher from the Houston Ballet Foundation saw her dance and invited her to enter the school, with a full scholarship.

When Debbie graduated from high school, she wanted to continue her dance training at the North Carolina School of the Arts. "My dancing at the audition was so good that they used me to demonstrate for the other kids," Debbie remembers. "But when we were finished, the dance director told me I hadn't made it, that I was 'built wrong' for dance. I was crushed."

After this rejection, Debbie stopped dancing for a year, but she didn't give up on her education. Her parents had divorced when she was seven, and although she lived with her mother, she remained close to her father. He felt strongly that she should go to college, and she agreed. She graduated from Howard University with honors—and with acting experience from theater classes and stage performances.

Debbie moved to New York to pursue her career. Her sister Phylicia (fə lē′ shə) had arrived there ahead of her. Phylicia had also trained as a dancer and an actress, but both women say there was only the normal sibling rivalry between them. "We grew up understanding that if one of us made it, we all made it," Phylicia says. "One success was a success for everybody."

In fact, Phylicia helped make some of Debbie's success possible. It was Phylicia who was first offered a role in the Broadway musical *Raisin*, based on the play *A Raisin in the*

In 1973 Debbie won critical praise for her portrayal of Beneatha in *Raisin*.

Vivian Ayers-Allen with her talented and famous daughters, Phylicia (left) and Debbie (right).

Sun. She turned the job down because she was about to have a baby, but she recommended her sister. Debbie started out in the chorus and later moved up to a lead. Years later, Phylicia was offered a role in Richard Pryor's semi-autobiographical movie *Jo Jo Dancer, Your Life Is Calling*. She had other commitments and had to say no again. Debbie wound up with the part. (Phylicia went on to become a celebrity, under the married name of Phylicia Rashad, in the role of Clair Huxtable on TV's "The Cosby Show.")

By 1980, Debbie had already appeared on Broadway, on television, and in the movies. She had credits for dancing, acting, singing, and choreography. Then she was offered a role as a student at the School of the Arts in the movie *Fame*. The part was supposed to be large—just right for the star she had already become. But before Debbie's scenes came up for filming, the focus of the movie changed. She was left with a single scene and a total of two lines.

When *Fame* turned into a TV series, the producers remembered Debbie's delivery of those two lines. She was offered the starring role of dance teacher Lydia Grant.

At that moment, Debbie may have remembered her own definition of luck: "when opportunity meets preparation." She was prepared, and here was an opportunity. Debbie decided to take a risk. She said she would take the part on "Fame" only if she could also have the job of choreographing the dance sequences. The risk paid off. She got both jobs.

The "Fame" series brought Debbie her greatest fame so far. Starting as actress/dancer/choreographer, she later became manager of the program's dance company. Her responsibilities covered everything from hiring and firing the dancers to approving the costumes they wore while performing the routines she worked out for them. She went on to direct and co-produce episodes.

In addition to working, she was learning. That meant she was creating more opportunities for herself, both on the series and elsewhere. While she was working on "Fame," she cut her first record album. She also returned to Broadway to star in the musical *Sweet Charity*, and she began making plans for other film and theater projects, some based on her own original ideas.

Debbie Allen is successful because she has been determined. She has had confidence in herself. She has had the support and help of people she could trust. She has been willing to work hard and to take chances. And she has always wanted a little bit more.

"Lydia Grant is a great character," she said once about one of the most important roles in her career. "But she certainly doesn't fulfill my ability as an actress. The degree of difficulty I need is just not there." When things weren't hard enough for Debbie, she found ways to make more demands on *herself*, by taking on more responsibility or by starting new projects.

"I would rather spend time with my daughter, Vivian, than do a lot of the things I do," Debbie insists. "If I have to make a choice, it's always going to be her."

Also in Debbie's favor is that she learned early what to do when she heard "No."

"Being a singer and dancer and actress meant there might be more work for me," she says. "But for a long time it just meant there were more ways I could get rejected." Debbie experienced rejection at some crucial points in her life. When she was just starting out, she was rejected by the Houston Ballet Foundation and the North Carolina School of the Arts. She received wonderful reviews in the movie *Ragtime*, yet it still took three years for another film offer to come along. When Debbie couldn't study with one teacher at one school, she found another. When she couldn't dance, she acted. When she couldn't perform, she taught. When movie roles didn't come rolling in, she concentrated on commercials and series TV. And when the theater didn't seem to have the right plays, she dreamed some up herself. She never gave up.

Debbie was also willing to pay fame's costs. "Sweat"— as Lydia Grant would repeatedly tell her students—is just one of those costs. Being famous is hard work. You work hard to achieve fame, to stay famous, and to protect the rest of your life from your fame. Fame eats into your privacy, your time, and your personal relationships. Says Debbie: "Being famous isn't *always* glamorous. Only the ones who are living it can decide if the costs are worth the rewards to them. Those who achieve fame and maintain it haven't just worked for it, they've chosen it."

Debbie Allen has been working hard on her choices since she was five years old. Her philosophy suggests that she doesn't mind the hard work. "It's almost as though you live so you can create," she explains. "You receive so you can give."

Questions

1. List four of Debbie Allen's achievements.
2. In what way did Debbie's sister play an important role in Debbie's early success?
3. Do you agree with Debbie's definition of luck: "when opportunity meets preparation"? Explain your answer.
4. Describe the goals you have for yourself. Explain what you have done so far to work toward those goals. How has encouragement or discouragement affected your attitude about your goals?

Applying Reading Skills

Read the incomplete sentences below, which are based on "Fame Is Not Enough." Write the phrase that best completes each sentence.

1. The author's main purpose in writing the selection was ____.
    a. to entertain
    b. to persuade
    c. to give factual information
    d. to describe
    e. to explain
2. From the viewpoint of the author, Debbie Allen ____.
    a. is a successful person
    b. has achieved more fame than her talents deserve
    c. has been very lucky
    d. should never have been discouraged in her ambitions
3. The author would probably agree with the opinion that ____.
    a. rejection helps weed out untalented performers
    b. family encouragement is the best means to achieve success
    c. talent, hard work, and perseverance are important elements in achieving success
    d. fame is always worth what it costs

To fling my arms wide
In some place of the sun
To whirl and to dance
Till the white day is done.
Then rest at cool evening
Beneath a tall tree
While night comes on gently,
Dark like me—
That is my dream!

To fling my arms wide
In the face of the sun,
Dance! Whirl! Whirl!
Till the quick day is done.
Rest at pale evening . . .
A tall, slim tree . . .
Night coming tenderly
Black like me.

Langston Hughes

DREAM VARIATION

WRITING ACTIVITY

WRITE A VITA

Prewrite

"Fame Is Not Enough" is a biographical sketch of Debbie Allen. A biography is the story of someone's life written by another person. In an autobiography, a person tells about his or her own life. When you apply for a job or for admission to a college or other school, you may be asked to write a brief autobiographical article. This kind of article is called a vita, from the Latin word meaning "life."

Before you begin, you will need to make a plan. An information map can help you choose and organize the information for your vita. The information map below shows you the four major kinds of information and supporting details usually found in a vita.

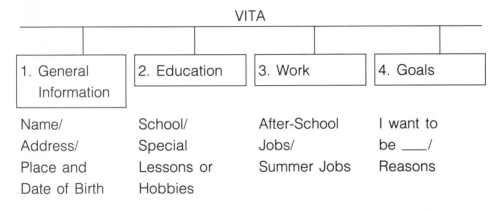

VITA

1. General Information	2. Education	3. Work	4. Goals
Name/ Address/ Place and Date of Birth	School/ Special Lessons or Hobbies	After-School Jobs/ Summer Jobs	I want to be ___/ Reasons

Part 1 includes the basic facts about you such as your name and address. You can see that Part 2, Education, includes information not only about your school but also about any other experience you feel has added to your education such as guitar lessons, working on the school newspaper, or interesting trips you have taken.

Part 3 gives information about your work experiences. Part 4 explains the goals you have, that is, what kind of a job or career you might like and the reasons you find it interesting.

Write

1. Each part of the information map will become the topic of a paragraph in your vita. The main idea sentence should identify the topic. The facts you choose will become the supporting details.
2. You can write your vita in any order; however, many vitas follow the order shown on the information map: General Information, Education, Work, and Goals.
3. Use your Glossary or dictionary for spelling help.

Revise

Read your vita. Did you include details about your life from each part of your information map? Pay special attention to the section on Work. Any job like babysitting or raking leaves is important to include because it shows that you are interested in work and can stick to a task. Reread your paragraph on Goals. Do your reasons explain some of the qualities you feel are important such as Debbie Allen's "go-for-it spirit"?

1. Proofreading is *very, very* important on your vita because the reader will judge whether you are capable of dealing with details. Proofread for end punctuation in your sentences, capitalization and spelling, and use of commas.
2. Be sure to use complete sentences and check to see that the subjects and verbs agree in number.
3. Rewrite your vita in your best handwriting to share.

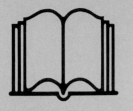

PREPARING FOR READING

Learning Vocabulary

1. Albert spoke freely and with refreshing <u>candor</u> about the play.
2. Mrs. Woodfin thought popularity, wealth, and importance were unworthy <u>ambitions</u>.
3. As a young girl, Mrs. Woodfin had read plays, made a theater of the attic, and <u>devised</u> scenery and costumes.
4. She had been <u>elated</u> when given the chance to play a famous role.
5. In a gesture of <u>vanity</u>, a rival actress arrived after the curtain had gone up on the play.

candor   ambitions   devised
elated   vanity

Developing Background and Skills
Main Idea

A writer usually has a point to make in a paragraph. This point, the most important information in the paragraph, is called the **main idea**. In a well-written paragraph, the main idea is supported by details that provide more information about the subject.

Sometimes the main idea of a paragraph is directly stated in a sentence at the beginning, in the middle, or at the end of the paragraph. Sometimes you have to combine information from two or more sentences to state the main idea. But many times, the main idea is only implied, or suggested, by the information given. To state an implied main idea, you must briefly sum up *all* the important details.

At times you may be asked to give the main idea of a passage made up of two or more paragraphs. To do this, first find the main idea of each paragraph. Then:

1. Ask yourself if the main idea of any one paragraph is the main idea of the entire passage.

IF NOT 2. Ask yourself if the main ideas of two or more paragraphs can be combined to state the main idea of the entire passage.

IF NOT 3. Ask yourself what main idea statement would sum up all the main ideas.

Read the passage below.

The last thing Albert wanted to do was to go into the weird old woman's house. But he was a person who could never say no. Before he knew it, he had gone inside with her.

The inside of the house was incredible. The ceiling was caving in, and the floors were rotted. Everything was covered with cobwebs and dust. But the amazing thing was that the entire place was stacked with books. There were books on the floor, on the tables, everywhere.

The woman invited Albert to sit down in the blue chair. She said it was the most comfortable. When Albert sat down, he nearly went through to the floor because the chair had no springs.

No one sentence states the main idea of the passage. What are the important details?

1. Albert didn't want to go into the house, but he did.
2. The inside of the house was incredible.
3. The ceiling was caving in, and the floors were rotted.
4. Everything was covered with cobwebs and dust.
5. The place was stacked with books.
6. Albert nearly went through the chair with no springs.

How would you state the main idea? As you read the next selection, think about how would you state the main ideas of the different groups of related paragraphs.

When Albert
Scully was four years old, his
parents sent him to nursery
school. Albert couldn't even
handle crayons. Ever since
then, people have been telling
him to "get with it." But Albert can't "get with" anything. He just isn't like
everyone else. And the more
he thinks about how different
he is, the more depressed
he gets.

On one of the lowest days
of Albert's life, his mother
sends him on an unpleasant
errand. An elderly neighbor
has been burning garbage in
her yard. Mrs. Scully wants
Albert to go to the woman's
house and tell her to stop—or
she'll call the police.

The Dream Watcher

I was pretty depressed as I walked over there, because about the last thing in the world I wanted to do was persuade some old lady to stop burning garbage. *I* didn't care if she burned garbage or not!

When I reached her house, there was nobody around. But this glow was coming from the backyard, so I went around to the back. There was this bonfire of garbage, stinking to high heaven. The old lady was throwing cereal boxes into it. She was really weird-looking. Very tiny and frail with bushy white hair and sort of bent over on a cane. But the weird thing was the way she was dressed. She was wearing a black velvet dress that came down to her ankles.

"Excuse me," I said. "I've come about the fire."

"Good!" she said. "Splendid blaze, isn't it?"

"What I mean is, my mother sent me about the fire."

"Fine, fine. Is she enjoying it?"

She was talking as though I were deaf, and on top of everything she had some sort of English accent. Man, did I want to beat a retreat. I could see that I was never going to get through to her.

"Look," I said, "I'm sorry to ruin your fire, but my mother is going to call the police if you don't put it out."

She didn't pay any attention to this, but hobbled up the back steps leaning on her cane. Then she turned and smiled at me. "You're shivering, sir. Come indoors."

The last thing in the universe I wanted to do was to go into this weird old woman's house. However, I am one of those people who can never say no. So before I knew it, I had gone inside with her.

The inside of her house was fantastic. It was so dilapidated that it looked like it had been designed or something. The ceiling was caving in and the floors were rotted and everything was covered with cobwebs and dust. But the really amazing part was that the entire place was stacked with books. On the floor, the tables, everywhere.

I guess it was rude, but I just didn't say anything. What could you say? Lovely place you have here? Meanwhile, she was smiling at me like I had just come off a spaceship and needed help.

"Do sit down, sir," she said. "The blue chair is the most comfortable."

I sat in the blue armchair and practically went through to the floor because there weren't any springs. She stared at me with these terribly blue eyes. "What would you like to talk about?"

"Well," I said. "I don't know."

"Don't know? How incredible, sir. The universe is filled with wonders, and you don't know what to talk about."

"What would *you* like to talk about?" I said.

"I will discuss anything that is beautiful," she said.

For a moment I thought she was kidding, but she wasn't. I looked around at all the books. "What about books?"

"Superb! Who is your favorite author?"

"Well, uh, Shakespeare."

"Superb!" she said again. "Which is your favorite play?"

I thought quickly. "*King Lear.*"

"Excellent. Why do you like it?"

"Well, I guess I like it because the story is so different. I mean, here's this great king who has everything in the world, yet he has to go crazy just to find out what the score is. The real score, I mean. I mean, he only becomes sane by going crazy first, if you see what I mean."

he nodded. "I certainly do. As a matter of fact, that is the most unusual interpretation of *Lear* I've ever heard. I shall send it to Sir Laurence Olivier."[1]

"You mean Olivier the actor?"

"None other. I knew him as a young man at the Old Vic."[2]

I was very surprised. "You mean you were an actress and everything?"

"I do."

"In London and everything?"

"London, Paris, Berlin, Rome. Do stop saying 'and everything,' my good man. It doesn't suit you."

"I'm sorry."

"Nothing to be sorry about. But as long as we are speaking English, we may as well speak it beautifully. Don't you agree?"

"Sure," I said. "Why not?"

I was beginning to feel a bit daring. As though I could say something very wild to her and she would understand.

"Listen," I said suddenly. "This will probably sound insane to you, but I have a very lousy life and it's nobody's fault but my own."

"Why do you think it's your fault?" She really looked interested.

"Well, I don't know. It *seems* to be my fault. I mean, I'm lousy in school and don't fit in anywhere and have all these peculiar tastes."

"What do you consider peculiar?"

"Well, like collecting recipes and going to museums and gardening. You know."

She tapped on the floor with her cane. She looked angry. "All you are saying is that you are different! A quality which puts you in the company of geniuses. Shakespeare was different. Beethoven (bā′ tō vən) was different. Edison was different. Need you complain?"

I had never thought of it that way before. "You mean I'm a genius?"

"I have no idea if you are a genius," she said. "However, you do have a certain candor that is refreshing, and your looks are superb."

This really amazed me. "They are?"

"Of course they are!"

I looked at my watch. "Oh, man! It's really late. I've got to go. I mean, I don't want to, but I have to."

"Very well," she said. "Come back tomorrow for tea at four o'clock."

---

1. **Sir Laurence Olivier** (ō liv′ ē ā): British actor.
2. **Old Vic**: famous London theater.

"OK. Great. I will."

"My name is Mrs. Orpha Woodfin."

I shook hands with her. "Mine is Albert Scully. And listen . . ."

"Yes, sir?"

"Burn all the garbage you like. Have a ball."

"I shall do that," she said softly, "in the fullness of time. Good night, Mr. Scully."

I got to Mrs. Woodfin's place the next day at exactly four o'clock. I knocked on the door and after a few minutes she opened it. She was wearing the same old velvet dress.

"Mr. Scully!" she said. "How good of you to come. You must be longing for your tea."

I didn't like tea, but the minute I got inside I could see that she had gone to a lot of trouble. There was a whole tea set laid out and a plate of crackers.

"Sit down, sir," she said.

I sat down, and she lowered herself into the broken rocker and poured my tea. "A biscuit?" she asked.

I took an old-looking cracker off the plate. "Thank you."

Mrs. Woodfin was staring at me. "Mr. Scully," she said, "I am eighty years old. When a person reaches that age, formalities are unnecessary. Let us get to the point. Why are you so unhappy?"

To tell you the truth, I didn't feel like going into this whole thing again. But then there was this long silence, so I said, "Well, I guess it's because I'm a failure or something."

She dropped the cracker she was eating and stared at me.

"I cannot believe my ears! You are sensitive and intelligent. Yet you tell me that you are a failure."

"Well, it's true," I said. "I am. Look, here's the picture. I'm a crummy student and a lousy athlete, and I don't have a single friend. I mean, I'm such a mess that I don't even have ambitions. Every other kid in the world has a million ambitions, and I don't. That's the picture."

"Very well. What are their ambitions?"

"They're very good ones!" I said. For some reason, my voice had gotten sort of loud. "First off, everybody wants to be popular. Then they all want to become something important after college. Then I guess they want to make a lot of money and get married and live in the suburbs. What's wrong with that?"

he shook her finger at me. "Everything, simply everything! Those are the deadliest ambitions I ever heard of. Only a coward could admire them."

"Well, I *do* admire them."

"Why?" she asked.

"I don't know why! And it isn't so marvelous to be 'different' as you said yesterday. It's lousy."

"Mr. Scully," she said. "Shall I tell you a story?"

"Sure," I said. "Fine." Which wasn't true, because I would have liked to go home.

She looked at me until I looked back, and then she held my eyes with hers.

"When I was your age, Mr. Scully, I had one ambition: to be a great actress. And so I read dozens of plays and recited them before a mirror. I turned the attic into a theater and devised costumes and scenery galore. My parents became so weary of this that they sent me to a dramatic academy, where I worked like a fiend. I stayed at the academy for two years. And then, sir, on November 1st, 1903, I played

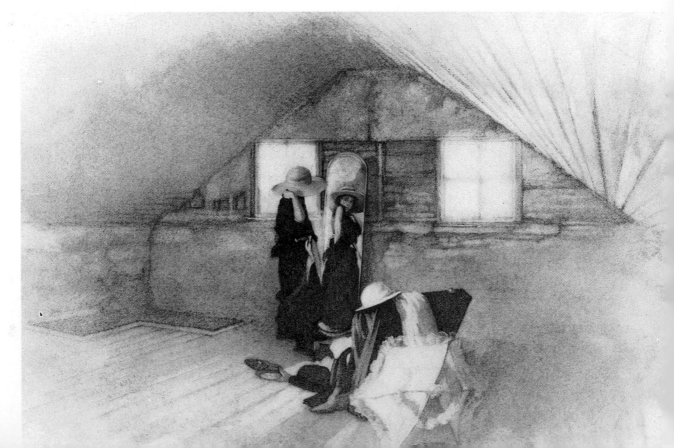

Ophelia[3] at the Haymarket Theater. After the curtain came down, the audience unhorsed my carriage and drew it through the streets of London, cheering. From that night on, the horizon of my life was illumined as though by skyrockets. Managers flocked to my door with contracts. Soon I was acting in every capital of the world. It seemed to me that I had achieved everything I had ever longed for. Then, Mr. Scully, the day arrived when I realized that I had achieved everything but happiness— and in one second, the glory turned to dust."

I was kind of bewildered by this. "Well. That's great."

"It was not great at all, sir."

"Look," I said. "You've obviously had a very unusual life, but I'm only a kid. I mean, I live in this crummy development and go to high school."

She smiled. "Rainer Maria Rilke[4] said, 'If your daily life seems poor, do not blame it; blame yourself, tell yourself that you are not poet enough to call forth its riches. . . .' "

I don't know how long we talked after that. It must have been hours. I calmed down and told Mrs. Woodfin my whole life, and she listened like she was really interested. Then she told me more about *her* life.

She had grown up in in London. She had become an actress when she was only sixteen and had acted everywhere in the world. She had traveled around in a special railroad car and had been admired by everybody. Kings, queens, everybody. Famous writers had written plays for her. But for some reason she had given up acting in her twenties and moved to America. She had bought this house in order to live simply and enjoy Nature. It was fantastic. Here was a famous person who had had everything in the world and given it up because it didn't make for "happiness." I couldn't understand it.

"It was 1906," Mrs. Woodfin was saying. "I had been invited to play Juliet[5] in Paris. It was a thrilling invitation because Madame Sarah

---

3. **Ophelia** (ō fēl' yə): a character in Shakespeare's play *Hamlet*.

4. **Rainer Maria Rilke** (ril' kə): (1875–1926) German poet.

5. **Juliet**: a character in Shakespeare's play *Romeo and Juliet*.

Bernhardt—the most famous actress in the world—had just played the role at the same theater. The tension was extreme. Here was I about to invade the artistic territory of the 'Divine Sarah.' "

"Were you scared?" I asked.

We were out in Mrs. Woodfin's yard. Mrs. Woodfin was sitting on a barrel, and I was sitting on the grass.

"Scared, Mr. Scully? I was elated. Madame Sarah was sixty-two years old. I was nineteen. I had everything in my favor: youth, beauty, talent."

"Man!" I said. "What happened?"

"A special box had been reserved for Bernhardt, but she did not enter it until the curtain was up and the play began. This gesture was typical of her vanity. Romeo was speaking, and the poor man's lines were almost obliterated by the spectacle of Madame Sarah's entrance. She swept into her box like a queen. And everyone's eyes were upon her. It was obvious that those of us on the stage were in for a contest."

"Man," I said. "Who won?"

"Wait and I shall tell you. I had begun the play badly, because of nervousness. My voice was unsteady and my hands were trembling. But by the time the third act arrived, I was in glorious command."

Mrs. Woodfin grabbed the sides of the barrel and pushed herself to her feet. Then she leaned on her cane and gazed into the distance with these very blue eyes she has. And it gave me chills, because suddenly she looked young.

"'Come gentle night . . . '" she said. "'Give me my Romeo; and, when he shall die, take him and cut him out in little stars, and he will make the face of heaven so fine that all the world will be in love with night and pay no worship to the garish sun . . . ' From that moment on, Mr. Scully, the evening was mine. When the final curtain came down there was no applause. People were too stunned to applaud. And then Madame Sarah Bernhardt, the Divine Sarah, the greatest actress in the world, rose to her feet and shouted, 'Bravo!' Her voice rang through the theater and was followed by a thousand voices shouting 'Bravo, Bravo, Bravo!' Yes, Mr. Scully, that night in Paris was my greatest triumph. And yet, four years later I left the theater and never acted again."

I gripped her hand, because all of a sudden I wanted to get through to her. To explain. I had never wanted anything so much in my life.

"But don't you see?" I said. "It was easy for you to leave the theater because you'd *been* there. You'd made it. But I've never made anything. And everyone is after me to get with it. And the more they tell me to get with it, the more paralyzed I become. It's awful. I'm the only person in America who doesn't belong to a group. I'm not square and I'm not hip. I'm not a hood. I'm not an intellectual. I'm not an athlete. And what else is there?"

"What else, sir? Why, yourself. Have you ever thought of just being yourself?"

Well, this one stopped me cold. Dead cold. "No," I said.

"There is a beautiful Jewish proverb," she said. "'If I am not for myself, who will be for me? And if I am only for myself, what am I?'"

I was starting to feel tired. Because I wasn't digging her, and the whole thing seemed so hopeless. Here was Mrs. Woodfin telling me to be myself, when myself was the thing that was wrong with me.

Suddenly Mrs. Woodfin stared over the back fence. I looked where she was looking, but all I could see was a United Parcel truck delivering a package to someone's house. For a moment I thought she was going to recite another Jewish proverb. But what she said was this:

If a man does not keep pace with his companions, perhaps it is because he hears a different drummer. Let him step to the music which he hears, however measured or far away.

And that was the very moment when I dug her. "*Henry David Thoreau!*"[6] I yelled.

I thought about what Thoreau had said for days. All of a sudden I didn't feel so embarrassed about my gardening. Or my recipe collection. Or the fact that I liked Shakespeare. I just started to accept these things, and it occurred to me that if Thoreau could have a different drummer, maybe I could, too. I know this doesn't make much sense, but I kept wondering if there wasn't a drummer for me somewhere. A kind of beautiful person who was beating a drum with my name on it. A kind of poet maybe, who was strolling through the world beating this very slow uneven beat that no one could hear but me.

---

6. **Henry David Thoreau** (thôr′ ō): (1817–1862) American writer.

Questions

1. How did Albert happen to meet Mrs. Woodfin?
2. Why do you think Albert confided in Mrs. Woodfin?
3. Which of the quotations recited by Mrs. Woodfin made the greatest impression on Albert? Why?
4. Have you ever met a person who had a positive influence on your life? Describe the person and the experience. Or describe a person you think would have an influence on your life.

Applying Reading Skills

Read the passages in "The Dream Watcher" listed below. Then write the answer to each question.

Page 279, from "Well, it's true . . . " to page 280, "It's lousy."

1. What is the main idea of this passage?
   a. Albert lacked ambitions.
   b. All of Albert's friends had ambitions.
   c. Mrs. Woodfin thought the ambitions of Albert's friends were deadly.
   d. Albert and Mrs. Woodfin disagreed about the value of popularity, wealth, and importance as ambitions.
2. Which two sentences support the main idea of this passage?
   a. Albert felt the ambitions were very good ones.
   b. Albert was a bad student and a bad athlete.
   c. Mrs. Woodfin thought the ambitions were not admirable.
   d. All Albert's friends had ambitions, but he did not.

Page 280, from "When I was your age . . . " to page 281, " . . . the glory turned to dust."

3. How would you state the main idea of this passage?

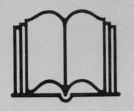

PREPARING FOR READING

Learning Vocabulary

1. Children can be very <u>credulous</u> about tales that grown-ups would question.
2. Jorkens said the tiger followed him <u>leisurely</u>, as though it did not want to run.
3. Jorkens saw a cave and decided to take <u>refuge</u> in it.
4. He searched for a small space he could <u>conceivably</u> squeeze into to save himself from the tiger.
5. Although he knew it was <u>absurd</u>, in fact silly, Jorkens preferred being chased by the tiger to being in a cave with it.

credulous   leisurely   refuge   conceivably   absurd

Developing Background and Skills
Author's Purpose and Point of View

The reason an author has for writing is called the **author's purpose**. Read the following and see if you can decide what the author's purpose is.

TEN WEEKS ON THE BEST-SELLER LIST!
500,000 COPIES SOLD!

Melissa Moss's

M U R D E R A T M I D N I G H T

A spell-binding thriller of love and revenge. The book *everyone* is talking about—and reading. "The season's best mystery," says *Herald* critic Carl Rich. "You won't put it down until you've read the last page," is the comment of the *This Week* reviewer.

Available at most bookstores   Also available
$9.95   in paperback—$3.95

Published by Cloak and Dagger Books
Riddlesdale, Ohio

You will probably agree that the author's purpose in writing the ad was to persuade people to buy the book. Persuasion is just one reason for writing. Authors may write to give factual information, to describe, or to explain. They may also write to entertain or amuse you. Can you think of an example for each of these purposes?

To figure out an author's purpose, ask yourself, "What reason did the author have for writing this particular piece?" Don't be misled by *what* is said. For example, the author of the ad gives a great deal of factual information, but his *purpose* in writing it is to persuade.

Writers often express a point of view in their writing. By **author's point of view**, we mean the author's manner of viewing things, or his or her attitude toward something. For example, from the point of view of the author of the ad, *Murder at Midnight* is a worthwhile book. A reader of the book may feel that the book is a waste of time. The ad-writer and the reader look at the book from different standpoints. They have different points of view.

Authors may state their point of view directly. But often it is stated indirectly. Asking yourself, "How did the author feel about what he or she wrote?" can be helpful in figuring out an author's point of view.

The selection that follows is an unusual story. As you read, try to discover the author's purpose in writing it. When you have finished, ask yourself if the author was successful in his purpose. Look for clues to the author's point of view. See if you can state his point of view in a sentence.

In A Dim Room

LORD DUNSANY

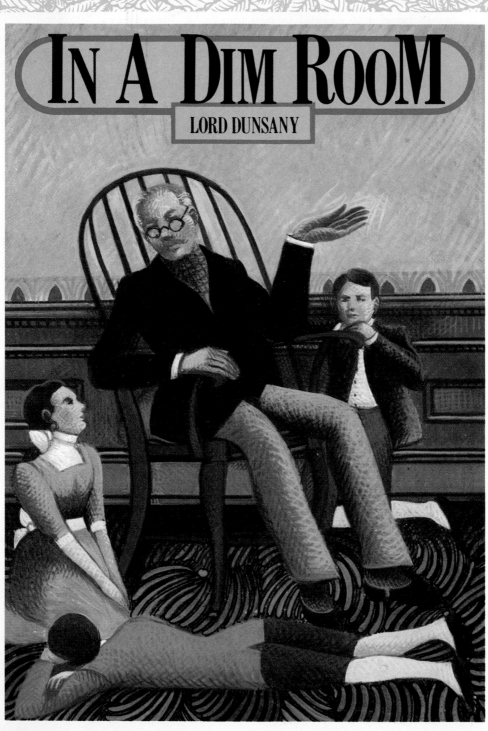

It is some while now since I have recorded any unusual experience that has come the way of my friend Jorkens. What happened was that a certain friend of mine said that his children liked thrilling tales, and I told them a few tales of lions and tigers, which had quite failed to thrill them. It suddenly occurred to me that there is something a little unusual in some of Jorkens' experiences, so that any tale of his might succeed where mine had failed. So I said to my friend's three children that I knew an old hunter of big game whose experiences were more out-of-the-way than mine, and asked my friend if I might one day bring him to tea.

I had no idea that there would be anything frightening about one of Jorkens' tales; nor did I think that the three children, ranging between ten and twelve years old, would be easily frightened. The permission to bring Jorkens was readily given, and the children unfortunately asked him for a thrilling tale, in those actual words, and Jorkens began at once as soon as they asked him. Now it is all blamed on me. I can only say that they asked for it, and they got it.

It should be borne in mind that they had never seen Jorkens before and had only his word for what kind of man he was; and then children can be very credulous. Well, here is the story, which he told almost as soon as he was seated in a comfortable chair, with the children standing before him.

It was about a tiger. But I was counting on his telling a straight story, such as I have so often heard him tell to grownups, and did not expect him to vary his style to suit his audience, if "suit" can be the proper word for the alarming effect he created.

"The tiger," said Jorkens, "had spotted me and was following me quite leisurely, as though it did not want to run in the hot weather, and knew perfectly well that I couldn't.

My story may serve as a convenient warning to you, when you grow up, never to go near an Indian jungle unarmed, and never to think as I did that just for once, on that particular morning, and for only a short walk, it wouldn't matter. It mattered more than you can guess. The tiger was there, coming slowly after me, and I was walking away, and the tiger was walking a little faster than I was. Well, of course I realized that, if he was only doing five yards in a hundred faster, I had no chance of escaping by walking. And I knew that running would only make it worse."

"Why?" asked the children.

"Why," said Jorkens, "because if I started a new game, the tiger would play it too. At walking he was only gaining five yards in a hundred, but at running he would have gained fifty. That's why I preferred walking, but it wasn't any better really, because it would end the same way. Unfortunately it wasn't actually in the jungle, but on some rocky land outside it; and there was no chance of a tree, because I was walking away from the jungle."

"Why?" asked another child.

"Because the tigers go outside the jungle at night and go back in the very early morning. All this was in the early morning, but the sun was well up, and I thought that the tigers would all have been back long ago. So I went for that walk unarmed, and, of course, I was quite mistaken."

"Why were you taking the walk?" asked the girl.

"You should never ask anyone," said Jorkens, "why he did anything that leads to disaster. All such things are done for the same reason, which one hates to admit. But there it is, they are all for the same reason, pure foolishness."

"Did it lead to disaster?" asked she.

"You shall hear," said Jorkens. "Well, I think I told you I was on rocky land; it was hilly too; and the tiger was getting

nearer. And then I saw a cave in the rocks, near the top of a little hill. Of course to go in there would cut off my retreat; but my retreat was doing me no good. It seemed to me that the small cave might get smaller, till there was no room for the tiger, or it might get larger and have ramifications amongst which I might dodge him. There were just two small hopes and nowhere else to go. So I stooped and went into the cave, and the tiger came in too.

"He was still some way behind me, and I saw the light go out as he entered, for he just about filled the entrance. The cave did get smaller, and soon I was on all fours. Still the tiger did not hurry. If it got smaller still, I might still conceivably squeeze on where the tiger could not. And it did get a little smaller, but not small enough. We went on over the smooth gray stone, and it got darker as we went, till I could no longer see the color of the floor, and the tiger seemed to absorb the whole of the daylight.

"A faint hope came to me from a story of a skeleton of a mouse, which had been found in a wall of a cathedral with the skeleton of a cat behind it. He had got where the cat could not follow, but it didn't do him much good. I hoped that, if ever I found such a refuge, the tiger would have more sense than that cat. But still the cave ran on, without getting as small as all that. Still the tiger wasn't hurrying, and that seemed to me to make the situation even more desperate. It seemed to show that the tiger was so sure. Of course I could smell him behind me, for he was still gaining; but the smell seemed almost too strong for a tiger nearly thirty yards behind, and the awful thought came to me that this cave which I hoped might shelter me was the tiger's own lair.

"Then came the hope, after going some distance, that the cave might soon come out through the little hill, though I don't know what good that would have done me. Still, absurd though it may seem, logically it seemed better to me to lose five yards in a hundred when walking in the open, if ever I could get there again, than what I was losing by going on all fours in a race with an animal to whom that sort of walking is natural. And then the uncertainties of the other side of the hill seemed better than those around me, and I thought I might find a tree. But there was no draught in my face; there was only the smell of the tiger in the darkness, and I realized I should never come to the open air."

I glanced at the children's faces to see if Jorkens was holding their attention any better than I had done. They were certainly listening intently, though I could not see that they were showing much more interest than they had shown in my poor story. The idea came to me that the sympathies of the girl were on the side of the tiger. But that of course, may only have been my fancy. I should perhaps say that it was in the autumn, and no lights had yet been turned on, and the room was growing dim. I repeat that it was no fault of mine: I had no idea what was coming.

"The tiger was gaining rapidly," Jorkens continued, "and the perfect smoothness of the limestone floor had made it quite clear by now that it must have for long been polished by soft feet, the large feet of a heavy animal: there was no roughness left on any edge upon which I had put my hand. And then the smooth floor came to a sheer smooth rock without crevice or crack in it, and no turn to the left or right. The cave had ended. I turned round in the dark and smelt, rather than saw, the tiger."

"What happened then?" asked one of the boys.

"He ate me," said Jorkens. "It is a ghost that is speaking to you."

And all the fuss that happened in that dim room was blamed entirely on me.

Questions

1. Why did the narrator ask to bring Jorkens to the children's house for tea?
2. What made Jorkens' story suspenseful?
3. Do you think the children really believed Jorkens was a ghost?
4. Describe the scene that might have taken place in the room after Jorkens finished his story.

Applying Reading Skills

The incomplete sentences below are based on "In a Dim Room." Choose the phrase or phrases that best complete each sentence. Write the complete sentences on your paper.

1. The author's purpose in writing the story was ____.
   a. to persuade   b. to inform   c. to describe
   d. to entertain   e. to give factual information
2. From the narrator's point of view, ____.
   a. Jorkens' story was more successful than any of his
   b. Jorkens' story was harmful
   c. Jorkens' story was believable
   d. Jorkens' story was quite humorous
3. From Jorkens' point of view, ____.
   a. his story was harmless
   b. his story was true
   c. his story was funny
   d. his story was thrilling

HOW TO TELL THE WILD ANIMALS

If ever you should go by chance
 To jungles in the East;
And if there should to you advance
 A large and tawny beast,
If he roars at you as you're dyin'
You'll know it is the Asian Lion.

Or if sometime when roaming round,
 A noble wild beast greets you,
With black stripes on a yellow ground,
 Just notice if he eats you.
This simple rule may help you learn
The Bengal Tiger to discern.

If strolling forth, a beast you view,
 Whose hide with spots is peppered,
As soon as he has lept on you,
 You'll know it is the Leopard.
'Twill do no good to roar with pain,
He'll only lep and lep again.

Carolyn Wells

PREPARING FOR READING

Learning Vocabulary

1. Alfred Hitchcock's childhood experiences <u>influenced</u> the kinds of films he made.
2. He set out to make <u>suspense</u> films that would have people sitting on the edge of their seats.
3. Hitchcock believed that fear is an <u>emotion</u> people actually enjoy when they are perfectly safe.
4. Hitchcock's <u>profile</u> became so well known that his side view became his trademark.

influenced   suspense
emotion   profile

Developing Background and Skills
Summarize

Read the passage below from *Brief Biographies*.

Alfred Hitchcock, the famous film director, writer, and producer, was born in London in 1899. He began his career as a director in England in 1925. The 1935 film *The 39 Steps* made him famous. He came to the United States in 1938 and began to work in Hollywood. There he became involved in directing, writing, and producing such brilliant suspense films as *The Man Who Knew Too Much*, *Psycho*, *Spellbound*, and *The Birds*. Although he is best remembered for his movies, Hitchcock also hosted a television series and published several collections of mystery stories. He died in 1980.

The passage is a summary of Hitchcock's life. A **summary** is a brief account that includes only the most important facts. The writer of the summary included only what she thought were the most important facts about Alfred Hitchcock.

Summarizing is a useful and important skill. How do you go about it? First of all, you must carefully consider all the information you have. Then you must decide what information is the most important—you must find the main ideas. You already know how to find the main idea of a paragraph. When you state the main idea, you are really summarizing. You can summarize several paragraphs, a long article, or even a book in the same way you go about summarizing a paragraph. Here are some rules to follow:

1. Be brief.
2. Include only the most important facts or ideas.
3. Leave out the unimportant details.

Now read the following paragraph.

"When I was no more than six years of age, I did something that my father considered worthy of reprimand. He sent me to the local police station with a note. The officer on duty read it and locked me in a jail cell for five minutes, saying, 'This is what we do to naughty boys.' I have, ever since, gone to any lengths to avoid arrest and confinement."

Which sentence is the best summary of the paragraph?
    a. An early experience gave the author a fear of jails and confinement.
    b. The author's father reprimanded him by having him locked in a jail cell for five minutes.
    c. The author has always gone to great lengths to avoid arrest and convinement.

Did you choose **a**? Explain why this is the best summary.

The following selection is about Alfred Hitchcock. As you read, look for the most important information presented. Think how you might summarize the information.

ALFRED HITCHCOCK
MASTER OF SUSPENSE

DEBORAH KUCAN WITKOWSKI

> *"When I was no more than six years of age, I did something that my father considered worthy of reprimand. He sent me to the local police station with a note. The officer on duty read it and locked me in a jail cell for five minutes, saying, 'This is what we do to naughty boys.' I have, ever since, gone to any lengths to avoid arrest and confinement. To you young people, my message is—Stay out of jail!"*

In the words above, Alfred Hitchcock described one of his earliest childhood memories. This memory continued to haunt the great movie director in later years. It also greatly influenced his films.

As a result of his childhood experience, Hitchcock was deathly afraid of the police. Throughout his life, he feared being arrested and accused of committing a crime by mistake. For this reason, he would not drive a car. He was afraid of having an auto accident and being locked away in jail.

Hitchcock's encounters with fear also included the stories he found in books. At the age of sixteen, he discovered Edgar Allan Poe. He was fascinated by the way Poe could scare him.

"I was afraid, but this fear made me discover something I've never forgotten since: fear, you see, is an emotion people like to feel when they know they're safe. When a person is sitting quietly at home reading a tale of terror, one still feels secure. Naturally you shiver, but since you're in familiar surroundings and you know it's only your imagination that responds to the reading, you then feel a great relief and happiness—like someone who has a cold drink after being very thirsty."

Hitchcock's reaction to Poe's stories encouraged him to make suspense films. He wanted to make whole audiences, not just one reader, feel the emotions of fear and suspense. He set out to make people sit on the edge of their seats.

His formula was a simple one. He would tell a story about ordinary people who get caught up in dangerous situations. Often, his characters are in danger of being hurt —or even killed—and they don't understand why. Hitchcock focused on ordinary people because he wanted moviegoers to identify with his characters and imagine themselves in their places throughout the action of the film. The audience was *always* the most important element in Alfred Hitchcock's filmmaking. He loved having the ability to make people react to what he showed on the screen.

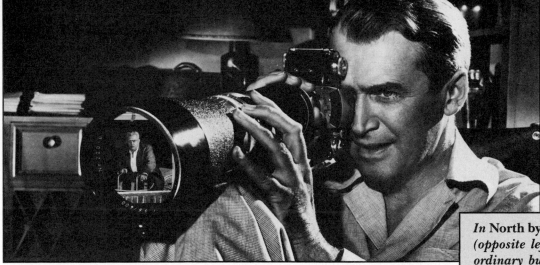

Many of his films are about an innocent person who is accused of something he didn't do. Once again, the source of his inspiration was his own childhood jail experience. He was also interested in crime stories and villains. He said, "The better the villain . . . the better the picture." And he created villains that audiences will never forget—from Norman Bates (*Psycho*) to hundreds of birds (*The Birds*).

Alfred Hitchcock made sixty-six movies between 1926 and 1980, the year he died. He was involved in every part of putting the picture together. He chose the stories that would be filmed. He directed the actors and actresses. He even approved the costumes and music. Hitchcock wanted suspense in his movies, but not while he was creating them. Everything was thought out before he started the actual filming. He used storyboards to plan all the details of a scene. Every camera shot, angle, and action was drawn out so that he knew exactly what image would appear on the screen.

Hitchcock had a playful nature as well as a calculating one. He used to play practical jokes on his cast and crew. "The best practical joke I ever played," he insisted, "was at a London hotel. I always thought blue was such a pretty color, but none of the food we eat is blue. So for the party, I had the soup dyed blue, the trout, the peaches, the ice cream." He wanted to make his co-workers react—the same way he wanted to make his audiences react to his movies.

In **North by Northwest** *(opposite left), an ordinary businessman is mistaken for a secret agent. He is pursued by spies who want to kill him because they think he knows too much.*

A news photographer (above) is the hero of **Rear Window.** *Confined to his apartment because of broken leg, he eases his boredom by gazing out the window at neighbors. His observations lead him to suspect that one of the neighbors is a murderer.*

Hitchcock also wanted to make strangers react. He would often get on a crowded elevator with someone and begin to tell a very suspenseful tale. Right before the ending, he would get off the elevator, leaving the other passengers in suspense.

Hitchcock was famous for making "guest appearances" in all of his movies. It was a "visual signature" he gave to each film. He only appeared on the screen for a very brief time. Fans had to pay close attention to catch him getting on a bus or passing by in a crowded street scene. In the movie *Lifeboat*, he had a unique problem. How could he make an appearance in a movie that involved a group of people stranded in a small boat on the open sea? The solution: He had one of the stranded passengers read an old newspaper that was found in the boat. One page included a weight loss advertisement with pictures of Alfred Hitchcock before and after reducing.

Playfulness aside, it was terror and fear that Hitchcock was really after. In *The Birds*, one of many memorable scenes takes place in a small schoolhouse. While the children are in class, the audience sees more and more birds flying around. Finally, the birds come to rest on telephone wires, rooftops, and playground equipment. The audience knows that something is going to happen as the children prepare to leave, but what, and when, and how? Hitchcock used real birds, mechanical birds, and animation throughout the movie to make each scene as real as possible.

Hitchcock was afraid of birds. He was also terrified of heights. In **The Birds** *(top)* and **Vertigo** *(bottom right)*, he used special effects and trick photography to make his audiences experience the same fears.

In **Suspicion** *(bottom left)*, the Master of Suspense placed a light inside a glass of milk. This forced viewers to focus on the glass and created the impression that it might contain poison.

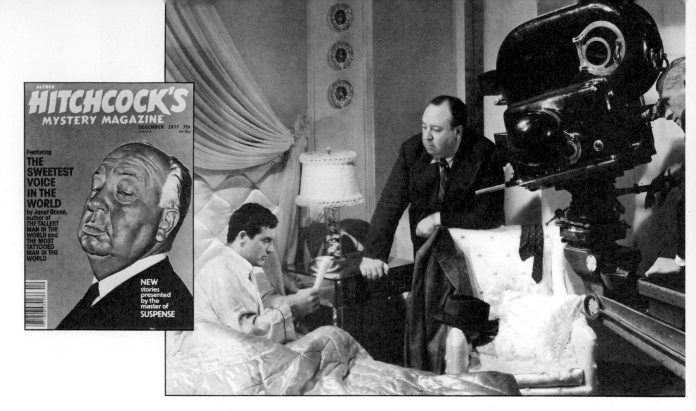

Hitchcock lent his name and his famous profile to more than the movies. He had a mystery magazine named after him. Although he didn't write or pick the stories that were included, people knew that they would experience suspense just because his name was on the cover. For six years, he hosted *Alfred Hitchcock Presents*, a television show that featured tales of suspense. The stories often had a twist that led to a surprise ending. In one show, a lady killed her husband with a frozen leg of lamb. She then cooked the evidence and fed it to the police when they came to investigate.

Most people, however, remember the Master of Suspense for his films. Many filmmakers admit that they have learned how to create suspense by studying his work. And many think that he was one of the best, if not *the* best, director of all time. If Hitchcock were alive today, he would feel greatly relieved by this response. Once someone asked him what he feared most. He listed in order: little children, policemen, heights, and that his next picture would not be as good as his last!

Questions

1. What was Alfred Hitchcock's "formula" for a suspenseful movie?
2. Why do you think people still go to see Alfred Hitchcock's movies?
3. Do you agree with Hitchcock's statement that "fear . . . is an emotion people like to feel when they know they're safe"? Explain your answer.
4. Summarize the plot of one of Alfred Hitchcock's films that you have seen or heard about.

Applying Reading Skills

A. Read each passage described below. Then write the answer to each question.

Second paragraph on page 301

1. Which sentence is the best summary of the paragraph?
    a. Hitchcock was involved in every aspect of his films.
    b. Hitchcock made 66 movies between 1926 and 1980.
    c. Hitchcock always left people guessing.

Third paragraph on page 301 and first paragraph on page 302

2. Which sentence is the best summary of the paragraphs?
    a. Hitchcock had a playful nature and played practical jokes.
    b. Hitchcock was interested in people's reactions.
    c. Hitchcock always left people guessing.

B. Read each summary below. Find the paragraph that each sentence summarizes. Write the paragraph number and page number on your paper.

1. Hitchcock gave his "signature" to every film he made by making "guest appearances."
2. Hitchcock relied on his own fears to create fear in his audiences.

PREPARING FOR READING

Learning Vocabulary

1. Adams had no <u>intention</u> of stopping to pick up the stranger on the lonely mountain road.
2. It seemed a strange <u>coincidence</u> that he had seen the same hitchhiker twice before.
3. The hitchhiker merely stood there, waiting. Nothing about him seemed <u>sinister</u>, or especially dangerous.
4. Only an occasional cabin broke the <u>monotony</u>, or dullness, of the wooded landscape.
5. As the train approached, Adams saw the stranger <u>beckoning</u> him across the tracks.

intention   coincidence   sinister
monotony   beckoning

Developing Background and Skills
Draw Conclusions

Read the paragraph below.

When she arrived home from school, Megan saw a strange, shiny new car parked in the driveway. She decided that the car belonged to a visitor. She went into the house to see who it was. A few minutes later, Ted came home and saw the car. He wondered whose car it could be. Then he remembered that this was the day his father was getting a new car. The car must be his father's new car. Ted rushed excitedly into the house.

Both Megan and Ted were **drawing conclusions**. A conclusion is a decision based on information and experience. Megan's conclusion was that the car belonged to a visitor. Ted's conclusion was different. Ted concluded that the car was his father's new car. You know that both conclusions cannot be right.

Ted had more facts than Megan did. As it turned out, Ted was right.

As you read, you will be presented with more and more information as you go along. You may find that your conclusions change as you continue. Read the following paragraph.

Roberto noticed the odd black car parked outside the school as he left. The next day, he noticed the same car parked across the street as he left his house.

On the basis of the information presented, you might conclude that it was a coincidence that Roberto saw the odd car twice in one day. But if you continue the story, you learn:

The following day, Roberto saw the car again as he left the practice field. It was in the supermarket parking lot when he picked up the groceries. It was there once more as he came out of the library. He began to see it everywhere—at the gym, outside the shop where he worked, at the post office, by the swimming pool.

By now you would probably conclude that it was *not* a coincidence that Roberto saw the car everywhere he went. The person driving the car was following him.

The following selection is a play. As you read, look for the conclusions the characters themselves reach. Think about what conclusions you can make about the characters and the events.

THE HITCHHIKER

A RADIO PLAY BY LUCILLE FLETCHER

CHARACTERS

ADAMS	MECHANIC	GIRL	OPERATOR
MOTHER	SLEEPY MAN	LONG DISTANCE	MRS. WHITNEY
VOICE	WOMAN	OPERATOR	

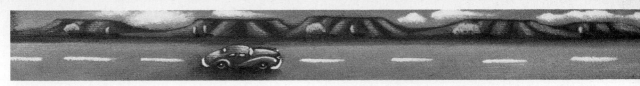

Sound: *automobile wheels humming over concrete road*

Music: *something weird and shuddery*

ADAMS: I am in an auto camp on Route Sixty-six just west of Gallup, New Mexico. If I tell it, perhaps it will help me. It will keep me from going mad. But I must tell this quickly. I am not mad now. I feel perfectly well. My name is Ronald Adams. I am thirty-six years of age. I drive a 1940 Ford V-8, license number 6V-7989. I was born in Brooklyn. All this I know. I know that I am at this moment perfectly sane. That it is not I who have gone mad, but something else—something utterly beyond my control. But I must speak quickly. At any moment the link with life may break. This may be the last thing I ever tell on earth . . . the last night I ever see the stars . . .

Music: *in*

ADAMS: Six days ago I left Brooklyn to drive to California . . .

MOTHER: Good-bye, son.

ADAMS: Good-bye, Mother.

MOTHER: I'll come out with you to the car.

ADAMS: No. It's raining. Stay here at the door. Hey, what is this? Tears? You promised me you wouldn't cry.

MOTHER: I know, dear. It's just— Ronald, I wish you weren't driving. Promise me you'll be extra careful. Don't fall asleep, or drive fast, or pick up any strangers. And wire me as soon as you get to Hollywood, won't you, son?

ADAMS: Of course I will. Now don't you worry. There isn't anything going to happen. It's just eight days of perfectly simple driving on smooth, decent, civilized roads. . . . (Fade)

Sound: *auto hum*

ADAMS: I was in excellent spirits. The drive ahead of me, even the loneliness, seemed like a lark. But I reckoned without *him.*

Music: *something weird and empty*

ADAMS: Crossing the Brooklyn Bridge that morning in the rain, I saw a man leaning against the cables. He seemed to be waiting for a lift. There were spots of fresh rain on his shoulders. He was carrying a

cheap overnight bag in one hand. He was thin, with a cap pulled down over his eyes. He stepped off the walk, and if I hadn't swerved, I'd have hit him.

Sound: terrific skidding

Music: in

ADAMS: An hour later, while crossing the Pulaski Skyway over the Jersey flats, I saw him again. He was standing now, with one thumb pointing west. I couldn't figure out how he'd got there, but I thought probably one of those fast trucks had picked him up, beaten me to the Skyway, and let him off. I didn't stop for him. Then, late that night, I saw him again.

Music: changing

ADAMS: It was on the new Pennsylvania Turnpike between Harrisburg and Pittsburgh. I was just slowing down for one of the tunnels—when I saw him—standing under an arc light. I could see him quite distinctly. The bag, the cap, even the spots of fresh rain spattered over his shoulder. He hailed me this time.

VOICE   (very spooky and faint): Hall-ooo . . .

ADAMS: I stepped on the gas like a shot. That's lonely country through the Alleghenies, and I had no intention of stopping there. Besides, the coincidence, or whatever it was, gave me the willies. I stopped at the next gas station.

Sound: horn honk

MECHANIC: Yes, sir.

ADAMS: Fill her up.

Sound: gas being put into car . . . bell tinkle, et cetera

MECHANIC: Nice night.

ADAMS: Yes. It hasn't been raining here recently, has it?

MECHANIC: Not a drop of rain all week.

ADAMS: I suppose that hasn't done your business any harm.

MECHANIC: Oh, people drive through here in all kinds of weather. Mostly business, you know. There aren't many pleasure cars out on the Turnpike this time of year.

ADAMS (casually):   What about hitchhikers?

MECHANIC (half laughing): Hitchhikers *here*? A guy'd be a fool to hitch on this road. It's two hundred and sixty-five miles long, there's practically no speed limit, and it's a straightaway. Now what car is going to stop to pick up a guy under those conditions? Would you stop?

ADAMS: No. (Puzzled) Then you've never seen anybody?

MECHANIC: Nope. Mebbe they get the lift before the Turnpike starts—just before the toll house—but then it'd be a mighty long ride. Most cars wouldn't want to pick up a guy for that long a ride. This is pretty lonesome country here. You haven't seen anybody like that, have you?

ADAMS: No. (Quickly) It was just a technical question.

MECHANIC: I see. Well, that'll be a dollar forty-nine—with the tax.

Sound: auto hum up

ADAMS: The thing gradually passed from my mind, as sheer coincidence. I had a good night's sleep in Pittsburgh. I did not think about the man all next day—until just outside of Zanesville, Ohio, I saw him again.

Music: dark, ominous note

ADAMS: It was a bright sunshiny afternoon. The peaceful Ohio fields lay dreaming in the golden light. I was driving slowly, drinking it in, when the road suddenly ended in a

detour. In front of the barrier, *he* was standing.

Music: in

ADAMS: There was nothing sinister about him. Nor was his attitude menacing. He merely stood there, waiting, the cheap overnight bag in his hand. Then he hailed me. He started to walk forward.

VOICE (far off): Hall-ooo . . . Hall-ooo . . .

ADAMS: I had stopped the car for the detour. I knew he must be thinking that I had stopped for him.

VOICE (closer): Hall-ooo . . . Halllll . . . ooo. . . .

Sound: gears jamming

VOICE (closer): Going to California?

ADAMS (panicky): No. Not just now. Sorry. . . .

Sound: starter starting

ADAMS (as though sweating blood): No. Not today. The other way. Going to New York. Sorry . . .

Sound: car starts with squeal of wheels on dirt

ADAMS: After I got the car back onto the road again, I felt like a fool. The thought of picking him up, of having him sit beside me was somehow unbearable. Yet, at the same time, I felt, more than ever, unspeakably alone.

Sound: auto hum up

ADAMS: Hour after hour went by. The fields, the towns ticked off, one by one. I knew now that I was going to see him again. And though I dreaded the sight, I caught myself searching the side of the road, waiting for him to appear.

Sound: car screeches to a halt . . . impatient honks . . . door being unbolted

SLEEPY MAN'S VOICE: Yep? What is it? What do you want?

ADAMS (breathless): You sell sandwiches here, don't you?

VOICE (cranky): Yep. We do. In the daytime. But we're closed up now for the night.

ADAMS: I know. But I was wondering if you could possibly let me have a cup of coffee—black coffee.

VOICE: Not at this time of night, mister. My wife's the cook, and she's in bed.

Sound: door squeaking on hinges as though being closed

ADAMS: No. Don't shut the door. Listen, just a minute ago, there was a man standing right beside this stand—a suspicious-looking man.

WOMAN'S VOICE (from distance): Hen-ry? Who is it, Henry?

HENRY: It's nobuddy, mother. Just a feller thinks he wants coffee. Go back into bed.

ADAMS: I don't mean to disturb you. But you see, I was driving along—when I just happened to look—and there he was.

HENRY: What was he doing?

ADAMS: Nothing. He ran off when I stopped the car.

HENRY: Then what of it? That's nothing to wake a man in the middle of his sleep about.

ADAMS: But I—

HENRY: You've been taking a nip, that's what you've been doing. And you haven't got anything better to do than to wake decent folk out of their hard-earned sleep. Go on.

ADAMS: But he looked as if he were going to rob you.

313

HENRY: I got nothin' in this stand to lose. Now on your way before I call out Sheriff Oakes. (Fades)

Sound: *auto hum up*

ADAMS: I got into the car again, and drove on slowly. If I could have found a place to stop . . . to rest a little. But I was in the Ozark Mountains of Missouri now. Only an occasional log cabin, seemingly deserted, broke the monotony of the wild wooded landscape. I had seen *him* at that roadside stand. I knew I would see him again—perhaps at the next turn of the road. I knew that when I saw him next, I would run him down.

Sound: *auto hum up*

ADAMS: But I did not see him again until next afternoon.

Sound: *railroad warning signal*

ADAMS: I had stopped the car at a sleepy little junction just across the border into Oklahoma—to let a train pass by—when he appeared, across the tracks, leaning against a telephone pole.

Sound: *distant sound of train chugging . . . bell ringing*

ADAMS (very tense): It was a perfectly airless, dry day. The red clay of Oklahoma was baking under the sun. Yet there were spots of fresh rain on his shoulders. I couldn't stand that. Blindly, I started the car across the tracks.

Sound: *train chugging closer*

ADAMS: He didn't even look up at me. I stepped on the gas hard, veering the wheel sharply toward him. I could hear the train in the distance now, but I didn't care. Then something went wrong with the car. It stalled right on the tracks.

Sound: *train chugging closer . . . car stalling*

ADAMS: The train was coming closer. I could hear its bell ringing, and the cry of its whistle. Still he stood there. And now I knew that he was beckoning—beckoning me to my death.

Sound: *train chugging close. Whistle blows wildly. Then train rushes up and by.*

ADAMS: Well, I frustrated him that time. The starter had worked at last. I managed to back up. But when the

314

train passed, he was gone. I was all alone in the hot dry afternoon.

Sound: train retreating. Crickets begin to sing.

ADAMS: I didn't know who this man was or what he wanted of me. I only knew that from now on, I must not let myself be alone on the road for one moment.

Sound: auto hum up . . . slow down . . . stop . . . door opening

ADAMS: Hello, like a ride?

GIRL: How far you going?

ADAMS: Amarillo . . . I'll take you to Amarillo, Texas.

GIRL: Gee!

Sound: door closes . . . car starts

GIRL: Gee, what a break this is. A swell car, a decent guy, and driving all the way to Amarillo.

ADAMS: Hitchhike much?

GIRL: Sure. Only it's tough in these great open spaces.

ADAMS: I should think it would be. Though I'll bet if you get a good pick-up in a fast car, you can get to places faster than say, another person, in another car?

GIRL: I don't get you.

ADAMS: Well, take me, for instance. Suppose I'm driving across the country, say, at forty-five miles an hour. Couldn't a girl like you, just standing beside the road, waiting for lifts, beat me to town after town—provided she got picked up every time in a car doing sixty-five?

GIRL: I dunno. Maybe she could and maybe she couldn't. What difference does it make?

ADAMS: Oh, no difference. It's just a crazy idea I had sitting here in the car.

GIRL: Imagine spending your time in a swell car thinking of things like that!

ADAMS: What would you do instead?

GIRL: Why I'd just *enjoy* myself. I'd sit back, and relax, and . . . (Sharply) Hey! Look out!

ADAMS (breathlessly): Did you see him too?

GIRL: See who?

ADAMS: That man. Standing beside the barbed wire fence.

GIRL: I didn't see anybody. There wasn't anything but a bunch of steers and the barbed wire fence. What did you think you were doing? Trying to run into the fence?

ADAMS: There was a man there, I tell you . . . a thin gray man, with an overnight bag. I was trying to . . . run him down.

GIRL: Run him down? You mean kill him?

ADAMS: He's a sort of . . . phantom. I'm trying to get rid of him—or else prove that he's real. But (desperately) you say you didn't see? You're sure?

GIRL: I didn't see a soul.

ADAMS: Watch for him. Keep your eyes peeled on the road. He'll turn up again—maybe any minute now. (Excitedly) There. Look there—

Sound: auto sharply veering and skidding. Girl screams.

Sound: crash of car going into barbed wire fence . . . frightened lowing of steer

GIRL: I'm gettin' outta here.

ADAMS: Did you see him that time?

GIRL (sharply): No. I didn't see him. And I don't expect to see him. All I want to do is to go on living— and I don't see how I will very long driving with you. So if you'll excuse me, mister—

ADAMS (frightened): You can't go.

Sound: door slams

ADAMS (desperately): Listen. Please. For just one minute. Maybe you think I am half cracked. But this man. You see, I've been seeing this man all the way across the country. He's been following me. And if you could only help me—stay with me—until I reach the coast—

Sound: door slams

ADAMS: No. You can't go.

GIRL (screams): Leave your hands offa me, do you hear!

Sound: struggle . . . slap . . . foot-steps running away on gravel . . . lowing of steer

ADAMS: She ran from me, as though I were a monster. A few minutes later, I saw a truck pick her up. I knew then that I was utterly alone.

Sound: *lowing of steer up*

ADAMS: I was in the heart of the great Texas prairies. There wasn't a car on the road after the truck went by. I was trying to figure out how to get hold of myself (Hall-ooo), when I saw him coming toward me (Hall-ooo), emerging from the herd of moving steers . . . .

VOICE: Hall-ooo . . . Hall-oooo . . .

Sound: *auto starting violently*

Music: *in*

ADAMS: I didn't wait for him to come any closer. Perhaps I should have spoken to him then, fought it out then and there. For now he began to be everywhere. Whenever I stopped, even for a moment—for gas, for coffee, a sandwich—he was there.

Music: *faster*

ADAMS: I saw him standing outside the auto camp in Amarillo that night. He was sitting near the drinking fountain in a little camping spot just inside the border of New Mexico.

Music: *faster*

ADAMS: He was waiting for me outside the Navajo Reservation, where I stopped to check my tires. I saw him in Albuquerque, where I bought twelve gallons of gas. I was afraid now, afraid to stop. I began to drive faster and faster. I was in lunar landscape now—the great arid mesa country of New Mexico. I drove through it with the indifference of a fly crawling over the face of the moon.

Music: *faster*

ADAMS: Now he waited for me at every other mile. I would see his figure, shadowless, flitting before me, over the cold and lifeless ground, flitting over dried-up rivers, over broken stones cast up by old glacial upheavals, flitting in the pure and cloudless air . . . .

Music: *strikes sinister note of finality*

ADAMS: I was beside myself when I finally reached Gallup, New Mexico, this morning. There is an auto camp here—cold, almost deserted at this time of year. I went inside, and asked if there was a telephone. I had the feeling that

if only I could speak to someone
familiar, someone that I loved, I
could pull myself together.

Sound: nickel put in slot

OPERATOR: Number, please?

ADAMS: Long distance.

Sound: return of nickel—buzz

LONG DISTANCE: This is long
distance.

ADAMS: I'd like to put in a call to
my home in Brooklyn, New York.
I'm Ronald Adams. The number is
Beechwood 2-0828.

LONG DISTANCE: Thank you.
(Pause) Gallup, New Mexico, calling
Beechwood 2-0828. (Fade)

ADAMS: It was the middle of the
morning. I knew Mother would be
home. I pictured her, tall, white-
haired, in her crisp housedress,
going about her tasks. It would be
enough, I thought, merely to hear
the even calmness of her voice. . . .

LONG DISTANCE: Will you please
deposit three dollars and eighty-five
cents for the first three minutes?
When you have deposited a dollar
and a half, will you wait until I have
collected the money?

Sound: clunk of six coins

LONG DISTANCE: All right, deposit
another dollar and a half.

Sound: clunk of six coins

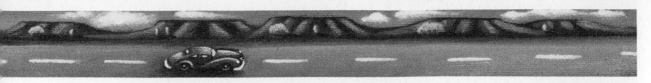

LONG DISTANCE: Will you please deposit the remaining eighty-five cents?

Sound: clunk of four coins

LONG DISTANCE: Ready with Brooklyn. Go ahead, please.

ADAMS: Hello.

MRS. WHITNEY (very flat): This is Mrs. Adams's residence. Who is it you wished to speak to, please?

ADAMS: Why, who's this?

MRS. WHITNEY: This is Mrs. Whitney.

ADAMS: I don't know any Mrs. Whitney. Is this Beechwood 2-0828?

MRS. WHITNEY: Yes.

ADAMS: Where's my mother? Where's Mrs. Adams?

MRS. WHITNEY: Mrs. Adams is still in the hospital.

ADAMS: The hospital! What's she in the hospital for?

MRS. WHITNEY: She's been prostrated for five days. Nervous breakdown. But who is this calling?

ADAMS: Nervous breakdown? But my mother was never nervous. . . .

MRS. WHITNEY: It's all taken place since the death of her oldest son, Ronald.

ADAMS: Death of her oldest son, Ronald?

MRS. WHITNEY: He was killed just six days ago in an automobile accident on the Brooklyn Bridge.

OPERATOR (breaking in): Your three minutes are up, sir. (Silence)

OPERATOR: Your three minutes are up, sir. (Pause) Your three minutes are up, sir. (Fade) Sir, your three minutes are up. Your three minutes are up. Your three minutes are up, sir.

ADAMS (in a strange voice): And so, I am sitting here in this deserted auto camp in Gallup, New Mexico. I am trying to think. I am trying to get hold of myself. Otherwise, I shall go mad. Outside it is night—the vast, soulless night of New Mexico. A million stars are in the sky. Ahead of me stretch a thousand miles of empty mesa, mountains, prairies—desert. Somewhere among them, he is waiting for me. Somewhere I shall know who he is, and who . . . I . . . am. . . .

The End

Questions

1. Where was Adams driving? Where did he start? How far did he get?
2. Why did Adams pick up the girl hitchhiker? Why did the girl run off?
3. Do you think Adams should have stopped and at least talked to the stranger? Why or why not?
4. If you had been Adams, what would you have done after talking with Mrs. Whitney? Explain your reasons.

Applying Reading Skills

A. Read the passages described below. Choose the phrase that best completes each sentence. Then write the complete sentence on your paper.

Mother's speech on page 309

1. Mrs. Adams speaks to Ronald as she does because ___.
   a. she knows something bad will happen to him
   b. she is concerned about him
   c. she doesn't want him to drive

Adams' part on pages 309 and the first column on page 310

2. Adams makes statements about himself because ___.
   a. he feels it will keep him from going mad
   b. he knows he is perfectly sane
   c. he feels perfectly well

Dialogue between Adams and Henry on pages 312, 313, and 314

3. Henry threatens to call Sheriff Oakes because ___.
   a. he thought the stranger was going to rob him
   b. he was annoyed at being disturbed
   c. he thought Adams might cause a problem

B. What conclusion did you reach about the identity of the hitchhiker? State your conclusion and give your reasons.

INCIDENT IN A ROSE GARDEN

Gardener: *Sir, I encountered Death*
Just now among our roses.
Thin as a scythe he stood there.

I knew him by his pictures.
He had his black coat on,
Black gloves, a broad black hat.

I think he would have spoken,
Seeing his mouth stood open.
Big it was, with white teeth.

As soon as he beckoned, I ran.
I ran until I found you.
Sir, I am quitting my job.

I want to see my sons
Once more before I die.
I want to see California.

Master: *Sir, you must be that stranger*
Who threatened my gardener.
This is my property, sir.

I welcome only friends here.

Death: *Sir, I knew your father.*
And we were friends at the end.

As for your gardener,
I did not threaten him.
Old men mistake my gestures.

I only meant to ask him
To show me to his master.
I take it you are he?

Donald Justice

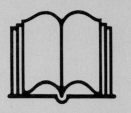

PREPARING FOR READING

Learning Vocabulary

1. In *The Alligator People*, a scientist transforms Richard Crane into a laughable version of an alligator.
2. In *The Twonky*, a television set manipulated by clearly visible wires becomes a menace.
3. In another monster movie, a woman confronts a vicious, power-hungry cucumber that takes control of a town.
4. The X from outer space is a giant chicken dinosaur who holds the world in peril until two heroes launch a cunning and successful counterattack against it.

transforms   manipulated   confronts
peril   cunning

Developing Background and Skills
Summarize

Let's review what you know about summaries and summarizing. A **summary** is a short statement that gives the most important information about a subject or topic. You may be asked to summarize a paragraph, several paragraphs, a long passage, or an entire selection. In order to summarize a paragraph, decide what information is the most important. To summarize several paragraphs or an entire selection, find the main idea of each paragraph and combine two or more main ideas. Remember these guidelines.

1. Be brief.
2. Include only the most important information.
3. Leave out unimportant details.

Read the two paragraphs that follow. Think about how you would summarize them.

324

The plot of the movie *Attack of the Killer Tomatoes* concerns the revenge of giant tomatoes who seek to punish housewives and corrupt politicians who steal from the government. During the reign of terror, the streets run red with tomato juice, or blood, or something.

The citizens of San Diego, where the tomatoes launch their attacks, manage to herd the tomatoes into the local football stadium. There the giant vegetables miraculously shrink back to normal size. The San Diegans squash them one by one and make a mess of the playing field. The title song adds color to the action. It includes such inspiring lyrics as "I know I'm going to miss her/A tomato ate my sister."

Which of the following statements is the best summary of the paragraphs?
    a. In the movie, giant tomatoes attack San Diego housewives and politicians, but the citizens overcome the tomatoes on the football field.
    b. The movie tells the story of a giant tomato attack on San Diego, where the streets run red with tomato juice.
    c. The movie's lyrics—"I know I'm going to miss her/A tomato ate my sister"—explain the plot of the movie.

Would you agree that the best summary is **a** because it combines the main ideas of the two paragraphs? Why are the other statements not the best choice for a summary?

The following selection includes eight sections, each describing a different monster movie. As you read, look for the most important information given in each section, and think about how you would summarize it. When you have finished reading, think how you might summarize the entire selection.

THE MOST RIDICULOUS MONSTER MOVIES IN SCREEN HISTORY

Harry and Michael Medved

THE ALLIGATOR PEOPLE [1959]

A mad doctor, fascinated by reptiles, transforms poor Richard Crane into a laughable creature vaguely resembling an alligator—the monster's costume only partially conceals the human identity of the wearer. The title of this film is misleading because Crane is the only "alligator person" to make an appearance in this Ultra Cheapie.

Lon Chaney, Jr., plays the scientist's crazed assistant, and provokes a fight and a few feeble explosions in a vain attempt to keep our interest. Beverly Garland is the long-suffering spouse who loses a husband and gains a strong distaste for alligator shoes.

GAMERA, THE INVINCIBLE [1962]

This Japanese saga tells the heart-warming story of a monster turtle, nearly 400 fcct long. If that's not bizarre enough for you, Gamera flies through the air like a snapping space shuttle and breathes fire when aroused. Though this curious airborne reptile wreaks havoc on the fair city of Tokyo, one small child takes a liking to him.

"Gamera doesn't mean to step on people," the Japanese boy explains. "He's just lonely. Even turtles get lonely sometimes." This sort of touching dialogue helped make the film so popular that the flying, fire-breathing turtle made a triumphal return in two sequels, *Gamera Versus Monster X* and *The Return of the Giant Monsters*.

THE TWONKY [1953]

The terrifying "Twonky" of the title is a boxy 1953 television set. It has menacing rabbit ears and tiny legs that carry it awkwardly from place to place. Its chief victim is Professor Kerry West (Hans Conried). He realizes too late that his TV has been possessed by the spirit of an evil robot from a distant planet. This mad machine takes over Conried's life, following him from room to room, and doing the dishes. Worst of all, or so the script informs us, it denies Conried's "right to be wrong."

This clunky machine is manipulated by wires so visible they would embarrass the Flying Nun. It is supposed to be incredibly powerful and intelligent, but in the end it proves no match for the wily Hans Conried. He eventually destroys his tormentor in an automobile accident.

ROBOT MONSTER [1953]

This 3-D fantasy presents a race of killer robots dressed in gorilla suits and deep sea diving helmets. They invade the earth and slaughter all of humanity, except for six very bad actors. We actually meet only two of the dreaded invaders—"Ro-Man" and his boss back on the moon, "Great One." Both parts are played by the same actor, George Barrows.

Barrows won the roles because he owned his very own moth-eaten gorilla costume. He offered an unbeatable bargain to director Phil Tucker, who couldn't afford the cost of renting a robot suit. Tucker explained the careful planning behind the film. "I thought, 'I know George will work for me for nothing. I'll get a diving helmet, put it on him, and it'll work!'"

THE X FROM OUTER SPACE [1967]

A Japanese "explorer rocket" returns from a space mission bearing a mysterious organism as part of its cargo. This itty-bitty blob quickly matures into "the X," a gigantic chicken dinosaur. It wobbles around on its spindly hind legs, flaps its wings at its sides, and sounds like an angry hippopotamus.

Our Boy X belches out deadly steel spears and crushes some of the shoddiest toy trucks ever seen in a monster movie. The world is in peril until two heroes lead a cunning counterattack. The counterattack succeeds, but this simpleminded soufflé definitely lays an egg.

THE CREEPING TERROR [1964]

A killer carpet from outer space devours a series of unsuspecting citizens. It gobbles up a girl who wears a bikini for a picnic in the woods, a folksinger and his followers, a platoon of the United States Army, a prom-full of teenagers, and one very fat fisherman. Oddly enough, these victims never run away from danger. If they did, this slow-moving rug would never catch up with them.

The paralyzed earth people summon the world's leading authority on space creatures. Dr. Bradford works closely with the heroic sheriff (who is actually the movie's director). Together, they solve the riddle of the slithering invader. Eventually they kill it with a hand grenade.

IT CONQUERED THE WORLD [1956]

A power-hungry cucumber lands on earth and establishes its headquarters in a cave. It then takes control of an Arizona town with the help of little rubber bats that bite their victims into surrendering. Also assisting is an earth scientist (Lee Van Cleef). He believes that the Big Green from Venus will establish an era of world peace. His wife knows better. She confronts the vicious veggie in its lair.

"I hate your living guts. . . . You're ugly!" she screams as she fires her rifle at the visitor from Venus. "You think you're going to make a slave of the world. Go on, try your intellect on me!" The cunning cuke comes rolling out of its cave on furniture casters. Sharp-eyed moviegoers can enjoy a good view of the gentleman who is pushing the creature from behind.

THE GIANT CLAW [1957]

"It's a bird!" declares brilliant young scientist Jeff Morrow. "A bird as big as a battleship!"

This squawking invader comes to earth from deep space and nests atop the Empire State Building. An invisible force field shields it from harm. It also travels with visible wires, stiff flapping wings, and google eyes.

The actors (Jeff Morrow, Morris Ankrum, and Mara Corday) react with exaggerated horror every time they hear the creature's telltale cackle. Jeff Morrow recalled: "We shot the film before we ever got a look at this monster. . . . The director just told us, 'All right now, you see the bird up there, and you're scared to death! Use your imagination.' But the first time we actually got to see it was the night of the premiere. The audience couldn't stop laughing. We were up there on screen looking like idiots, treating this silly buzzard like it was the scariest thing in the world. I was never so embarrassed in my entire life."

Questions

1. Choose two of the movies described in the selection and explain the plot of each.
2. Explain why each of the movies you chose might be described as ridiculous.
3. Which two of the movies described seem most nearly alike to you? Give the reasons for your answer.
4. Describe a monster movie you have seen (not one of the ones described in the selection). Briefly explain what it was about and tell whether you felt it was successful or not. Explain your reasons.

Applying Reading Skills

A. Reread the section about *Gamera, the Invincible*. Then choose the statement that is the best summary of this section.

    a. This heart-warming saga of a monster turtle was so successful that two sequels were made.

    b. A small child takes a liking to the giant turtle Gamera and explains that the turtle means no harm.

    c. A child's touching defense of a giant turtle who wreaks havoc on Tokyo made *Gamera* a popular film.

B. Write a one- or two-sentence summary of the two sections listed below.

1. *The Giant Claw*
2. *The Creeping Terror*

C. In three or four sentences, write a summary of the entire selection "The Most Ridiculous Monster Movies in Screen History."

WRITING ACTIVITY

WRITE A DESCRIPTION

Prewrite

Monster movies are popular with people of all ages. Real fans will go to see even ridiculous monster movies such as those described in "The Most Ridiculous Monster Movies in Screen History." Moviemakers have created some memorable monsters, including King Kong and Godzilla.

You are going to write a description of a memorable movie monster. Before you write, try these activities.

1. Review the information about summarizing on pages 324 and 325. Then reread the article on ridiculous movie monsters. Notice the way the writers described the monsters. Summarize the kinds of information you will need for your description.

2. Look in your media center for magazines or books about the most popular movie monsters. In a list, summarize the things that you think make these monsters so memorable.

3. Do a survey of ten students in your class. Since students are the audience for your description, you need to find out what they like. Ask questions such as:

   What is your favorite movie monster?

   How would you describe that monster?

   What made the monster believable?

   Summarize the results of your survey.

4. Try drawing a sketch of your monster.

5. Reread all your notes and make a plan for writing. Think about including these things in your description.

   a. Physical appearance of the monster

   b. Personality of the monster

   c. Special powers or abilities

   d. The monster's motive, or reason, for acting the way it does

Write

1. Introduce your monster in the first paragraph. You may want to contrast a very *ordinary* setting with the arrival of an *unordinary* monster. For example, a quiet summer day in Iowa changes drastically when a giant corn borer appears.
2. Develop two or three paragraphs that describe the appearance, personality, powers, and motive of your monster.
3. Use your Glossary or dictionary for spelling help.

Revise

Read your description. To help your readers develop a clear picture of your monster try to use lively adjectives. For example, would a horrifying monster or a scary monster sound more frightening? Use antonyms to develop contrast. For example, the monster had an unbelievably ugly body but beautiful green eyes.

1. Proofread for capitalization and end punctuation in all your sentences.
2. Make sure that the subject and verb in each sentence agree in number. (The monster's size and its strength were awesome. NOT: The monster's size and its strength was awesome.)
3. Rewrite your description to share.

UNIT FOUR
LEVEL 13

ANCIENT AGES

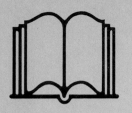

PREPARING FOR READING

Learning Vocabulary

1. Geeder was <u>fascinated</u> by her neighbor, a mysterious woman named Zeely.
2. Zeely's <u>extraordinary</u> height and beauty made her seem like a queen to Geeder.
3. Geeder became convinced that Zeely was a queen <u>descended</u> from the Watutsi tribe of Africa.
4. Zeely, who raised razorback hogs, told Geeder that the animals knew her <u>scent</u>.
5. As Zeely spoke to Geeder, she looked deeply at her, as if Geeder's <u>image</u> were fading away.

fascinated	extraordinary	descended
scent	image	

Developing Background and Skills
Sequence of Events

Sequence of events is the order in which things happen. In real life, events take place in chronological order; that is, they follow one another in time. Writers do not always describe events in chronological sequence, however. As they plan the events in their stories, writers may arrange them in different ways.

In newspaper stories, reporters often start out by describing an event and then explaining the actions that led up to it. They tell about the most dramatic event first in order to attract a reader's attention and interest. Read the example below.

—LOCAL GIRL WINS CONTEST—

Dressed in a shimmering robe of vibrant colors, Elizabeth Morris dazzled the entire audience at the First Annual Storytelling Contest last night and walked off with the first prize. With a voice that ranged from a soft whisper to a piercing call, Morris was spellbinding as she told an African folk tale about the sun and the moon.

Morris first became interested in storytelling because of her grandmother. . . .

Some writers choose to interrupt the plot of a story by using a flashback. The events described in the flashback took place in the past. By describing past events in the life of a character, writers can help readers better understand the character's motives and feelings in the present. Read the example below.

As Ray watched his brother Tommy run toward him through the field, he felt a special joy and pride. He thought back to the night when Tommy was born. There had been a terrible storm, and the bridge had been washed away by the swollen river. Despite the fear he felt, Ray had set out to bring the doctor. . . .

Another way writers arrange plot events is by creating a story-within-a-story. An important part of the plot in these stories involves a character in the main story telling a story to another character.

The story you will read next is a story-within-a-story. One main character, Zeely, tells the other main character, Geeder, a story about herself. As you read, think about the story Zeely tells. How does it help you learn more about her?

ZEELY

VIRGINIA HAMILTON

Elizabeth, who has given herself the nickname Geeder, is spending the summer on her uncle's farm. She becomes fascinated by her uncle's neighbor, Zeely Tayber, a mysterious young woman who raises prize razorback hogs. To Geeder, Zeely's extraordinary height and beauty make her seem like a queen. When Geeder finds a magazine photograph of a Watutsi princess who looks remarkably like Zeely, she is convinced that Zeely is indeed a queen, descended from the Watutsi people of Africa. After Geeder tells this story to the neighborhood children, Zeely arranges a meeting with Geeder in a clearing in the woods.

"You are very much the way I was at your age," Zeely said.

"You were like *me*?" Geeder said. "Were you just like me?"

Zeely smiled. "I mean that because you found the picture, you were able to make up a good story about me. I once made up a story about myself, too."

"Miss Zeely!" Geeder said. "I wouldn't have told a soul if I hadn't found that picture. It is proof!"

Carefully, Zeely ran her long fingers over her robe. "My mother's people were Watutsi people out of Africa a long time ago," she said quietly.

"Just like the lady in the picture!" Geeder said.

"Yes," said Zeely, "and I believed that through my veins ran the blood of kings and queens! So it was that my mother came to make this robe for me," Zeely said. "I had asked her many questions about her people—I talked of nothing else for quite a while. She made this robe exactly like the ones they wore." Then she added, "I put it on today because wearing it, I can be more the way I was. You may touch it, if you like."

And gently, Geeder touched it.

Zeely didn't say anything for a time. Then, she began again. "I was tall," she said. "The children laughed at my skinny arms and my long legs. I wore my robe all the time, for I thought it beautiful and I wanted the children to believe

about me what you have come to believe."

"But you *are* a Watutsi," Geeder said.

"Yes," said Zeely, "but wait . . . "

"You just said you came from Africa," Geeder said.

"Wait!" Zeely said. "We all came out of Africa—what of it?"

Geeder was quiet. She wasn't sure what was happening.

"I remember," Zeely began, "I wore my robe every day. My mother didn't like that. She would say, 'Zeely, you must wear clothes like other children, you must play and be like other children!' I would say, 'No, mama. No!'"

Geeder sat quite still, with the photograph of the Watutsi woman on her lap. She had held her hand pressed against it when Zeely first began speaking. Now, she smoothed her fingers over the photograph.

"Oh, Miss Zeely," Geeder said, "I thought you were special even before I found the picture." It was as if she spoke to herself and not to Zeely. "You are the most different person I've ever met," Geeder said.

Zeely laughed softly. She drew her long legs up under her chin and folded her arms around them. In this way, she rocked slowly from side to side. Her eyes closed and there was a smile upon her lips.

"Where I came from," Zeely said, "Canada, there was a lake.

"Oh, it was not a large lake," she said. "You could swim it, going slowly, in about fifteen minutes. I have done that. I have swum it when there was no moon or stars to light my way.

"You see," Zeely said, looking at Geeder now, "the children wouldn't often swim in that lake, even in the daytime. A tiny old woman lived beside it. She wore a big bow in her hair that was very dirty. On top of the bow she wore a man's straw hat. She walked, bent forward, with a big cane for support. Often, she cackled to herself and pointed her cane at things. The children were afraid of her, but I was not. Sometimes, I'd be swimming in the lake in the daytime, and she'd come upon me. 'Zeely Tayber,' she would call, 'I see you!' And I would call back to her, 'And I see *you*!' Then, she would call again. 'One of these times, I'll catch you!' she'd say, and she would cackle and point her cane at me.

"One night," Zeely said, "I had finished swimming and was pulling on my clothes when I heard footsteps on the path. I heard a cackle, and I knew who it was. All at once, fear took hold of me. I had not ever thought of that little woman walking around at night, you see. At that moment, I was terrified. Quickly, I gathered my clothes and stood between a bush and tree, well hidden in the darkness, I thought. And there she came along the path."

"Oh," said Geeder, softly. Her eyes were wide.

"She did nothing for a moment," Zeely said. "She stood there beside the lake looking at the dark water. Then, she looked around. She went up to a stone lying there beside her and touched it with her cane. It moved. It was a turtle and it scurried into the water."

"No!" said Geeder.

"Oh, yes," Zeely said. "And there was a fallen branch, twisted upon itself there, right next to the path. Vines grew over it. She poked one vine with her cane. It rippled. It was a snake, and it slithered off into a bush near where I stood."

"No!" said Geeder.

"I couldn't believe my eyes," Zeely said, "I was so amazed by what I had seen. The woman kept cackling. Her back was turned to me. But I must have choked out loud on my fear, for suddenly she was silent. She spun around and stood there, facing the darkness where I was hidden."

343

"'Zeely Tayber,' she said, 'I see you!' And I remember, I began to cry.

"'Zeely Tayber,' she said again. She raised her cane right at me, and she was coming toward me. I could see her bow moving in the air. Suddenly, she had me by the arms. She was cackling again—I thought she would never stop.

"At last, she spoke," Zeely said. "'Zeely Tayber,' she said, 'you have made a poor soul happy. You are the night and I have caught you!'

"Soon, the woman let me loose and went on her way, laughing and singing to herself. I was stunned by what she had said to me and I stood there in the darkness for many minutes. All at once in my mind everything was as clear as day. I liked the dark. I walked and swam in the dark and because of that, I was the *night*!

"Finally," Zeely said, "I told my mother about what had happened. My mother said that I simply had not known darkness well enough to tell the difference between a stone and a turtle and a vine and a snake. She said the snake and the turtle had been there all the time. She said that since the woman was not quite right in her head, she had decided that I was the night because my skin was so dark."

"Did you believe what your mother said?" asked Geeder.

"I came to believe it," Zeely said. "I believe it now. But I was sorry my mother had said what she did. It meant I was only myself, that I was Zeely and no more."

Geeder sighed and looked down at her hands. "Things . . . are what they are, I guess," she said, quietly.

"Yes," said Zeely. "No pretty robe was able to make me more than I was and no little woman could make me the night."

"But you *are* different," Geeder said. "You are the most different person I've ever talked to."

"Am I?" Zeely said, her voice kind. "And you want to be, too?"

Geeder was suddenly shy. She took hold of her beads and ran her fingers quickly over them. "I'd like to be just like you, I guess, Miss Zeely," she said.

Zeely smiled. "To be so tall that wherever you went, people stared and questioned? You'd like to be able to call a hog to you and have it follow you as though it were a

puppy?" She laughed. The sound of it was harsh. "Hogs see me as just another animal—did you know that? Their scent is my scent, that is all there is to it. As for being so tall, I would like once in a while not to have people notice me or wonder about my height. No," Zeely added, "I don't think you'd enjoy being like me or being different the way I am."

"I guess not, then," Geeder said. "I mean, I don't know." She stopped in confusion. She would never have imagined that Zeely didn't like being tall. "I want to be . . . to be . . . " She paused.

"Whoever it is you are when you're not being Geeder," Zeely said, finishing for her. "The person you are when you're not making up stories. Not Geeder and not even me, but yourself—is that what you want, Elizabeth?" Zeely looked deeply at Geeder, as if the image of her were fading away. "I stopped making up tales a long time ago," she said, "and now I am myself."

Geeder was so startled she could not say anything. And the way Zeely called her Elizabeth, just as though they were the same age, caused a pleasant, quiet feeling to grow within her. What she had promised herself at the beginning of the summer crossed Geeder's mind. *I won't be silly. I won't play silly games with silly girls.*

But I *was* silly, she thought. I made up myself as Geeder, and I made up Zeely to be a queen.

She let go of her bright necklaces and smoothed her hands over her hair.

"Myself . . . " she whispered. "Yes, I guess so."

Zeely Tayber ruffled the creases from her long robe and then stood up to leave. She was tall and beautiful there, before Geeder. Her expression was soft.

She touched Geeder lightly on the hair. Her long fingers fluttered there a moment, as lithe as the wings of a butterfly, before they were gone. Zeely knew before Geeder did that Geeder was close to tears.

"You have a most fine way of dreaming," Zeely said. "Hold on to that. But remember the turtle, remember the snake. I always have."

Geeder didn't see Zeely leave the clearing. The colors of bush and tree swam in her eyes and Zeely melted away within them.

Questions

1. What opinion does Geeder have of Zeely as the story begins?
2. What did Zeely mean when she told Geeder to remember the turtle and the snake?
3. In what ways is Geeder's impression of Zeely similar to Zeely's childhood impression of the old woman?
4. Have you ever wanted to be someone other than the person you are? Describe the person you wanted to be and tell why you wanted to be that person.

Applying Reading Skills

A. List in chronological order the important events described in the introduction to "Zeely."

B. Look at the two time lines below. The first is a time line for Zeely's childhood story of the past. The second is a time line for the story of Zeely and Geeder in the present. Copy and complete each time line.

- Zeely's story of the past

  1.   2. Sometimes the woman would come upon me while I was swimming in the lake.   3.   4. The old woman poked the vine.   5.

- The story of Zeely and Geeder in the present

  1.   2. Geeder said, "But you *are* a Watutsi."   3.   4. Geeder was suddenly shy and took hold of her beads and ran her fingers over them.   5.

GO, MY CHILD

Go, my child,
  to the lands of your people.
Awaken them.
They have slept too long.
Many years have passed.
Traditions have been carried away
  by the wind.
Old tales have fled into the night.
The way of the Ancient Ones is dying.
Wash away the evil and harm
  that have befallen them.
Lead them in traditional song.
Lead them in ceremonial dance.
Send them forth to the far edges
  of the earth
To find all that has been lost.
Let those among us
  who have left us to die
Know that we only slept,
And now,
We live again.

ALONZO LOPEZ

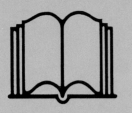

PREPARING FOR READING

Learning Vocabulary

1. Some African women paint the walls of their houses with colorful abstract <u>murals</u>.
2. <u>Elaborate</u> beaded clothing made by the women is used in special ceremonies or <u>rituals</u>.
3. When girls reach womanhood, they are kept apart, or <u>secluded</u>, for a time in their homes.
4. They learn to do beadwork, a <u>cherished</u> pastime that is highly respected.
5. In her art each woman follows her own <u>innovative</u> spirit, so there are many new and different styles.

murals	elaborate	rituals
secluded	cherished	innovative

Developing Background and Skills
Make Generalizations

A **generalization** is a general statement that is a kind of conclusion. Generalizations are based on many particular facts or specific examples. Read the paragraph, question, and answer choices below.

Wood is the most widely used material in African sculpture. Wood sculptors often work with simple tools such as axes, knives, chisels, and scrapers in carving. Wood, however, is not the only sculpturing material. Ivory, stone, clay, and mud are often used. The sculpturing of bronze and brass works of art began in Nigeria and spread to nearby areas. Iron, though not in widespread use, is employed in certain regions. Fibers and twigs are frequently used in the sculpturing of masks—if the word *sculpture* can include materials of this kind.

What generalization can be made on the basis of the information in the paragraph?

    a. African sculpture involves the use of simple tools.

    b. Sculptors mostly use metals in their work.

    c. Many materials are used in African sculpture.

If you read the paragraph carefully, you discovered that most of the information had to do with the kinds of materials used in African sculpture. Wood, ivory, stone, clay, mud, brass, bronze, fibers, and twigs were all mentioned. These examples are sufficient to make the generalization *Many materials are used in African sculpture* (**c**).

A generalization based on facts and evidence is said to be valid. To be valid, a generalization must be supported by many specific examples. Generalizations that are not supported by facts or that are supported by too few facts are said to be invalid. Choice **a** makes a general statement about *African* sculpture. The facts in the paragraph, however, only refer to *wood* sculpture. Is choice **b** supported by the facts in the paragraph?

A generalization is a kind of rule, and like a rule it usually has exceptions. For this reason, avoid words such as *all*, *every*, and *none* in making a generalization. For example, there are hundreds of leading museums that have collections of African art, but there are several that do not. A valid generalization based on this information would be *Many leading museums have collections of African art*.

As you read the next selection, notice the generalizations the author makes. Think about the generalizations you can make.

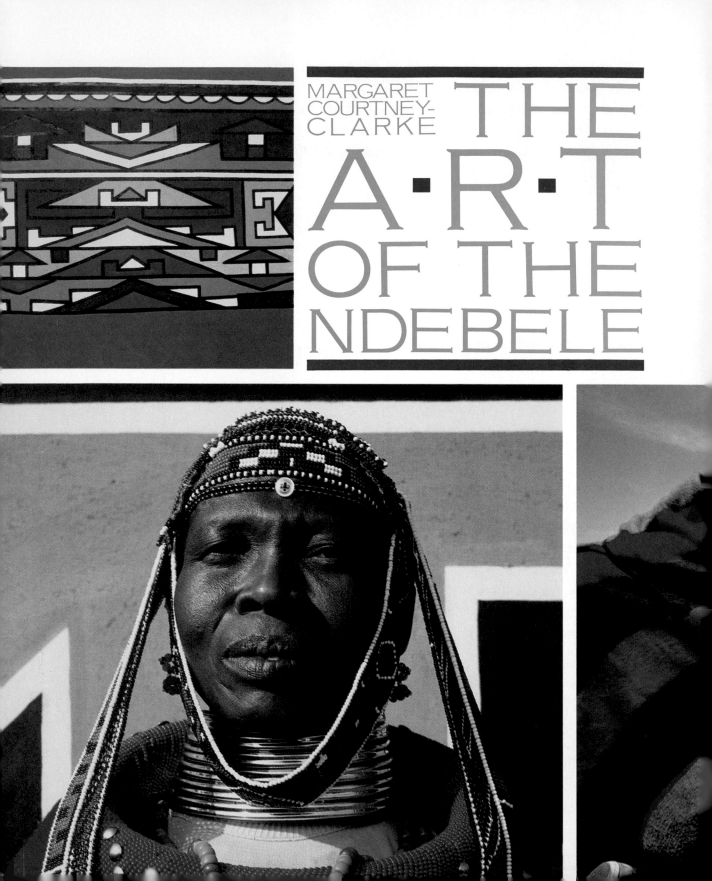

MARGARET
COURTNEY-
CLARKE

THE
A·R·T
OF THE
NDEBELE

The Ndebele (en deb′ ə lē) are a people of southern Africa. Once they were nomads and warriors, but about a hundred years ago they gave up this way of life to become farmers. Today, because of South African government policy, the Ndebele in the region known as the Southern Transvaal are being relocated from their native lands and farms to a recently created homeland, KwaNdebele.

For generations, the women of the Ndebele have created a rich and beautiful abstract art. They paint the walls of their houses with colorful murals. They also make elaborate beaded clothing to wear for the special rituals that are important to their life. Margaret Courtney-Clarke photographed and described this art created by the Ndebele women of today.

Young women help prepare the food for a wedding feast. They wear the red, yellow, green, and blue blankets that are customary for such an occasion.

351

PAINTING AND BEADWORK

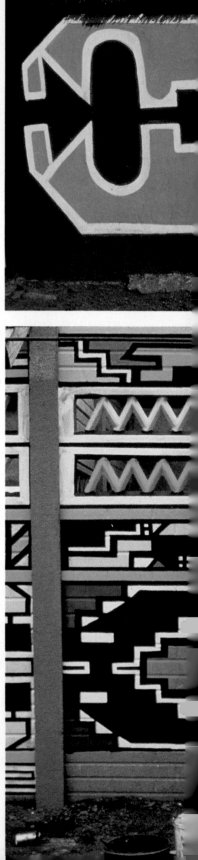

For the Ndebele, the most important ritual is the ceremony of manhood. Every four years young men between the ages of eighteen and twenty-two are sent away for three months to attend a special school, *wela* (wā′ lə). During *wela*, the young men learn their responsibilities toward their families and their community. Special training hardens them, and songs of praise give them courage. These events, along with teachings by the elders on customs and culture, create a strong bond among them.

Wela is the most important occasion for the Ndebele woman's role as artist. Before the young men leave for the schools, the women carefully replaster the outside walls of their homes and reconstruct the entranceways. Then they paint—and repaint each year—their impressions of everyday life, in geometrical designs, on the wall surfaces. While the young men are away, their families proudly welcome all visitors and relatives. A white flag hoisted on a tall pole outside the front entrance shows that the mother has a son at *wela*.

When girls reach womanhood, they too are secluded for three months. During this time, in the privacy of their homes, they perfect the arts of beadwork and painting. Painting is not taught in schools, so it is only through this mother-daughter tradition that the art survives.

For these and other ritual occasions, the Ndebele women wear elaborate outfits. Beautiful blankets with beaded trimmings; long beaded strips attached to headbands; beaded

Ndebele designs are geometric and abstract. The motif shown here is typical. *Below:* An Ndebele woman paints market stalls using commercial paints.

skirts; and copper leg, arm, and neck rings are all worn. In contrast, the men are dressed mainly in plain Western clothes. Though most women still wear traditional clothing, men have worn Western clothing since the turn of the century.

Ndebele children wear beads before they wear clothes. Their first ornament is put on shortly after birth—a simple string of white beads around the waist, worn for luck. As they get older, they wear beaded anklets, wristlets, and necklets. As boys approach an age of responsibility, they adopt Western-style pants. Girls wear cotton skirts, often stitched in brightly colored beads. For their "coming out" celebration, the girls wear stiff rectangular aprons completely beaded in geometric three-dimensional patterns.

Young girls, maidens, and married women continue to wear beadwork throughout their lives on special occasions. Married women in the homeland and remoter areas still wear beaded aprons and an all-purpose blanket. Beadwork is a cherished pastime for Ndebele women. After completing their day-to-day tasks, women gather under the shade of a tree or inside their homes in the heat of summer, or around the hearth in winter, spending their spare time sorting, stringing, and stitching beads.

MURALS

When the summer rains have ceased and the crops have been harvested, mural decoration begins. Mural decoration is a personal art. A woman's style of mural decoration and her choice of colors set her apart from other women.

Throughout Africa, the traditional family homestead consists of an enclosure of several buildings. The Ndebele call this compound *umuzi* (ù mü′ zē).

The *umuzi* consists of a main hut and several outbuildings, encircled by a low wall. There is either an elaborate entrance or a simple gatepost. Other low walls divide areas within the *umuzi*, creating courtyards.

The Ndebele use building techniques similar to those used throughout Africa. Both men and women take part in the building. The men do the heavy construction, and the women gather the materials and do the manual labor. First wooden poles are placed into the ground, and twigs and sticks are woven between them to form walls. The men lay down the roof beams over the walls, and tie down bundles of grass to form the thatched roof. The women then plaster the framework for the walls on both sides with a mixture of clay and cow dung. This takes several months to complete. After the basic structure is finished, surrounding low walls and solid benches are added. After the dwelling has dried, painting begins.

In the past, a woman was limited to the colors she could find in the earth—brown, ocher, red, and black. As bluing for washing became available, this, too, was used to complement the other colors. The designs were bold, linear, and abstract, becoming more complicated on the front of the

The white flag flying in front of this home shows that the family has a son attending *wela. Below:* Detail of a front facade.

house. The side and back walls were painted with much simpler, more subdued shapes outlined in black.

The women traveled long distances to obtain natural colors. In earlier days it was not unheard of for a woman to walk as far as one hundred miles to reach an area known for its deep red soil. In the past, the women used animal-hair brushes, feathers, and chewed twig ends to apply the annual coat of paint. Another common technique was to use the fingers to apply wet clay to a darker dry surface, creating a three-dimensional textural pattern.

Feathers and earth are still used today, but more women now use commercial brushes and water-based acrylic paint. These are often mixed with slaked lime or earth to obtain pastel tones. The choice between natural colors and new paints is an economic one. Commercial paints are expensive but last several years. Earth colors are continually washed away and must be reapplied after the rains.

Ndebele painting is composed freehand, directly onto the surface of the wall. There is no preliminary drawing, measuring, or use of any other tools except the painter's hands, her brush, and her innovative spirit.

A two-story house, electric light poles, and even a blue swimming pool are incorporated into this design for the front wall of a house.

THE OLD AND THE NEW

Although Ndebele murals are primarily abstract, they often include designs based on animals, light bulbs, and razor blades. The Ndebele intermix traditional designs, such as the sun and trees, and Western symbols, such as letters of the alphabet.

Telephone poles, wrought-iron work, airplanes (*ufly*, the Ndebele call them), and staircases and steps all appear—dramatically changed—on Ndebele walls and in their bead-work. The artists look around them and choose the most graphic and geometric forms and shapes to use in their artwork. Ndebele women are interested in cars, for example, not because of the cars themselves, but because they are fascinated by the designs of license plates. Animals and figures, which are difficult to reduce to geometric shapes, are rare in Ndebele art.

The Ndebele style continues to grow and change, as the women adapt Western images, blending new with old to use them in their art. Today, South Africa is a troubled country. But it is important that despite the problems, a small group of people stubbornly continues an age-old and distinct artistic tradition.

Questions

1. What customs, traditions, ceremonies, and rituals give the Ndebele women a chance to display their skills?
2. Why do you think the author chose to photograph and write about the women artists of Ndebele?
3. Do you think it is important to keep alive customs and traditions such as those practiced by the Ndebele? Give reasons to support your answer.
4. Choose one of the photographs in the selection and describe it.

Applying Reading Skills

Copy each sentence below that is a valid generalization based on the information presented in "The Art of the Ndebele." List at least two facts or examples that support each valid generalization.

1. The ceremony called *wela* is an important ritual for the Ndebele.
2. Most Ndebele women dress in highly decorated, elaborate outfits.
3. The customs and way of life of the Ndebele have always remained the same.
4. The building of houses is a job shared by men and women of the Ndebele.
5. Several different tools and painting materials are used in decorating Ndebele houses.
6. Many Western symbols are incorporated into the designs of the Ndebele murals.

PREPARING FOR READING

Learning Vocabulary

1. Hiram Bingham, a young American <u>archaeologist</u> visiting Peru in the early 1900s, came across the tomb of Pizarro.
2. In the 1500s, Pizarro had conquered the Inca <u>empire</u> of South America.
3. Pizarro had a <u>ruthless</u> plan to kill the Inca leader and carry off the Inca treasures.
4. Legends told that the Incas still lived and would one day seek <u>vengeance</u> for Pizarro's crimes.
5. Bingham became <u>obsessed</u> with these fabulous stories and began to search for the Incas and their cities.
6. He marveled at the genius of the <u>architects</u> who had designed fabulous cities in the mountains.
7. His Indian guides would not approach the sacred sun stone; <u>reverence</u>, not fear, held them back.

archaeologist   empire   ruthless   vengeance
obsessed   architects   reverence

Developing Background and Skills
Maps

A **map** is a drawing that shows all or part of the earth's surface. A historical map, like the one on the next page, gives information about places in the past.

The **arrow** shows you which way north is. If you know which way north is, you can easily find the other directions. The **scale bar** indicates scale, or relative size. You can use the scale bar to figure out distance.

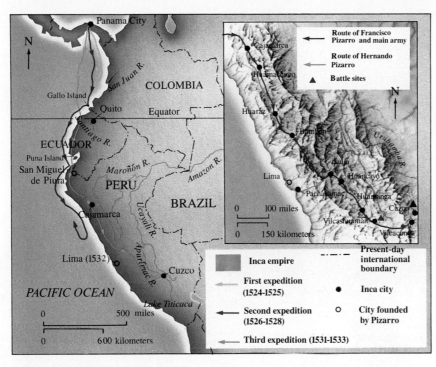

Notice the map in the upper right-hand corner of the main map. This map, set into the main map, is called an **inset map**. What part of the main map is shown in the inset map? Does one inch on the main map represent a smaller or a greater distance than one inch on the inset map? Does the inset map show greater or less detail than the main map?

To save space, information on a map is shown by symbols. A symbol is something that stands for something else. The meaning of the symbols is explained in the **key**, or legend. Notice that both the main map and the inset map have a key. When using a map, it's a good idea to check the key. How is the Inca empire indicated on the map? How many expeditions did Pizarro make?

As you read the next selection, use this map and the map in the selection to find the places visited by Pizarro and Bingham. See if you can trace their routes as you follow the story.

Machu Picchu, the fortress-city of the Incas, built high in the Andes Mountains.

ON THE TRAIL OF THE
INCAS

HEINZ SPONSEL

A young American archaeologist named Hiram Bingham was strolling through the streets of Lima, the capital of Peru, at the beginning of this century. He stopped in front of an old cathedral. After admiring the ancient white-washed structure from the outside, he entered. A dim light filtered through the stained-glass windows. Bingham entered a small side chapel. Next to a window, imbedded in the wall, hung a tablet bearing an inscription in gold letters.

CAPTAIN GENERAL
DON FRANCISCO PIZARRO
FOUNDER OF LIMA—
JANUARY 18, 1535
DIED JUNE 26, 1541

Bingham examined the glass window. Behind it, in an open marble coffin, lay a skeleton, the eyes filled with cotton. It was the mummy of Pizarro, conqueror of Peru, who had destroyed the empire of the Incas.

It had happened in 1532. Pizarro had made a daring march through Peru with scarcely two hundred men. Now he longed to capture the golden empire of the Incas. Atahualpa (ät ə wäl′ pə), the ruling chief of the Incas, was not aware of the strangers' real intention. At that time, Atahualpa had his residence in Cajamarca (kä hə mär′ kə). In the city stood the royal palace and the Temple of the Sun. It was here that the greedy white men met this great ruler.

Surrounded by noble warriors and women in gowns of gold, Atahualpa sat under a canopy of feathers. A curtain veiled his head from view. Around his neck he wore a golden disk. To the Incas, he was a living god. But all the Spaniards could see, or perhaps all they wanted to see, was gold, and gold was everywhere. At that moment Pizarro devised his ruthless plan. It would be carried out when Atahualpa returned the visit a few days later.

The chief arrived in a sedan chair adorned with gold and diamonds. Nobles, wearing beautiful feathers of tropical birds, were gathered around him. Servants went ahead to clear the way for the Son of the Sun with plumes and palm branches. Six thousand warriors followed, bearing no arms.

Pizarro took note of their lack of weapons with satisfaction. He gave a sign to his men. Suddenly, guns the Spaniards had hidden till now were fired directly into the crowd of peaceful Indians. Pizarro himself rudely pulled the king off his sedan chair and took him prisoner. The Sun God surrendered to his fate with the calmness of true royalty. By now he understood that the vicious strangers wanted only his vast fortune. Atahualpa promised to give them as much gold and silver as it would take to fill his prison. Pizarro readily agreed. After fulfilling that promise, the Incas could be assured of the safe return of their chief, Pizzaro told them.

Atahualpa ordered his subjects to collect gold and silver and to pile it up in the prison where he was being held. When Pizarro noticed how easily the Incas could collect the ransom, he greedily demanded more. Again the people collected gold and silver to buy their chief's release. But Pizarro still hesitated to set his prisoner free. He wanted to seize the country's entire store of riches and decided to get rid of Atahualpa.

To do this, Pizarro came up with a false charge of treason. A few weeks later, a Spanish court sentenced the chief to death by fire. This was soon changed to a more "merciful" sentence— death by strangulation. Thus after an imprisonment of ten months, Atahualpa, the last of the Incas, the last of the reigning gods of the sun, was choked to death.

In the meantime, the Spaniards marched from Cajamarca to Cuzco (kü′ skō), then the capital of the Incan civilization. The conquerors marched along the most perfectly built roads they had ever seen. They entered Cuzco without meet-

An engraving made in 1595 shows Atahualpa negotiating with Pizarro.

ing any resistance. Once again they resumed their shameless criminal looting. Gold! Ever more and more gold!

But the spirits of the murdered Incas finally took revenge. The Spaniards began to fight among themselves. Francisco Pizarro was stabbed to death in his palace by a fellow countryman.

All this had happened almost four hundred years before Hiram Bingham had come to Lima. He found himself unable to get the memory of the Incas out of his mind. He became obsessed by the story of their fabulous past and of their empire. Legends told that their cities still existed, hidden somewhere in the jungles of the towering Andes Mountains. According to these legends, the Incas still lived there and would one day seek vengeance for Pizarro's unspeakable crimes.

Bingham knew that he must search for the traces of the Incas. He gathered five Indians as guides, a dozen llamas, and several mules. Then he started out to cross the wilderness and rocky mountains of Peru.

Nothing was left of the old roads, of course. The men found some broken stone walls and a few steps cut into the steep mountain sides. The path followed the Apurímac (äp′ ə rē′ mäk) valley upward. Terraces of stone had been cut into the walls of sheer rock. Bingham realized that these must have been fertile fields centuries ago. The Incas had lifted the good earth from the valley. The stone terraces had been designed to hold it fast. The Incas had also built irrigation canals so that grain could grow in the middle of a stony wasteland.

Bingham and his men were able to make only ten or twelve miles (16–19 km) a day. They traveled through the jungle for weeks.

Eventually they reached a height of twelve thousand feet (3,600 m). Bingham found it difficult to breathe the thin air at this altitude. The Indians, used to life on the high mountain ranges, showed not the least sign of fatigue. In the evenings, they somehow found places to pitch their tents. Then the campfire was started and some wild game roasted on a spit. Sometimes an Indian would play a strange folk melody on a handmade flute. Was it an old song from the Incan past?

Months had gone by, but they had still not come upon any trace of the Incas and their ancient city. An inner force drove Bingham on. He never lost faith in his hunch that hard work and patience would bring him success.

The Urubamba (ėr′ ə bäm′ bə) river foamed wildly between the steep slopes of the Andes as the party continued to make its way along its bank into the unknown. Gradually the valley widened. They came upon a small plain on which stood a cluster of clay huts. The Quechua (kech′ wə) Indians lived here. Their faces, darkened by the sun, appeared almost black. The men and women wore thick ponchos with colorful belts, from which hung knives and flutes.

For seven days Bingham stayed on as a guest in the forgotten village of the Quechuas before continuing his march. No white explorers had ever journeyed so deeply into this area. Again weeks and months went by. Again dangers beset the men everywhere.

The weary column had almost given up hope when the miracle occurred. A sharp white light pierced the dense jungle. Through

the thickness of the trees they could make out high slopes. Then they saw walls, houses, and towers of white granite shimmering in the sunlight. Bingham was certain he had come upon the long-lost city of the Incas.

"The city of the Incas—right in the jungle," he whispered in astonishment. He stood stock-still, gazing at the sight which was so like a dream.

But one of the Indians murmured, "Machu Picchu (mäch' ü pēk' chü)!"

"Machu Picchu!" Bingham repeated the name.

There it was—the city in the middle of the jungle. Houses, steps, walls, gates, and columns reached high up into the sky.

The explorers noticed that the houses were roofless. The roads lay deserted. The sharp wind from the Andes blew through the holes in the windows. Bats swung on jasmine bushes. Poisonous spiders crawled over stones.

The Indians stood motionless, watching in silence. Then they bent down and removed their sandals. They believed they stood on holy ground.

A new camp was set up in the middle of this city full of ancient ghosts. These men had been

The royal tomb at Machu Picchu shows the incredible masonry skills of the ancient Incas.

looking for it for months. Now they would rest here just as long. Was this city a thousand years old, or even older? Bingham wondered as he roamed through it day after day, each time making new discoveries. Would he ever find out?

The city had been built at an elevation of almost seven thousand feet (2,100 m). At this height a strong wind blew constantly. It shook, but never shattered, the immense walls of white granite. More and more questions went through Bingham's mind. How had the Incas been able to build this city? They had neither horses nor carts to transport the rocks. He marveled at the genius of the ancient architects as he studied Machu Picchu more closely.

He climbed to the highest point of the city—to the top of the tower at the mountain's peak. Here the wind blew stronger than ever. The Indians who had followed him remained on the last stairway. One of them pointed at the stone pillar rising up from the rocks and murmured in awe: "Intihuatana (in' tē wä tä' nə). Now Bingham understood; he knew that word. It meant "sacred stone of the sun." So this was the reason the Indians would not advance

closer to him. It was not fear holding them back, but reverence. Bingham was standing on the spot where the priests of the Incas had worshipped the sun god.

Far below shone the white walls of the city. Bingham descended the slopes slowly. At nightfall he was again seated around the campfire with the Indians. One of them confided to him: "Incas are still living in the Urubamba valley."

Several days later, Bingham continued his exploration. Eventually the men sighted white buildings in a wide valley. Countless towers and church spires clutched at the sky. It was Cuzco, the capital city of the Incas!

Bingham and his companions spent that night on the hills above Cuzco. It was the night of their farewell—to each other, and to their incredible discovery. That night an Indian recounted the age-old legend of this sacred golden city. Once the sun god Manco Capac (män' kō kä' päk) had sent his sister to found a city and an empire. He gave her a golden stick and said: "Where the staff is held fast in the earth, there you must build your city." Manco Capac soon joined his sister in her search for the exact site, which took many years. They would throw their staff into the ground over and over again, but it never remained stuck. Then they finally entered this valley. They threw their staff high in the air. As it fell it dug itself deep into the earth. Cuzco was founded on that very spot. Manco Capac himself became the first chief of the Incas. Cuzco was made the capital of their great empire. In the center of the city they built the House of the Sun, called Intichacha (in' tē chä' chä).

After the Indian had told his tale, he looked down upon the valley and the ancient city. His own face seemed to have been carved out of rock. Suddenly its expression changed. His eyes blazed, and he said in a bitter voice: "Pizarro destroyed all of it—the city, the House of the Sun, and the whole empire."

He rose and went off into the night by himself. Bingham followed his Indian friend. He put an arm around his shoulder and led him back to the campfire. To comfort him he told the Indian: "Pizarro was unable to destroy all of it. Descendants of the Incas still live in the jungles. And their majestic city of Machu Picchu, still standing on its rock, has been watching over the Urubamba valley for all these centuries since."

A shadow of a smile spread over the man's face. The campfire crackled, and a song rang out in the wind over the hills. It was the song of the moon, the sun, and the earth, the song of the timeless trail.

Questions

1. Who was Francisco Pizarro and what "unspeakable crimes" did he commit?
2. Why did Bingham refuse to give up his search even after months without any discoveries?
3. Why had the perfectly built roads Pizarro followed to Cuzco disappeared by the time Bingham began his search?
4. If you had been Hiram Bingham, what things would you have done to prepare for your search for the Incas and their lost city?

Applying Reading Skills

Use the maps on page 365 to answer the questions below.

1. On what continent is Peru? Describe its location.
2. Does the main map or the inset map show greater detail?
3. In what direction is Machu Picchu from Cuzco?
4. About how far is it from Cajamarca to Cuzco?
5. In what direction do the Andes Mountains extend?
6. What geographical feature might make travel from Lima to Machu Picchu difficult?
7. About how much farther is it from Cajamarca to Cuzco than it is from Lima to Cuzco?

WRITING ACTIVITY

WRITE AN OBITUARY

Prewrite

Hiram Bingham stared at the remains of Francisco Pizarro in the Lima cathedral, wondering what kind of person the living man must have been. Surely the Incas and the Spanish viewed him quite differently. What do you suppose would be the difference between an obituary, or death notice, of Pizarro written for an Incan newspaper of the time and one written for a Spanish newspaper? You are going to write those two obituaries.

First, review the obituaries of well-known people in your local newspaper to check the basic facts included in any obituary. Such facts usually include information on the date of birth and death, place of birth, and family members. You will have to check an encyclopedia for the basic facts about Pizarro.

What other kinds of information might be found in an obituary? Can you add to this list?

1. Major job or career
2. Most memorable character trait
3. Contributions to the community

Remember, you are writing two obituaries of Pizarro. One will present the Incan point of view. The other will present the Spanish point of view. Reread "On the Trail of the Incas." Use the list above and make a chart like the one below. One item has been given on the chart to get you started. List other points of view on the chart by working with your teacher and members of your class.

370

Don Francisco Pizarro	
Incan Point of View	Spanish Point of View
Monstrous murderer of innocent people	Courageous defender of Spanish colonists

Write

1. Reread your notes from the chart and review your list of basic facts about Pizarro. One way to organize each obituary is given below.
2. **Paragraph 1:** Give the basic facts of Pizarro's life. This paragraph will be the same for both obituaries.
3. **Paragraph 2 or more:** Write a description of Pizarro based on a specific point of view using information from the chart.
4. Write a headline for your obituary to attract the attention of your readers.
5. Complete the second obituary from the contrasting point of view.
6. Use your Glossary or dictionary for spelling help.

Revise

Read your obituaries. Does each one contain a paragraph giving the essential facts of Pizarro's life and death? Remember your original purpose. Could your readers tell immediately from reading the obituary the newspaper's point of view about Pizarro?

1. Proofread your sentences for correct punctuation, especially of dates.
2. Check the spelling of the names of people and places.
3. Rewrite and share your obituaries.

PREPARING FOR READING

Learning Vocabulary

1. The old man thought it was a good <u>omen</u> when the boy arrived just as the sun rose.
2. The old man was thin and bent with the years, but he spoke with the <u>vigor</u> of a young man.
3. The boy's voice was never proud or <u>arrogant</u>, but rather <u>wistful</u> and pleading.
4. The old man told the boy that he must be very sure before repeating the words of the sacred <u>vow</u>, because the promise was <u>irrevocable</u>, and he would have to keep it until death.

omen	vigor	arrogant
wistful	vow	irrevocable

Developing Background and Skills
Sequence of Events

Read the following passage and see if you can decide the correct (chronological) order of events. Then read the lists.

Chuto (chü′ tō) appeared at the head of the trail. Cusi (kü′ sē) ran to him, and together they walked to the hut. They ate supper, and afterward Cusi put a package into Chuto's hands. He had bought the present for Chuto several days before in Cuzco. But even before that, Cusi had known he would return to the valley. Now Chuto opened the package. When he saw what was inside, he was pleased.

The two lists show the sequence of events as they really happened and as they were narrated or described in the passage.

1. Chuto appeared at the head of the trail.
2. Cusi ran to Chuto.
3. Together they walked to the hut.
4. They ate supper.
5. Cusi put a package into Chuto's hands.
6. He had bought the present for Chuto several days before in Cuzco.
7. He had known he would return to the valley.
8. Chuto opened the package.
9. When he saw what was inside, he was pleased.

1. Cusi knew he would return to the valley.
2. Cusi bought the present for Chuto in Cuzco.
3. Chuto appeared at the head of the trail.
4. Cusi ran to Chuto.
5. Together they walked to the hut.
6. They ate supper.
7. Cusi put a package into Chuto's hands.
8. Chuto opened the package.
9. When Chuto saw what was inside, he was pleased.

When writers describe events out of sequence, they often use words such as *then*, *afterward*, *before*, and *when* as clues. The word *when* tells you that *Chuto saw what was inside* and *Chuto was pleased* took place at the same time. *As* and *meanwhile* are other words that signal events that happen at the same time.

Verb tense, too, is a clue to order. The verb forms *had bought*, and *had known*, are in the past perfect tense. They indicate events that took place earlier than those described in the simple past tense (*appeared*, *ran*).

See if you can determine the sequence of events in the story that follows. Understanding the sequence of events can help you understand the story.

Secret of the Andes

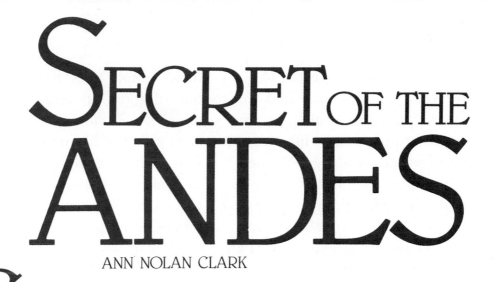

ANN NOLAN CLARK

Cusi (kü′ sē), an Inca boy, had lived all of his life in Hidden Valley, high in the mountains of Peru, with old Chuto (chü′ tō), the llama herder. Cusi loved the mountains and his special pet llama, Misti. Yet he was disturbed by questions that no one would, or perhaps could, answer for him. Why does he wear golden earplugs, the sign of royal blood? Who were his parents? Who is he? By whose order do Chuto and he care for the llamas? Cusi longed to know the answers almost as much as he longed to belong to a family.

One day Cusi followed Misti along a trail he had never seen before. It led to a hidden canyon and the ruins of an ancient temple. There he found a pair of tiny golden sandals. In some way he did not understand, Cusi knew the sandals were his. Taking the sandals as a sign, Cusi set out for Cuzco, the sacred city of the Inca, to search for his heart's desire.

On his way he found an Ayllu (ī′ lü), a village of the Ancient People. There he rested, before continuing his journey to Cuzco.

In Cuzco, Cusi found an Indian family which adopted him. It seemed his dream had come true. But Cusi soon realized he did not belong with them. He headed back to his home in the high mountains, his questions unanswered. On his journey, he met an old man.

The old Indian greeted Cusi. "I saw you coming, you and your llamas. The Sun came just then. You and the Sun came into the new day together. It is a good omen."

Cusi laughed. He felt happy, so happy that everything else seemed unimportant. Now he said, natural and serious and quietly glad, "I am a good omen. I know it. You see I am going home."

The Indian looked at him for a long time, saying nothing, but the silence was not heavy. It was restful and right, as everything about this new day seemed restful and right. Cusi returned the old man's gaze frankly and with interest. He saw a thin old Indian, bent with the years and the vigor of living. The brown face was wrinkled with age, but the hair above it was black as a young man's, and the black eyes were young and bright and keen. Then Cusi started and looked again. Massive, heavy gold earplugs hung from the man's ears, lengthening the earlobes to fantastic length. The man nodded. "Yes," he said.

Although the answer was short, it carried a wealth of meaning. The man's simple "Yes" told Cusi, "I am one of them, as you are. We belong." A month ago Cusi would have tortured his mind asking himself, "Who are they? To whom do we belong? Why do a few of us wear them?" Now such questions seemed unimportant.

After another time of silence the man spoke. "You have been to Cuzco. Did you bring the golden sandals back with you?"

"Yes." It was Cusi's turn to answer simply. The man seemed satisfied with the answer, as Cusi had been.

"They call me Keeper of the Fields. His Fields. Chuto and I and you too, perhaps, follow the same trail." To Cusi's look of surprise the Indian explained, "I know Chuto as I know you. As I knew you had gone down the mountain trail to Cuzco.

"And the sandals, did you bring them with you?" the Indian asked again.

"Yes, it was the sandals that made me know that the people I met could not be my family. I could not share them. If it had been Chuto who needed them, or Misti,

I could have given them because —because—" The boy struggled for the right word and suddenly leaped to his feet, his eyes black and deep with excitement. "They would have had a right to them because we are part of each other. We are a family. We belong to one another, and everything we have can be shared together."

Cusi stood still and tense. There was the answer! What he had been looking for had been his. He had not known it. He had almost lost it. He had almost gone away, leaving all that mattered behind him. "But I guess deep in my heart I knew," he said aloud, "because when I traded for one thing at the market, I always traded for two, two knitted caps, two pairs of cotton trousers, two alpaca sweaters. Always one for Chuto, one for me."

The old man was laughing softly. "Of course you knew, but you had to find out that you knew. You will get your heart's desire." He quoted, "Grieve not if your searching circles."

"Oh!" Cusi cried. "I understand now. My trail circles back to Hidden Valley. To where I belong."

The Old One pointed skyward. It was midday. Cusi had talked away the hours of morning. "But you did not waste them, Cusi. Their coming was a spring thaw in a mountain river. The ice in your heart has melted. The flood of your feeling has washed clean your life-way of its deadwood of misunderstanding."

Misti's llama bell tinkled impatiently. "It is time that you take the trail again," the old man said kindly. "I will help you load your llamas and find the way."

"I know the trail," Cusi told him. "I traveled it not many days ago."

The Indian shook his head. "That trail is gone. A landslide wiped it away. Almost half a mountain slid down into the valley where the trail forked."

"No! It cannot be. It must not be. That would mean the Allyu town was gone—and the woman who fed me, who called me son—" Cusi stared with unbelieving eyes.

"Perhaps. Year by year our number grows fewer."

"The Inca will never die!" Cusi returned hotly.

The Indian sighed. "Forget us

not," he repeated softly, and it was a farewell for those of his blood who had gone on the trail of no returning. Cusi felt a need for getting home, for being safe again with those he loved and those who loved him, safe again in Hidden Valley.

"Time passes," the old man said.

When the shadows of evening fell with purple softness over the bleakness of the bare brown mountains, the Keeper of the Fields said good-by to the highland shepherd. "This is for Chuto," he said, handing Cusi an ear of corn. "It is from the Lake," he said, meaning Lake Titicaca (tit′ i käk′ ə), the Sacred Lake of the Ancient Inca. "Chuto will prize it. And this—this is for you. Learn to make it talk, and its voice will heal your heart's loneliness." It was a long reedlike flute that highland people use to sing to themselves and to their flocks. Cusi was pleased. It was the first gift that anyone had given him, and he felt the sting of tears in his eyes. "Today has been the greatest day of your life, for you have learned to read your own heart." With that the old man turned and went back

over the trail by which he had come. He was lost quickly in the purple shadows, and only his memory remained like the small glow of an evening campfire.

Cusi went on. His llamas followed. Somewhere a night bird chirped his evening prayer. Somewhere an old man sat by the blackened chips of a supper fire. Chuto. Waiting.

Night closed in, thick and still, mysterious and cold. Bright stars twinkled down, and a pale moon. On a lonely trail a young boy slept by three tired llamas.

As he neared Hidden Valley, Cusi got out his flute and gave the flute call. He had been practicing it all day, and although it was far from perfect it delighted him. Suncca began a wild barking. Chuto appeared at the head of the trail.

Cusi was alarmed at the weariness in the Old One's face, but when Chuto spoke, his voice sounded as it always did, soft and patient and kind. "You have come back," the old man said and repeated himself as was his habit. "You have come."

He touched briefly Cusi's shoulder. Together the man and the boy walked to the hut before the supper fire. "Deep in my heart I think I knew you would come back. I think I never doubted it, deep in my heart."

Cusi smiled at him. "Deep in my heart I must have known, too, because look, I bartered for these at the marketplace. One for you. One for me. This is for you. This is for me." As he talked Cusi unloaded Misti and gave Chuto the things he had brought for him.

Chuto was pleased. He put the trousers on. He put the sweater on. He put the cap on. Then he helped Cusi unload the two other llamas.

While they were eating supper Cusi got out the corn from Sacred Lake, gift to Chuto from the Keeper of the Fields. Chuto's eyes lighted when Cusi gave it to him. "Ah, you saw him, then? You saw him," he said as he thoughtfully turned the corn over and over in his strong brown hands.

"I saw him," Cusi answered. "He showed me the new trail around the landslide. Did you know there was a landslide?"

Chuto nodded. "They told me. How good that you saw her, now that the sliding mountain has, perhaps, destroyed all that you saw." This was what Cusi had wanted—some word, some sign, some token that the Old One wanted to talk.

Cusi moved nearer the small fire flame. The night was hushed with waiting. There were no stars. There was only blackness, velvet blackness, thick and soft, blanketing the mountain peaks, blanketing the wind, hushing the noises of the night.

Cusi spoke. "Chuto, my Chuto, I want to stay here with you. You are my family. This is my home. I never want to go away again."

Chuto did not answer. The llamas were not humming. Even the whining Suncca was still.

"Chuto, let me stay."

"Why do you say that? Why?"

"Because it is what I want. I learned that this is my heart's deep wish."

"Are you certain? Are you sure? Think before you answer. Do not speak quick words that will run away once you have set them free."

Cusi shivered, but he did not falter. "I want to stay. I want to share your days and give you mine."

Again Chuto repeated, "Think, Cusi. Be careful of your words."

"I want to stay."

"You are too young to know what you want."

Cusi stood up. "I am old for my years. The woman of the Allyu who gave me food and called me son thought it; I could tell. The Keeper of the Fields acted toward me as if I were old enough to talk with. I am old for my years. I am old enough to know what I want. You only question me, doubt me, turn me back when my feet ache to walk the manhood trail."

Cusi's young voice broke. It was not arrogant. It was not proud. It was a wistful, pleading cry. "Chuto, my father. Father of my choice, believe in me."

Chuto too was standing. "Son of my choice, I believe you now. You are ready. It is I who falter because I love you. Give me time to open this door to you that, once opened, closes itself forever."

Cusi waited. He stood erect and firm. He did not move. Neither excitement nor fear made his heart beat faster or his pulse race. He was relaxed. He was ready. He was not afraid.

At last Chuto spoke. "Four hundred years have lessened our numbers, but have not diluted our blood. For four times four hundred years our blood will flow in its destined channel across our conquered land. Cusi, repeat after me these words I say:

"I Cusi, Son of the Ancients,
Son of Nobility,
Son of Royalty,
Son of the Last Mighty Inca,
I, Cusi, shepherd boy of Peru,
making my sacred, my lasting,
my irrevocable vow . . . "

Cusi's voice did not stammer, did not waver as he said:

"I, Cusi, . . .
make my sacred, my lasting,
my irrevocable vow
for now and for my tomorrows
until Death takes Life from me."

Chuto asked again, "Are you ready? Are you sure?"

The reply came promptly and clearly. "I am ready. I am sure."

"It is well. Repeat the words I say. Repeat them slowly. Repeat them distinctly. Each word must cut itself into your heart until life's end.

"I vow to keep the secret of the cave.

Now and forever I keep the secret.

Never will I show it

except to the Chosen One.

Never will I speak of its hidden

bounty except to him who will

be chosen to follow me.

Never will I speak

of this hidden spot.

I will not think of it

lest my dreams betray me.

I will not think of it

lest my thoughts escape me:

With my blood I will defend my

knowledge.

With my blood I make this vow.

With my blood I will keep it."

Cusi repeated the words. He felt a sharp stab of pain, and a drop of blood slowly dripped to the ground beneath his feet.

Again Chuto told him to repeat words that he said to him. This vow was to keep the Inca's llama flock intact, breeding them with wisdom, tending them with knowledge, giving them out with judgment. Again Cusi felt the small sharp stab of pain and knew his life's blood was hostage to his vow.

The third time Chuto recited the vow the boy answered as clearly as he had the first time. This was his promise to serve, to guide, to train, to protect the chosen novice who would be sent to shepherd the flock when Cusi would be taken to rest in the place of his Ancients.

As Cusi repeated the words, "With my blood I make this vow. With my blood I will keep it," the moon thrust the clouds away and lighted the mountain valley in silver gray.

Chuto motioned for the boy to follow him. They went down the trail to the Sunrise Rock. Chuto touched the stone wall behind the rock. With the flat palms of his hands he touched it. Slowly the massive wall pivoted. Slowly it turned. Slowly it turned, forming an opening to a great cave.

The man and the boy went inside and the rock closed itself behind them. They were in a gigantic rock-hewn room, which was piled from floor to roof with woven bags upon woven bags filled to bursting with powdered gold.

Chuto spoke, but it did not sound like Chuto's voice. The words were precise. They were deadly and cold. Cusi, listening, shivered.

"They, the Conquerors, came.
They came swarming into the land
  with hate and with weapons.

They came.
They captured the mighty Inca,
  holding him with chains.
They captured him.
Down the trails of the Andes
the Indians sent
    ten thousand llamas,
    carrying bags of gold dust
    to ransom their King.

But they, the Conquerors,
  killed him.
They killed the Inca,
  fearing his wrath
  if they set him free.
And the ten thousand llamas
  marching down the trails of the
  Andes vanished from the land,
  and with them vanished the
  gold dust, ransom for the King.

Four hundred years men have
  searched to find the llamas
  and to find the gold.
Only two men shall know
  where the llamas are herded.
Only two men shall know
  where the gold is hidden.
Only two men shall know,
  one whose footsteps approach
  the end of the trail,
  one whose young feet stand
  at its beginning.
Only two men shall know.
Only two men shall know.
This has been written in the stars."

The voice stopped. It did not trail away. One second its icy tone filled the room. The next second all sound had stopped and life stood still.

Cusi's wrist hurt, but he was too proud to touch it. He would not even glance at its wound.

Slowly the cave wall opened, although Cusi had seen no move on Chuto's part. Slowly the old Indian and the young one went out into the cold gray of just before the dawn. They sat in the shelter of the rock and listened to the wind wailing the night's departure.

Chuto talked, and Cusi listened. "Herdsmen of the Inca's llamas must be wise and widely traveled. If you like, you are free to go over the trails."

"How could I go and leave the llamas?" Cusi asked him.

The old man answered with dignity. "I would be here. There are many years left for me."

"But if something happened to you?" Cusi asked.

"You would be told."

"Yes, I would be told," Cusi said quietly. "Perhaps some day I'll go, but not tomorrow or tomorrow or tomorrow."

The dawn sent forth its herald colors to let men know that day was due. Cusi and Chuto rose to face the east and to salute the Sun for a new beginning.

385

Questions

1. Why did Cusi leave Hidden Valley? Why did he later return?
2. Whose fields did the Keeper of the Fields take care of?
3. Do you think Cusi was ready (was old enough and had enough experience) to take the sacred vow? Explain your answer.
4. If you had been in Cusi's place, what questions would you have asked Chuto about your origins, the sacred vows, the secret cave, and choosing a successor?

Applying Reading Skills

The sentences below describe events from "Secret of the Andes." They are not listed in correct order. On your paper, write and number the events in the order in which they actually occurred. Two of the events took place at the same time. List them under the same number.

1. A landslide destroyed the Ayllu village.
2. Cusi slept by three tired llamas.
3. Cusi found a pair of tiny golden sandals.
4. Cusi and Chuto rose to face the east and to salute the Sun for a new beginning.
5. Cusi rested at the Ayllu village.
6. The old man gave Cusi an ear of corn for Chuto.
7. The conquerors captured the mighty Inca.
8. A drop of Cusi's blood dripped to the ground.
9. Cusi traded at the market for caps, trousers, and sweaters.
10. Cusi and Chuto went down the trail to the Sunrise Rock.
11. Cusi and Chuto sat in the shelter of the rock.
12. An old woman gave Cusi food and called him her son.
13. Cusi repeated the words of the vows.
14. Cusi felt a sharp stab of pain.
15. Chuto and Cusi listened to the wind wailing the night's departure.
16. Cusi got out his flute and gave a flute call.

EL CONDOR PASA

I'd rather be a sparrow than a snail.
Yes, I would
If I could, I surely would.
I'd rather be a hammer than a nail.
Yes, I would
If I only could, I surely would.

Away, I'd rather sail away
Like a swan that's here and gone.
A man gets tied up to the ground,
He gives the world it's saddest sound,
    it's saddest sound.

I'd rather be a forest than a street.
Yes, I would
If I could, I surely would.
I'd rather feel the earth beneath my feet,
Yes, I would
If I only could, I surely would.

Paul Simon

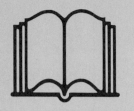

PREPARING FOR READING

Learning Vocabulary

1. Jamie's leg ached with an angry and <u>persistent</u> pain.
2. He <u>resolutely</u> limped to the crest of the ridge to stare at the ruins.
3. In the darkness of the cave, Jamie saw the <u>vague</u> outline of an object.
4. As Jamie left, he saw the house on the far <u>horizon</u>, faintly <u>illuminated</u> by the rays of the setting sun.

persistent   resolutely   vague
horizon   illuminated

Developing Background and Skills
Context Clues

Suppose you did not know the meaning of *promontory* and came across it in the following context:

The <u>promontory</u> extended out into the plain. Its outline resembled a crouching animal. Surely this was the landmark used by the Indians following the trail to their hunting grounds.

Were you able to figure out the meaning of *promontory* by using semantic context clues? **Semantic context clues** are words, phrases, and sentences that can help you determine the meaning of an unfamiliar word.

When you use semantic context clues, you use words and phrases you *do* know to understand words you *don't* know. You know that the promontory extended out into the plain, that it resembled a crouching animal, and that it might have been a landmark for a trail. These clues let you know that a promontory is a high piece of land that sticks out.

Another kind of context clue is called syntactic. **Syntactic context clues** are found in word order and sentence structure. In order to use syntactic clues, you must be able to recognize the common parts of speech—nouns, verbs, adjectives, and adverbs—and understand how sentences are put together.

To see how syntactic clues work, look at the incomplete sentence below. See if you can figure out what the missing word is.

The highest and most easily seen peak in the range was Deer Mountain. Its _____ shape stood out against the skyline.

Which of the words below fits the sentence?
    a. minimal: smallest in amount
    b. minimize: to make as small as possible
    c. massive: exceedingly large
    d. greatness: largeness

If you read the sentence carefully, you will see that the missing word comes before a noun. Adjectives, words that describe nouns, often come before nouns. If the missing word is an adjective, you can eliminate **b** (verb) and **d** (noun) as choices. Both **a** and **c** are adjectives. Which word best fits into the meaning of the sentence? The first sentence gives semantic clues that help you decide that the right word is *massive* (**c**).

Try to figure out the meaning of the unknown words you encounter in the next selection by using both semantic and syntactic context clues. Use the strategies described above.

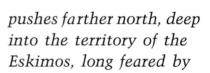

Jamie MacNair is staying in northern Canada with his friend Awasin (ə was' ən), son of the headman of a Cree Indian village. While he is there, the Crees are visited by a group of Chippeweyans who live near the wilderness area known as the Barrens. The Chippeweyans are facing starvation and have come to the Crees for help.

The two boys accompany Denikazi (den' ə kä' zē), the Chippeweyan chief, on a hunting trip to the summer range of the caribou. But when Denikazi fails to find the deer at the spot known as The Killing Place, he pushes farther north, deep into the territory of the Eskimos, long feared by the Indians as enemies. Jamie and Awasin are left behind at The Killing Place in care of two of Denikazi's braves, Etzanni (et zan' ē) and Telie-kwazie (tē' lē kwä' zē). The Chippeweyans tell them legends of a Great Stone House farther north, which is said to be older than any white settlements in the region. Jamie and Awasin decide to look for the house, and, leaving a message in the sand for the two Chippeweyans, they set off down the Kazon River. But the boys lose their canoe and most of their gear in rapids, and

THE GREAT STONE HOUSE

FARLEY MOWAT

Jamie wrenches his knee. What is worse, they spot Eskimos on the lake! They hide near the Stone House, realizing that Etzanni and Telie-kwazie will have given them up for lost.

Awasin awakened first the following morning, and, after a worried study of the river for signs of Eskimos, he turned to look at the surrounding plains. On all sides the Barrens were empty of motion. The only sound was the distant whistling of curlews. Nevertheless, the fear of the Eskimos was still strong in his heart.

The Stone House stood on the crest of a long ridge that stretched westward and upward into a range of hills. On the skyline at the end of this range stood the massive shape of Deer Mountain. Under its western slopes Denikazi was at that moment probably preparing to meet the herds of caribou.

By the time Jamie wakened, the panic of the previous day had worn away. He had never really believed the tales of Eskimo ferocity, and this morning he felt foolish at having allowed himself to be so badly frightened. Also he was hungry, and his leg hurt with an angry and persistent pain.

"Well," he said, "whatever happens, we have to eat. What about it?"

Awasin shook off his nagging fears and rummaged through the pile of gear. He found the fishline.

"The trout may have begun their autumn run by now," he said, "and they will be as hungry as we are. I'll go down to the river and see."

Carrying the rifle, Awasin started off. Jamie set about making a fire.

An hour later, Awasin returned, carrying a huge trout. In a few minutes the morning air was heavy with the smell of roasting fish, and the boys began to stuff themselves.

When they had eaten their fill, they smoked and dried the remaining fish. As the boys sat watching the fire, the words that neither one had wished to speak came unbidden to Jamie's lips.

"We'd better face it," he said quietly. "We're in a mess right to our necks. And through my fault. Telie-kwazie and Etzanni will never find us now—and we'll never find them either."

Though the boys knew that no Chippeweyans would dare come up the river while the Eskimos were about, the situation was not yet hopeless. Jamie's leg was better. The weather was still good, and it would be possible to travel across the plains on foot for another two or three weeks without serious difficulty. But in which direction should they go?

The Killing Place would certainly be deserted by the time they could get through. And to attempt on foot the long journey all the way south to the forests was out of the question. There was only one alternative.

There was a strong probability that Denikazi was still in the vicinity of Idthen-seth. Even if he had

met the deer, he would need several days to make his hunt and to dry the meat for transportation home. From the ridge by the Great Stone House the boys could clearly see the mountain called Idthen-seth. They estimated it was not more than thirty miles away.

Sitting by the fire in gloomy silence, both Awasin and Jamie separately came to the conclusion that their only hope lay in traveling west to intercept Denikazi.

"Things may not be so bad," Awasin said. "I think we stand a chance of meeting Denikazi if we can get across to Frozen Lake River. It's high ground all the way, so we wouldn't have trouble crossing streams as we would going south."

"It's the only thing we *can* do, I suppose," Jamie replied. "But if we get there too late . . ." He left the sentence unfinished.

"We won't!" Awasin reassured him. "Anyway, we can't wait here."

The boys discussed the plan in detail and decided they'd have to move as soon the crest of the ridge and stood staring at the strange ruins that lay before him.

as they could, and at top speed. However, there was no use starting until Jamie's leg was a little better. In the meantime Awasin undertook to catch more trout so they would be sure of having food once they left the river.

Left alone at camp, Jamie limped about gathering twigs and moss for use in drying the fish. On one trip from the campfire he came under the shadow of the stone structure on the ridge. He stopped now to glance up at it.

His curiosity about the Great Stone House had died abruptly at the time of the accident. Until this moment he had deliberately ignored the massive stone ruin which had once been his goal, and which now lay close at hand.

Now he looked at it, looming mysteriously above him. "I came here to see you," he thought, "and got in a mess doing it. I might as well take a good look while I'm here!"

Resolutely Jamie limped to

Whatever the structure had once been, it was now hardly more than a rough rectangle of rocks about fifteen feet square and ten feet high. Jamie was sure that no Eskimo or Indian would have constructed anything so massive and so regular in outline. He was also sure that no white man had come this way before. "Funny," he thought as he hobbled closer, "it looks like a fort or a watchtower without any doors or windows."

He began to poke about among the moss-grown rocks at the base. Arctic hares had been using the crevices between the stones as hiding places. As Jamie fumbled among the rocks one of the big hares leaped out almost at his feet and fled like a gray ghost. Jamie got to his feet and circled the building looking for an opening. But he found none. The whole thing seemed to be one solid mass of masonry. Jamie began to think it was only a huge cairn, or monument, and not a building at all.

He went back to the place where

the hare had jumped out, and here he found a deep crevice in the rocks. He peered in, and what he saw made his heart beat faster.

The crevice led into a cave, and in the semidarkness Jamie saw the vague outline of something that was certainly not stone. He lowered himself to his knees and squeezed his head and shoulders through the opening.

His body blocked out the light, but his outstretched hands touched something cold and rough. He gripped it and backed out of the hole, dragging the object with him.

As the sunlight fell upon it Jamie's eyes grew wide with wonder, for in his hand he held a sword! And what a sword it was. Four feet in length, it had a double-edged blade and a two-handed hilt. It was the sort of weapon that only a giant could have handled. The blade was deeply pitted and rusted. On the hilt were broad rings of gold, turned greenish by centuries of weather.

Fascinated, Jamie hefted the heavy weapon, then he laid it down and crawled back into the hole. Again his hands touched something, and he scrambled out, bringing with him a bowlike helmet of some metal that had resisted the attacks of rust.

Two hornlike studs were fastened to the sides of the helmet.

Jamie had seen pictures of such a helmet as this in his schoolbooks, and he recognized it at once.

"This is the kind of helmet Eric the Red[1] and Leif the Lucky[2] wore!" he whispered. "And that means— that the ancient Vikings must have built this place!"

Unable to contain his excitement, Jamie hobbled to the edge of the hill and began calling for Awasin.

Down by the riverbank the Indian boy heard the cries, and the ever-present fear of Eskimos returned. Grabbing the three trout he had caught, he raced full tilt up the long slope to the camp.

Jamie was not there! He dropped the fish and grabbed the rifle, then a scuffling noise from the crest above him made him turn.

Awasin was levelheaded, but this time he almost panicked. A huge, horned head, dull green in color, peered over the summit of the hill.

---

1. **Eric the Red:** Viking explorer who discovered Greenland in 982 A.D.

2. **Leif the Lucky:** son of Eric the Red, who landed on the coast of North America about the year 1003 A.D.

An unseen hand brandished a mighty weapon such as Awasin had never seen before in all his life. He raised the rifle with shaking hands and was on the point of firing blindly at the apparition. His finger tightened on the trigger.

Fortunately, in that instant the spell was broken. Jamie caught his foot between two rocks and fell. The helmet rolled away revealing his shock of blond hair and the sunburned face.

"Hey!" he yelled. "Help me up, you dope. And watch where you point that gun!"

A few minutes later Jamie was trying to explain his treasure find to a confused Awasin, who only vaguely understood what it was all about.

"It must have been like this," Jamie said, running his words together in his excitement—"hundreds of years ago some of the early Viking explorers must have wandered into Hudson Bay and then tried to come south up the Kazon. Maybe it was a thousand years ago. The Vikings came west from Greenland in open boats and some of them must have come through Davis Strait. This *proves* it!" Jamie continued. "I'll bet this sword and helmet are worth a thousand dollars to a museum!"

The thought of so much money left even Jamie breathless for a moment, and in the silence Awasin asked a question. The talk of Vikings and Greenland and museums was above his head, but one thing was clear to his practical mind.

"Perhaps you're right about all this," he said, "but just *how* do we get these things home?"

The question brought Jamie back to reality. "You *would* think of that!" he said bitterly. Then suddenly cheerful again: "Listen, Awasin. We'll leave the stuff right here, then next summer we'll come back and get it. Come on, let's see what else is in this old stone house!"

His enthusiasm restored, Jamie once more crawled into the crevice while Awasin, curious despite himself, stood ready to take the objects Jamie might hand out.

Worming his way downward, Jamie disappeared completely, but a few moments later his hand appeared. In it was clutched a dagger whose blade was rusted away to a thin sliver of metal. Awasin was examining it when Jamie's muffled voice called him back to the tunnel mouth. This time the object was a flat, square piece of gray metal about the size of an old-fashioned school slate. Its weight made Awasin grunt in surprise. "This is made of lead!" he called to Jamie.

Jamie was busy tugging one more object out of the litter of fallen rocks and decayed moss. Finally he got it free and shoved it outside, calling at the same time, "What's this?"

For answer Awasin yelled as if he had seen a ghost. In fact he had. As he emerged into the daylight Jamie saw the object lying where Awasin had dropped it. It was a human skull.

Awasin was trembling. "That is a grave," he cried. "I'll take my chances with the Eskimos! We're moving camp!"

Jamie was in no mood to argue. Hurriedly he pushed the ancient weapons back into the crevice and rolled a rock over the entrance. The skull he left alone. Then he hastened after Awasin.

As he hobbled away he saw the small square of lead, and rather than go back to the grave again he picked it up and took it with him.

Already Awasin had the camp gear rolled in the blankets. He was stuffing dry fish into a bag he had made from an old deerskin robe. His dark face was tense and anxious. Awasin wanted nothing so much as to put many miles between himself and the white skull beside the Great Stone House.

As night fell they made a new camp on the narrow ridge that ran westward like a ramp toward the bulk of Idthen-seth. After a skimpy meal of fish, Jamie sat silent for a little while staring curiously at the thin sheet of lead he had brought with him from the tomb.

At last Jamie spoke. "It's covered with some kind of writing," he said wonderingly. "Queer-looking, like picture writing." He paused, looking back at the distant crest of the hill where the ruins stood. "I'll bet if we could read it, we'd know the story of those old Vikings at the Stone House."

Faintly illuminated by the last rays of the evening sun, the shape of the Great Stone House hung on the far horizon—a mystery still; but Jamie felt he held the key.

Jamie and Awasin eventually were forced to spend the winter in the Barrens. The story of their survival is told in Two Against the North *by Farley Mowat. The answer to the Stone House mystery is finally revealed in its sequel,* The Curse of the Viking Grave.

Questions

1. Why were Jamie and Awasin alone in the wilderness?
2. Why did the boys have to hurry to carry out their plan to meet Denikazi?
3. Do you think the boys' decision to travel west to meet Denikazi rather than to return to the Killing Place was a good one? Give the reasons for your answer.
4. Write the letter Jamie might have written to a musuem about his discovery. Think carefully about the information you will include.

Applying Reading Skills

A. Use context clues to determine the correct meaning of each underlined word. Write the word and its meaning.

1. There was no way to ascertain how long the trip would take. It might be weeks, it might be months.
   a. shorten   b. explain   c. determine   d. inquire

2. Jamie was annoyed and worn out. He spoke testily in reply to the questions.
   a. quickly   b. crossly   c. softly   d. politely

B. Use context clues to choose the word to complete each sentence. Write the complete sentence.

1. The boys were full of _____ as they set out. The weather was mild, they had plenty of food, and they felt sure they would find Denikazi soon.
   a. opportunity: a good chance or occasion
   b. confident: self-assured
   c. optimism: belief that things will turn out for the best

2. Soon after the boat entered the rapids, it overturned in the _____ waters.
   a. turbulent: not calm or smooth
   b. agitation: the act of moving or shaking roughly
   c. perturb: to disturb or excite

PREPARING FOR READING

Learning Vocabulary

1. Eric the Red sailed west to explore Greenland when he was <u>exiled</u> from Iceland.
2. When Eric's son Leif later sailed farther west, he began to wonder if another explorer had actually seen land or only a <u>mirage</u>.
3. The Vikings who settled in Greenland found boats, stone axes, and other <u>relics</u> of earlier <u>inhabitants</u>.
4. The Greenlanders who attempted to start a colony in Vineland were forced to <u>abandon</u> it after two years.

exiled	mirage	relics
inhabitants	abandon	

Developing Background and Skills
Context Clues

Context clues can often help you figure out the meanings of unfamiliar words. Semantic context clues can be synonyms, antonyms, and direct definitions. They can also include familiar words, phrases, and sentences that describe or give examples.

Another kind of context clue is called a syntactic context clue. Syntactic context clues are found in word order and sentence structure. The position of a word in a sentence and the words around it can help you to determine what part of speech the word is. The main parts of speech are nouns, verbs, adjectives, and adverbs. Each of these is identified in the sentence that follows.

| NOUN—names a person, place, thing, or idea; often follows *a, an, the*, another adjective, or a preposition |

The Vikings later established many thriving colonies.

| ADVERB—describes an adjective or a verb; often tells, how, how much, when, in what way | ADJECTIVE—describes a noun; often comes before a noun or after verbs such as *is, was, became* |

| VERB—describes an action, existence, or occurrence |

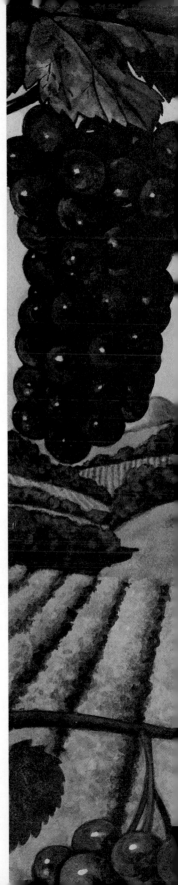

Read the sentences below and the answer choices for the meaning of the underlined word.

Grapes grew in <u>profusion</u> throughout the region. Wine was an important product, and large quantities were exported.

a. lavish: more than necessary   b. abundance: plentiful amount

c. moderation: avoidance of extremes   d. flourish: to thrive

The position of *profusion*, following the preposition *in*, is a clue that *profusion* is a noun. Only two answer choices are nouns—**b** and **c**. (You should recognize that **a** is an adjective and that **d** is a verb.) Which noun—*abundance* or *moderation*—fits the meaning of the sentence? The semantic context clues in the second sentence should help you choose *abundance*.

As you read the following selection, try to determine the meanings of unfamiliar words you encounter by using both semantic and syntactic context clues.

LEIF THE LUCKY

The people we call the Norsemen, or Vikings, were from the Scandinavian countries of Norway, Sweden, and Denmark. Around the year 800 A.D., some of these Norsemen began leaving their homelands to trade, raid, and find new lands. Some sailed westward, discovered Iceland, and settled there.

Eric the Red was an Icelander. In 982 A.D., he was exiled from Iceland for three years as punishment for killing a man. Eric decided to sail westward to explore a land sighted—but never explored—a century before. Eric landed on Greenland. After his exile was over, Eric went back to Iceland, then returned to Greenland with colonists to settle the new land. In 986, an Icelander named Bjarni Herjolfsson (byär′ nē hėr′ yōl′ sən) was driven off course by a storm while on his way to Greenland. He drifted several days in the fog. When the weather cleared, he sighted land to the west. He sailed along the coast several days without landing before sailing east to Greenland.

Fifteen years later, Leif Ericsson, the son of Eric the Red, decided to sail west to find the land Bjarni had sighted.

The story of Leif's voyage (and those of Bjarni and Eric) are known to us from the Icelandic sagas, stories learned by heart and passed down from generation to generation. The following story is based on those sagas. It is historical fiction. Some of the characters, like Brendan, and much of the conversation is made up. But Leif, Bjarni, and Tyrker (tir′ kər) really lived.

ELIZABETH JANEWAY

HELLULAND

GREENLAND

route of Leif Ericsson

MARKLAND

VINELAND

After they had sailed five days—a day longer than Bjarni—and still had seen no land, it occurred to Leif that Bjarni had once thought he was enchanted. Leif sat up in the dark and thought about this. There *was* something a little magical about Bjarni's story. He had seen three lands, and three is always the magic number in a fairy tale. Bjarni had got home safely, but Bjarni had not set foot onshore.

Leif felt a sudden shiver up the spine. Everyone had always believed that Greenland lay at the end of the world and that past it there could only be enchanted isles. Where were they going? Or—was there really nothing there? Had Bjarni seen not land, but a mirage? Sitting in the dark, Leif thought about this. He wished he could talk to someone about it, but he knew he could not. Not even to Brendan. Not even to Tyrker. He was the commander. He must not show his doubts to *anyone*.

Slowly he lay down again. Bjarni had said that he ran before an unusually strong wind on the last leg of his journey. His ship must have covered a good many more miles daily than the average day's sail, which was the unit by which the Norsemen measured their trips. That was why they had not yet seen land. Leif repeated this to himself until daylight. Then he sat up and peered ahead. There was nothing there.

When land was sighted at last, the next afternoon, it was in the most matter-of-fact way that could be imagined.

He almost couldn't believe it. He'd looked so often . . . . "It's there, all right," said Brendan.

"I see it is," said Leif. All doubts, all worries dropped away, and Leif became the commander. "Keep the oar, Brendan. Tyrker, have the men make a small boat ready and then come forward to me."

He strode up to the prow of the ship. Ahead, to the west, the land grew steadily clearer.

It was barren land. Bjarni had said so, but Leif thought he had never seen anything quite so useless. The ground was covered with flat stones, and in the distance a glacier glittered in the sun. Leif, Brendan, and Tyrker spent a day onshore. No one could think of a reason for spending more.

"Well, we landed," said Leif. "It's more than Bjarni did. But I can't say it's much more." He kicked one of the stones. "Helluland—Stoneland," he said. "Let's go back to the ship." So they rowed out.

"Now what do we do?" Brendan asked.

"Coast the land south, of course. We don't know if Bjarni's landfalls[1] were islands or a mainland. We must see whether they are joined together."

So, through the height of summer, they sailed along the land to the south, using oars when they had to, keeping the land on their right. Not knowing the shore, they did not keep too close, and at night they anchored. The nights were fairly short, though longer than summer nights in Greenland. They were definitely moving into a new climate.

After some days, the character of the land began to change. One fair morning Leif rowed in again, to a white sandy beach, where thick woods came down to the sea.

"Now this is a land!" cried Brendan, leaping ashore. "Look at the timber, Leif! We can fell enough trees here to make our fortunes twice over when we sell them in Greenland!"

"That we can," Leif agreed. "And yet, Brendan, I think we'll sail on. We can return here on the way home if we want. But let's sail to the south while the good weather lasts. Bjarni saw three lands. Let's not go home having seen less!" Brendan

---

1. **landfalls:** lands reached or sighted. Bjarni Herjulfsson reported sighting three lands to the west of Greenland.

and Tyrker agreed and they returned to the ship. This country Leif called Markland, or Wooded-land.

Again they traveled along the shore. It is likely that they came down between Newfoundland and the mainland of Canada through the Strait of Belle Isle. At one time, crossing the Gulf of Saint Lawrence, they seemed to be out in the open ocean again. But they picked up the shore again after two days. Following it, they marveled at its richness, at the enormous trees that stood above the long white sandy beaches of what we now call New England.

At last, one perfect summer day, Leif determined to land and make camp. He had decided to pass the winter in this new country, and he wanted time to build shelters, gather food, and explore the neighboring land.

In the early morning, just as the sun rose, they steered the ship into a sound that lay between the island and the mainland. The tide ran out surprisingly fast—Leif had never seen such a swift tide—and since the bay was shallow, the ship ran aground! A fine captain I am! Leif thought to himself, surveying the tidal flats around the ship. He had never done such a stupid thing before. But Tyrker laughed him out of his shamed feeling. No harm was done after all, for Viking ships were built for beaching, and the rising tide would float them again.

The men were so eager to be onshore that Leif let them wade across the sand to where he could see a river emptying into the bay. They came back to report a lake lying upriver. It was a perfectly protected anchorage. When the tide rose, they rowed the ship up the river and into the lake, which was deep even at low tide. There they cast anchor and prepared to make themselves at home in the New World Leif had led them to.

That first night Leif spent ashore he never forgot. Tyrker had taken two men and gone hunting. They came back with a deer. Brendan had sent other men to fish in the river. They caught three enormous salmon, salmon bigger than they had ever seen. They built a huge fire and roasted the venison and fish and ate their fill of the good fresh food they'd been longing for.

As darkness fell—much earlier than the men were used to in Greenland summers—a chorus of birds sang in the trees over their heads and an enormous moon swam slowly up the sky. Leif sat up by the dying fire, his hands clasped about his knees, too happy to sleep. At last the birds were silent, all was still, and only a fragrance of pine and sea freshness mingled in the air. Leif stretched out his arms and lay back.

"Brendan," he said.

Brendan gave a sleepy grunt.

"If the Irish came here," Leif told him, "it's no wonder they stayed."[2]

---

2. Irish legends told of monks who had sailed westward and discovered a wonderful land.

The first thing Leif and his party did was to make sure of shelter. It did not take long to build sleeping quarters, but Leif had his men cut down trees all about their camp to the distance of a bowshot. He had seen no evidence of people, but that did not mean there *were* no people in this paradise. He did not intend to allow any enemy to creep up on his camp unseen and unheard. Everyone approaching had to come either across the lake or across a wide cleared space onshore.

It was not really the Irish he expected to find. This land was so enormous, just the part they'd seen so far, that Leif knew the chances were very small of stumbling on the traces of any earlier party of settlers. But what stuck in his mind were the skin boats and the stone axes that the Greenlanders had found in their own country. He had always believed them to be relics of primitive people native to Greenland. Where had those people come from? Where had they gone to?

We know now that the Eskimos had, at that time, withdrawn far to the north in Greenland, leaving it almost empty. Experts who have studied the subject believe that this was because the climate in Greenland was milder when Eric settled there than it is today. Eskimos need a cold climate, for they are used to living on Arctic animals. In pursuit of the game they were used to, then, they had moved out of southern Greenland.

Leif, of course, knew nothing of this, but he did know that people had lived in Greenland before the Norsemen. It seemed most likely that, if they had lived in Greenland, they had lived also in this much richer land. Why should they not live here still? In the virgin forests it was impossible to find traces of them, except by chance.

But Leif took no chances. His camp faced the woods across a space that his men could command with bows and spears. He kept a constant watch. During his explorations, he was careful to keep his camp always guarded by a party strong enough to hold it.

While they were building their houses and clearing the land, Leif sent out advance scouts. They reported that there were no traces of inhabitants for a day's journey anywhere around the camp, but Leif continued to be watchful.

When the wooden huts had been made strong and secure, Leif divided his men into two groups. The first stayed by the settlement. Their duties were fishing, setting traps, smoking fish and meat for the winter supplies they would need, and keeping a guard on ship and shore. The second group went exploring. With axes and knives they hacked their way through the woodland. The scouts moved ahead to serve as eyes and ears.

Sometimes Leif went with the explorers. Other times he stayed in camp to supervise the work there. Brendan took command of the men spying out the land. They had arrived too late in the year to plant any crops, but Leif could see that the land would bear well. The soil was rich, the growing season much longer than it was even in Norway. Wheat, which they could not grow at all in Greenland, would do well here. And as for cattle, they could grow fat on rich pastureland for months longer than in the north.

Leif dreamed many dreams as he moved about his work. Why should he not return with a party of colonists to settle here, as his father had settled Greenland? How much better and richer life could be here than in the north where just to stay alive was a struggle!

Food crops would grow here; cattle and sheep would thrive; wool could be woven; fuel was plentiful. Of course, they would need iron for tools and weapons. But why should they not find that here, too, and set up their own smithies?

If only the land was as empty as it seemed! If only they would not have to fight for it! Each time Leif went exploring he rejoiced anew over the emptiness as well as the richness of the country. Each time that he waited in camp he was again relieved to hear from the returning party that no inhabitants had been discovered and that all the men had come back safely.

And then one day Tyrker, of all people, disappeared! Canny, wise old Tyrker, who had come to keep an eye on the young men, was missing.

Leif was worried and decided to lead a search party himself. He called a dozen men who had been in camp all day. They got ready quickly for it would be dusk in an hour or so. They started out, calling as they went, then pausing to listen for an answering shout. The scouts went ahead to retrace the path Tyrker had traveled. On and on they went while the shadows grew longer. Leif was just about to give up, afraid of losing himself and his search party in the dark.

Then out of the woods to the right, with a crackling of twigs, came a figure.

"Tyrker!" shouted Leif. The man halted and the ones ahead turned back. Leif ran to the old man and took him in his arms. "Tyrker, foster-father, where have you been? What's kept you out so late? It's nearly dark!"

It was Tyrker all right—but when Leif let him go and looked at him he felt his heart sink into his boots. Tyrker gave a roar of laughter and burst into speech in a tongue Leif could not understand! But after a moment he passed his hand over his face and spoke at last in Norse.

"Leif, my good boy, look what I've made! Here, take a drink!" He waved at a big wooden cask at his feet. "It's wine, Leif, it's wine! I made it!"

"Wine! What was that language you were shouting?"

"German, naturally," said Tyrker. "It's my native tongue, isn't it? Where did I learn to make wine but in Germany? So when I think of wine, I think in German. Not in Norse, not in the language of men who know nothing about wine, don't even know grapes when they see them! The woods are full of wild grapes, Leif, wherever there's a bit of clearing. I've been watching them ripen for a month, and for a week I've had this nice little brew fermenting . . . "

"And you've gone off every now and then to see if it was ready."

"Laugh if you want," said Tyrker. "But without me you'd never have known there were wine grapes here."

Leif was delighted with Tyrker's discovery, and he named the country Vineland. So it was known for centuries in Icelandic sagas.

The winter amazed them by its warmth and by the height of the sun. The saga writer recorded, and it is still there to be read, Leif's astonishment at having breakfast in full daylight. Compared to Greenland, it almost seemed as if cattle could pasture out all winter. There was plenty of game all winter, too.

It was even more amazing that not once did Leif and his party see another human being. And yet Leif did not believe the land vacant. It was too rich, too good. Sometimes he had a feeling that something, someone was watching. Never, therefore, did he relax the care with which a guard was kept. Perhaps it was just this care that kept him from seeing Vineland's inhabitants.

Then it was spring, and time to go. On the return trip, they followed the same course by which they had come. Sailing along the coast, Leif noted every landmark for later trips. At length, when the wooded shores gave place to barren ones, Leif left the land and struck for home across Davis Strait. He had a fair wind, and it was not many days before he saw the Greenland glaciers before him.

eif did not return to Vineland, but his brother Thorvald (tür′ vəld) did. He reached Leif's camp without difficulty and explored for two years. The sagas tell that Thorvald found a wooden building that was used to store grain. The party was attacked by Skraelings.[3]

Another Greenlander, Thorfinn Karlsefni (tür′ fin kärl′ sef′ nə), and his wife Gudrid (who was the widow of Thorstein, another of Leif's brothers) attempted to start a colony in Vineland. They sailed with a party of sixty men and five women and landed at Leif's camp where they lived for two years. Gudrid gave birth to a son, Snorri, before Skraelings forced the Norse to abandon the colony.

---

3. **Skraelings** (skrā′ lingz): the name the Norse gave to both the Eskimos and Indians.

Questions

1. According to the Icelandic sagas, who was the first Viking to sight land west of Greenland? The first to explore the land west of Greenland? The first to attempt to start a colony?
2. Why did Leif continue south after he sighted what he called Helluland and explored it?
3. Do you think Leif was especially brave and adventuresome? Explain your answer.
4. If you had been offered the chance to go with the Greenland colonists to Vineland, would you have gone or not? Give reasons to explain your answer.

Applying Reading Skills

Use semantic and syntactic context clues to choose a word to complete each sentence. Write the complete sentence.

1. Although Leif and his party kept a constant watch for enemies and looked for signs of settlers, they saw nothing. The inhabitants were able to _____ the Vikings.
   a. extinguish: to destroy; to put an end to
   b. elude: to avoid or escape
   c. implication: that which is hinted or suggested
   d. subtle: secret; mysterious
2. Things went well and the colony progressed for two years, when suddenly _____ struck.
   a. nutrition: the study of the foods people eat and need
   b. cooperative: willing to work together with others
   c. disperse: to break up and send off in different directions
   d. adversity: misfortune; hardship

DIK BROWNE'S
Hägar
THE HORRIBLE

WRITING ACTIVITY

WRITE A FRIENDLY LETTER

Prewrite

The historical story "Leif the Lucky" is based on sagas, oral stories passed down from generation to generation. What other ways can we learn about history? You are probably used to reading history books, but old newspapers, letters, and diaries are also sources of historical information. These sources are called original sources because they were created by people who actually lived at the time. Have you ever thought that a letter or diary you are writing now may someday be an original historical source for students in the future?

Suppose you were a passenger on the voyage described in "Leif the Lucky." During the voyage you write a letter to a friend describing the people, places, and events of the trip.

Before you begin, you need to make a plan for writing the body of your letter. An outline can help you organize the information you might include. Reread the story. Then complete the outline below.

I. Traveling South
   A. Sailed south with Leif and my friends, _____.
   B. Sighted land after six days' sail and named it Stoneland.
   C. Sailed south again and landed at beach with forests and named it Markland.
   D. Sailing south looking for a place to winter, beached the ship but finally found an anchoring spot in deep lake upriver.
II. Wintering (Add the major details.)
III. Naming Vineland (Add the major details.)

Write

1. Look up the correct form for a friendly letter in your English book.
2. You can figure out a year for your **Heading** from the information in the introduction to the story.
3. Choose a name for the friend to be used in the **Greeting**.
4. Each part of the outline will be a paragraph in the **Body** of your letter. Remember, the outline contains major points to include in your letter. Why not do some research and add some other information, such as what a Viking ship was like?
5. Choose a **Closing**, and don't forget your **Signature**.
6. Use your Glossary or dictionary for spelling help.

Revise

As you read your letter, imagine you are on that voyage so long ago. Besides the information from your outline, did you add a personal note to make your letter more interesting to your reader? For example, did you get tired of taking your turn at the oars or standing guard? Were you worried about never returning home alive? Transition words such as *first*, *then*, *next*, and *soon* will help make the order of events clear to your reader.

1. Proofread for correct punctuation and capitalization in each part of your letter.
2. Do the subject and verb in each sentence agree in number?
3. Rewrite your letter to share.

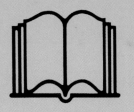

PREPARING FOR READING

Learning Vocabulary

1. To Greenlanders, the climate of Newfoundland would be <u>comparatively</u> mild.
2. Traces of houses and a smithy were revealed when the ruins of the early settlement were <u>excavated</u>.
3. The <u>location</u> of the settlement suggests it might have been a base for voyages of exploration.
4. <u>Deposits</u> of anthracite coal are unknown in Greenland.

comparatively   excavated
location   deposits

Developing Background and Skills
Maps

A drawing of the earth or part of the earth on a flat surface is called a **map**. To show the curved earth on a flat surface requires a system of transferring locations on the earth to locations on the map. This can be done by using a grid system. A grid system is a network of lines of longitude (meridians) and lines of latitude (parallels) used on a map or globe. Meridians extend north and south. Parallels extend east and west. Meridians and parallels meet, or intersect.

The map on the next page shows part of a polar region. Notice the grid pattern. The grid lines marked 100° W., 90° W., 80° W., and so on to 90° E. are meridians. How are the parallels labeled?

You know that north is the direction toward the North Pole. The **north arrow** on the main map is on the 0° meridian, but it could have been placed on any meridian. All the meridians meet at the North Pole.

Notice the **inset map** in the corner of the main map. This
inset map shows a small part of the main map in greater
detail. The scale of the inset map is different from that of
the main map. Does one inch on the inset map represent a
greater or a smaller distance on the earth than one inch on
the main map? Look at the **key** on the inset map. What do
the areas with short blue lines indicate?

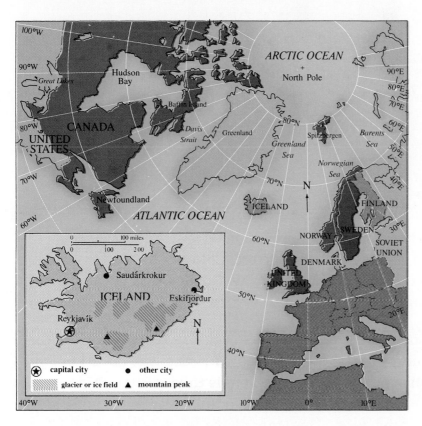

As you read the following selection, refer to the maps. You
will probably find that using a map will make the story more
understandable and interesting to you.

VINLAND THE GOOD

PATRICIA LAUBER

Scholars now believe that Viking explorers landed on the coast of North America about 500 years before Columbus. The sagas tell about Vinland (or Vineland) the Good. But just where was this land?

Somewhere on the eastern coast of North America there is a pleasant region with rich soil that was once known as Vinland the Good. The problem is to identify it. Norse visits to Vinland were made by handfuls of people who stayed only a brief time. They must have left few traces. The most we could hope to find are a few foundations, some tools or weapons, a grave, or a stone with a few words carved in the Vikings' ancient runes.[1]

The evidence may lie over a huge area. Vinland could be anywhere from northern Newfoundland to Chesapeake Bay. That is one of the few things on which scholars who study the sagas agree.

1. **runes:** the alphabet used by the Vikings.

What the Sagas Say

Over the years, the sagas have been the chief source of clues in the search for Vinland. Scholars have tried to match landmarks of the sagas with present-day places along the coast. They have tried to match the Skraelings with particular groups of Eskimos or Indians. Most of all, they have tried to find a place that matched the description of Vinland. None of this is easy, because the clues in the sagas can be read in many ways.

For example, Vinland is described as a land of mild climate. No snow fell, and cattle could graze in the open all winter. Does that mean that it was a southerly land? At first glance, the answer seems to be yes, but it could be no. The men who explored Vinland were used to the winters of Greenland, Iceland, and Scandinavia. Compared with these, a New England or Newfoundland winter might seem very mild. It is also true that animals from Greenland were as hardy and used to cold as their owners. The sagas may simply be saying that Vinland's winter was milder than Greenland's. They do say that no snow fell, and they may mean just that. Or they may mean that compared with Greenland, little snow fell. Or perhaps the tellers of the sagas emphasized the mildness of the climate by saying no snow fell.

Vinland is described as a land where wild grapes grew. Today, wild grapes grow along the coast only as far north as Portland, Maine. Does that mean Vinland must have been south of Maine? Some scholars would say yes. Others say no, and their reason has to do with the meaning of the word *Vinland*.

Grapes or Pastures?

Some scholars point out that *vin* is a very old Norse word that originally meant "pasture" or "grass." They think that Vinland was named for its grassy pastures and that there were no grapes. Later on, when writers such as Adam of Bremen[2] heard about Vinland, they gave *vin* its newer meaning of "grapes" or "wine." They thought that because the new land was named Wineland, it must have grapes. So they added grapes and grapevines to the story.

Other scholars, however, do not agree. They say that *vin* had ceased to mean "pasture" long before the discovery of Vinland. They also think that the grapes are too important to be an invention and that Vinland was indeed a land of wild grapes. If they are right, then Vinland must have been at least as far south as New England.

There are probably almost as many opinions about Vinland as there are scholars studying this subject. Nonetheless, a number of archaeologists and historians have come to think that Vinland was at least partly a northern land. They think that the forbidding land of mountains, glaciers, and flat stone named Helluland can only have been the southern part of Baffin Island. If so, then the second land, named Markland for its woods, must have been Labrador. And the third land, Vinland, was Newfoundland.

2. Adam of Bremen wrote an early world geography in 1075 A.D. Adam learned of Vinland from Svein, king of the Danes.

The Case for Newfoundland

To us, Newfoundland does not seem much like Vinland the Good. It is a chilly, rather barren island. No grapes grow there. To Greenlanders, however, it may have looked very different. They were not farmers looking for farmland, but hunters, fishers, and keepers of livestock looking for a place to continue this way of life. They were also people from a treeless arctic land. To them, Newfoundland may have seemed good beyond their dreams. Game and fish were plentiful. There was good pasture on the northern coast. There were great forests of spruce, balsam fir, and birch. The climate was comparatively mild. And the earth held something else they needed—iron ore for making tools and weapons.

Another reason for thinking that Newfoundland was Vinland is its geographical position. An explorer from Greenland, following the Labrador coast southward, would have to come to Newfoundland. And there the explorer would have to make a choice. Turn east and sail along the island's Atlantic coast. Or turn west and sail through the narrow strait that separates the northern tip of Newfoundland from the mainland.

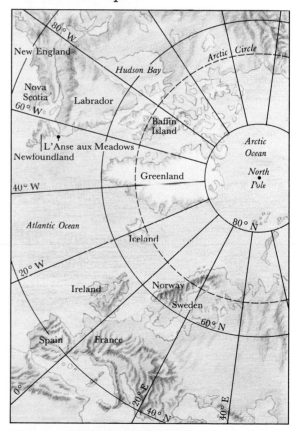

The map above shows the North Atlantic from the point of view of the Vikings.

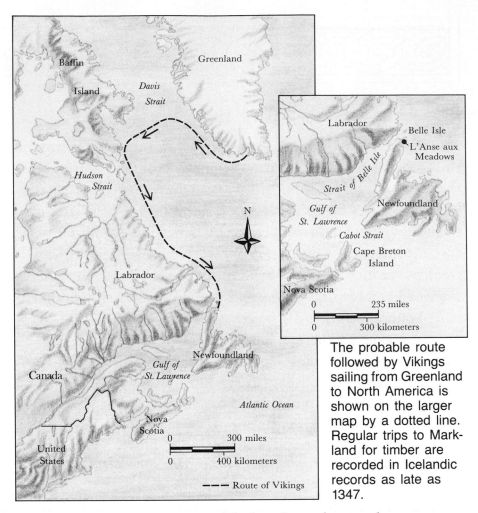

The probable route followed by Vikings sailing from Greenland to North America is shown on the larger map by a dotted line. Regular trips to Markland for timber are recorded in Icelandic records as late as 1347.

A turning point is a likely place for explorers to go ashore. Since Newfoundland was the most attractive place the Greenlanders could have seen up to then, they may well have decided to build a base there and to explore other areas from it. A base on the tip of Newfoundland would also be easy to find again on later voyages. In *The Greenlanders' Saga*, Thorvald, Karlsefni, and Freydis[3] were all able to find Leifsbudir[4] easily.

3. **Freydis** (frā' dis): Leif Ericsson's sister, who organized a voyage to Vinland before Karlsefni's.
4. **Leifsbudir** (lēfs' bü' dir): "Leif's booths," the name the sagas gave to Leif's camp in Vinland.

A Viking Village

It was this reasoning that led a Norwegian explorer, Dr. Helge Ingstad (hel′ gə ing′ stä), and his wife, archaeologist Anne Stine Ingstad, to a major discovery. Thinking that the tip of Newfoundland was a logical place for Leif to have made his camp, they began a search. They came upon the ruins of an early settlement near the tiny fishing village of L'Anse aux Meadows (lans′ ō med′ ōz). Digging revealed traces of houses and of a smithy, where bog iron had been processed into metal.

The remains of the houses are no more than beaten earth floors, the outlines of turf walls, and hearths. But the houses were built in the Norse style. They were like the remains of houses found in Greenland. One had a great hall like the ones Viking houses had. Since the Indians and Eskimos did not build houses of this kind and did not know how to forge iron, there is no doubt that the settlement was built by outsiders.

Eight house sites like this one were excavated at L'Anse aux Meadows. Some were as large as 15 by 20 meters (49 by 65 feet). *Left:* Dr. Helge Ingstad and Dr. Anne Stine Ingstad on board their ship *Halten,* which was used during their expeditions to Newfoundland.

Who were the outsiders? Few clues have been found. There are some very rusty nails and some pieces of iron, but the acidity of the soil has probably destroyed other clues of iron. Archaeologists have also found a small piece of smelted copper, a stone lamp of the kind that was used in Iceland, a whetstone[5] for needles, and a piece of bone needle. The most important find to date is a soapstone spindle whorl, exactly like the whorls used in Norway in the early part of the eleventh century by women spinning wool. The discovery of the whorl suggests that there were women in the settlement. There is no soapstone found near L'Anse aux Meadows, so the whorl must have been brought in, either from Norway or from Greenland, where there were many Norwegian goods.

The style of the houses, the spindle whorl, and other clues have convinced archaeologists that the settlement was Norse. Carbon-14 dating[6] of charcoal from the forge also points to a Norse settlement. The charcoal came from wood in trees that died between the years 860 and 1060 A.D. (Carbon-14 dating does not give an exact date, but shows a span of time.) So far there is no way of telling exactly who these Norsemen were. But there is a chance that the little settlement was once known as Leifsbudir.

---

5. **whetstone:** a stone for sharpening knives or tools.
6. **Carbon-14 dating:** a method used by archaeologists to date remains of plants or animals.

The brass ring-headed pin and the soapstone spindle whorl found at L'Anse aux Meadows prove the site was settled by the Norse.

A Larger Vinland

The location of the settlement suggests that this was the base from which the Greenlanders made voyages of exploration. Some of these voyages were to the south. So it is possible that Vinland became the name not just for one place but for a region that started in Newfoundland and reached south into New England. If this is so, many problems would be solved.

Grapes grow wild in New England. In the hardwood forests of southern New England, the Greenlanders would have found large numbers of grapevines. The same hardwood forests might have supplied the *mösurr* (mŭ' shər) wood that the sagas mention. Although no one is sure about what *mösurr* wood was, the best guess is that it was bird's-eye maple. *Mösurr* is an early German word for "spotted," and bird's-eye maple is a kind of spotted wood. It has markings that resemble birds' eyes, and it has long been prized by cabinetmakers.

A larger Vinland would also solve the problem of the Skraelings. Most scholars think that the Skraelings of the sagas were Indians because they had bows and arrows, which Eskimos did not have at that time. But the Indians of Newfoundland were the Beothuks (bā' ə thuks), a people who lived by hunting in the woods and collecting food along the coast. Later explorers found that they were shy people, who were not warlike. So scholars wonder whether the Beothuks could have been the Skraelings whose attacks forced the Greenlanders to give up the idea of colonizing Vinland.

These Skraelings sound more like one of the Algonquin (al gong' kwin) groups, which were widespread in eastern

North America. Later French and English settlers described the Algonquins as skilled hunters, trappers, and fishers. Some groups were farmers, and they stored corn in dome-shaped houses made of poles lashed together and covered with bark. This description fits the wooden storehouse discovered by Thorvald's men. Algonquins were often friendly in their first meetings with white settlers, coming to meet them with bundles of furs to trade or to offer as gifts. But if they were met with hostility, they could and did fight bravely, attacking in yelling war parties and shooting arrows as they came.

Apart from what the sagas tell us, there is another reason to think that Vinland reached south into New England. In 1930, archaeologists excavated the house where Karlsefni lived in Greenland after his marriage to Gudrid. In one of the rooms a lump of coal was discovered. The find surprised the archaeologists, because no coal ash has ever been found in the hearths of the Greenland colonists; there is only wood ash. The coal proved to be a kind of anthracite, and this was even more surprising. No deposits of anthracite coal have ever been found in Greenland. There are none in Iceland or Norway, the two countries with which Greenland was linked by ship. There are none in eastern Canada or northern New England. This kind of anthracite occurs in only two places on the east coast of North America. Both are in Rhode Island and near the sea.

The most likely explanation of the coal is that Karlsefni sailed as far south as Rhode Island and landed. Like many other travelers, Karlsefni and his companions collected some souvenirs before sailing for home. One was a lump of coal. Perhaps others will yet be found in Greenland.

Questions

1. What is the chief source of clues in the search for Vinland? Why has the search been difficult?
2. What two interpretations are there for the *vin* in Vinland?
3. What information in the selection do you think is the strongest evidence that Vinland was Newfoundland? What problems about Vinland are solved by considering Vinland a large region that stretched from Newfoundland to New England?
4. If you had a chance to go on an archaeological expedition, what people or events would you choose to learn about? What part of the world would you travel to?

Applying Reading Skills

Refer to the maps on pages 423 and 424 to answer the questions below.

1. Describe the route taken by the Vikings from Greenland to Newfoundland by giving directions, distance, and landfalls.
2. About how much longer is the Vikings' route than the most direct route from Greenland to Newfoundland?
3. Which strait is narrower, Hudson Strait or the Strait of Belle Isle?
4. In what direction is Cape Breton Island from Baffin Island?
5. Does the main map on page 424 show less detail or greater detail than the inset map?
6. About how far from L'Anse aux Meadows is Belle Isle?
7. In what direction is Newfoundland from Iceland?
8. What land would you first reach if you sailed directly west from the southern tip of Norway?

Castaways
on the
Sea of Time

JOHN CHRISTOPHER

Brad had been visiting his cousin Simon in England, when a weird fireball appeared. The boys found themselves transported to a different world—an "If" world. In this altered world, the Roman Empire had survived into the late twentieth century. The result was a total lack of social or technological progress. The boys' arrival touched off a revolution, followed by a dictatorship worse than the Empire. Brad and Simon found themselves in danger.

The cousins, along with Bos and Curtius, two Roman friends, decide to head west, sailing to a yet undiscovered America. They land in territory inhabited by Algonquin Indians. When the Algonquins prove to be unfriendly, the boys escape on a raft constructed from the remains of their wrecked boat. They push out to sea, but they soon find themselves lost in fog. Then suddenly, out of the mist, looms a Viking ship. The friendly Vikings seem happy to have rescued them. But what are Vikings doing on this side of the Atlantic? And why do they speak Latin instead of Norse?

The Vikings didn't seem concerned about being immobilized by the mist; the sea was flat calm and longships were provisioned for long periods at sea. Food was provided: dried meat, salt fish, and a kind of biscuit. Simon suddenly realized how hungry he was and ate ravenously.

Their rescuers clearly knew of the lands on the far side of the ocean and assumed they were castaways from a ship which had gone astray. But they showed no real curiosity about them. They were more interested when Bos spoke of the pack of whales. It seemed that whale hunting had been the object of their expedition, but they had found none.

The sun was below the horizon and the day fast darkening when the captain aroused cheers with the cry of "Land in sight!" The mist had now completely cleared, and despite the dusk a low line of coast was plainly visible on the port bow.

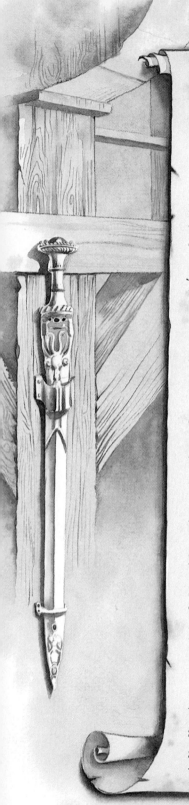

"The harbor's unmistakable," Brad said. "Yankees went whaling from here, too. That's Nantucket island."

"Home," the Viking captain said, smiling broadly. "Warm hearths, warm hearts, good food, and good cheer! Welcome, friends."

Women and children thronged out to welcome their menfolk back. They, too, were blond, the women large-boned with braids of yellow hair that framed plump pink cheeks. They favored the strangers with curious looks. One who, judging from the way she embraced him, was the captain's wife, asked where they came from.

He roared laughter. "From the sea—a gift from Odin.* But in truth, wife, they come from beyond the great water, as our forefathers did. They are Romans! Romans will grace the winter feast this year. Is that not good news?"

She answered his laugh with one equally hearty. The other women crowded close, staring at the Romans. One patted Brad's cheek and another twined fingers in Bos's beard. Then Simon saw something which took his mind off the women around them.

She stood back from the rest. She was about fourteen but as tall as he was. Her hair was a brighter, more buttery gold than that of the others, her eyes a purer cornflower blue. And there was a charming earnestness about her gaze. Simon returned the look and thought she colored slightly. Then she turned and went, disappearing behind one of the huts. Following her with his eyes, Simon noticed something: Brad was doing the same.

They feasted that night in a large building, which was used as a general meeting place. A stone hearth at the center supported a big log fire; the men sat at tables on either side, and the women brought round food and drink.

---

* **Odin** (ō′ din): the Norse god of wisdom and war.

hey had been given seats of honor close by the chief, and Bos now addressed him. He said: "It is not just for food and drink that we owe you thanks. Death would have found us, had you not found us first."

"The finding was our good fortune," Wulfgar said. He wagged a greasy fist clutching a chunk of meat. "I have been favored by the gods before, but never so greatly."

That seemed excessive, Simon thought, but it was probably just a fashion of talking. He decided to follow the custom of the country and weigh in with a little hyperbole himself.

"For all these things," he concluded grandly, "we are most deeply in your debt, and not least for being honored as guests at your winter feast."

"Our winter feast?" The chief's face broadened in another laugh. "But this is not our winter feast, Roman! It wants another month till Yule. Then we have *real* eating and drinking, in celebration of the turn of the year and, thanks to your coming, the turn in our fortunes."

Brad and Simon set off next morning on a trip of exploration. At the edge of the village, one of the huts was being rebuilt, with timber being taken from a run-down hut nearby.

They started to move on, then stopped. The girl they had seen the previous day appeared from behind the hut which was being dismantled. It seemed a good opportunity for introductions. Simon told her his name and Brad's and she gave hers. She was Lundiga, daughter of Sigrid. Simon would have been glad to talk longer, but an older woman called her to help. When Simon tried to assist, Lundiga shook her head firmly. "It is not proper."

As they walked on, Simon said: "Isn't she terrific?"

"Great," Brad said. "But I'd watch it if I were you. Lundiga daughter of Sigrid . . ."

"Well?"

"If you'd been paying attention yesterday, you'd know Sigrid is Wulfgar's wife. Which makes Lundiga the daughter of the chief."

"Ah." Simon thought about it. "On the other hand, where's the harm in making friends with the boss's daughter?"

The Viking women were hard workers. Apart from tidying and cleaning, preparing food, looking after children and animals, and tending things in general, they kept the huts in repair, and brought in fuel for the fires. They even laid fishing lines in the harbor and mended the sails of the longships.

And yet Simon had an impression, from looks and occasional critical remarks, that their attitude toward their menfolk was more one of mild contempt than submission. A reply by Lundiga to a question tended to confirm Simon's idea.

In olden days, she said, the men had been true warriors, and explorers and traders, taking their longships on frequent voyages to the mainland. Whaling, too, had been more keenly pursued, and more successful. Nowadays they were increasingly loath to put to sea, and returned empty-handed as often as not.

When they were alone, Brad said to Simon: "You'd think with the women doing all the work they would be totally subservient, but it's not like that. The men are served by the women, and boast about their whale hunts, and make the big noises generally. But children are identified through their mother, not their father. Lundiga, daughter of Sigrid—even though Wulfgar's the chief. And did you hear what she was saying this morning: that where marriage is concerned the women do the choosing?"

"Yes, I heard."

Whaling was a constant preoccupation with the Vikings. At last, on a bright morning with a stiff wintry breeze from the south, they actually got going. Lundiga had told Simon and Brad her mother was worried about stocks, in particular oil, and they thought she might have had a private word with Wulfgar. At any rate all three seaworthy longships were manned by the full complement of men. The newcomers had been split up, but Simon and Brad found themselves together on Wulfgar's ship.

It was not long after lunch that Wulfgar raised the cry of *"Balleinus!"* indicating a whale in view. The Vikings roared approval, and Wulfgar chanted a time for the oars, breaking off now and then to give a command to the helmsman. Simon found himself caught up in the excitement of the chase. The Vikings were yelling like madmen, and he along with them.

Two had detached themselves from the forward oars and stood on the platform beside Wulfgar, holding harpoons attached to lines. Wulfgar also had a harpoon.

Then a squall swept in suddenly from the starboard quarter, stinging them with darts of cold rain, and the sky darkened. For perhaps a quarter of an hour, rain was intermittent, but then it turned into a steady, chilling downpour. Not long after, Wulfgar called to them: "We have lost him. This expedition is ill-fated. We will set course for home."

Wulfgar, though, was not downcast. "Our luck will change," he cried. "After the winter feast, we shall take whales by the dozen. Odin will provide for his children. At the winter feast, the eagles will spread their wings, and then we shall live prosperously on Odin's bounty. Now, home!"

There was an increasing mood of anticipation in the village. The women spent a good deal of time preparing for the feast. They were very cheerful, with one exception. That was Lundiga, who seemed preoccupied and withdrawn.

One day, while they were taking turns tobogganing on a slope outside the village, Simon said, "You're looking prettier than ever today, Lundiga."

It wasn't a particularly stylish compliment, but he did his best to improve things by gazing earnestly into her eyes. He was disconcerted to find them brimming with tears. He was even more taken aback when she burst into loud sobs.

Surveying them both through tears, Lundiga said: "You must go."

"Go?" Simon stared at her. "Go where?"

"Away from here. From the island."

"But why?"

She looked at him, then turned to Brad.

"You asked me once about how it was my people came here, and I said I did not know. That was not true, Bradus."

He said: "I wondered at the time. There's always some story or legend, even if it's not very accurate."

"It was because of you Romans. A long time ago—more than thirty generations."

She paused. "My people were part of the empire. We spoke the language of the empire, obeyed the Emperor's commands. But in the northern mountains there were those of our race who had not submitted to the Romans. They had many children and not enough food. They came south, and called on my people to rise against the Romans. Our ancestors joined with them, and together they won a great battle against the Roman army. But the Emperor had other armies. In the next battle, our ancestors were defeated, with great slaughter.

"In one town, hearing what the Romans had done in other places, the people took their longships and set sail. Four longships sailed, and three were lost. The fourth found safe landing here.

"For many generations my people prospered on this island and were happy. In the last hundred years it has been harder. We have less of everything: ships, huts, food."

Simon said, "But your people talk of good times to come. They say Odin is going to help them, after the winter feast."

She began to cry again.

In a strange, wary voice, Brad said: "Just what is this stuff about Odin, and the winter feast, and the eagles?"

"We have a legend passed down from the early days. It spoke of hard times to come, very hard, and said they would not pass until Romans came to the island."

"Well," Simon said, "that's all right, isn't it? Here we are."

She stared miserably at them. "The legend said the Romans would come—to be a sacrifice to Odin at the winter feast. After that, Odin will bring good times again."

Simon could not believe what he was hearing. He said: "But the flying eagles . . ."

"I remember now," Brad said. "It's something that's been at the back of my mind, but I didn't make the connection.

A very old form of Scandinavian ritual killing. The eagles don't fly: they simply spread their wings. What that means, precisely, is that someone cuts the victims' chests open, and slowly bends the ribs outwards till they look like wings. It was called the bloody eagle."

He looked at Lundiga. "And we are to be the eagles?"

"They are treacherous curs," said Curtius when they told him. "Let us go at once and kill them."

"Four of us," Simon said, "against roughly a hundred? I don't like the odds."

Bos asked: "What do you say we should do?"

"The winter feast," Brad said, "takes place at the full moon. The moon's half full now, so we have time. Our best plan is to escape by night in one of the longships."

"How soon?" Bos asked.

"Not right now, certainly. We want a clear night."

The weather had been dull for days, with a sharp east wind and low clouds. Curtius said: "What if there is no clear night before the feast?"

"Then we'll have to take a chance on getting away in the dark. But it'll be a lot easier with a moon."

"And there's the question," Simon put in, "of when Lundiga can get away."

"She is one of them," Curtius said, "and therefore not to be trusted."

"Lundiga betrayed her people when she warned us," Brad said. "If we disappear, they're bound to suspect her of telling us. We have to take her."

After a week of cloudy weather, they woke one morning to find a blizzard sweeping in from the west. It snowed all day, and as night came with snow still falling, Simon realized that the invisible moon would be three-quarters full.

440

Next day the snow had ceased, and the clouds were breaking; patches of sunlight made the whiteness dazzle. Bos and Curtius were jubilant, seeing this as the signal to go. "Another day may mean another blizzard," Curtius said. "It must be tonight."

Before supper that evening Bos slipped away; on a reconnaissance, he said. Brad urged him not to do anything suspicious.

When at last they went back to the hut, the night sky was bright with starlight and the light of a moon close to full. They set out again, their footsteps crunching on the packed snow. The things they needed for the voyage had been hidden in one of the abandoned huts. It was not far from there to the chief's hut. From a distance, Bos gave the owl hoot which was the signal to Lundiga.

It sounded exactly like an owl; if she were asleep it would scarcely wake her. And they were committed now; they could not wait. Bos hooted again. At that moment Lundiga slipped out of the shadows.

They had earmarked Wulfgar's own longship for the enterprise. As they made their way down the hill, they could see its dragon head swaying against the moonlit waters of the bay. The noise of their footsteps on the snow seemed very loud, and Simon was glad when they were clear of the village. Despite the cold, he was sweating.

When they were not more than fifty yards from the quay, there was a sudden outburst of wild screeching behind them. Simon glanced back quickly. The din was coming from the chief's hut, or rather from a figure just outside it: Lundiga's mother.

Even at this distance the sound was shattering; up among the huts it must have been ear-piercing. Viking men came running out.

C urtius spoke sharply. "Into the boat!"

The Vikings were wasting no time; within seconds they were piling into the remaining longships and casting off. Visibility was excellent across the silvery bay; the moon, for which they had waited so impatiently, was an enemy now.

"Pull!" Bos roared. "For your lives . . ."

Heaving on his oar, Simon was aware of the hopelessness of it. There were three of them against dozens in the other two longships. The leading one was closing; within minutes it would be alongside.

The men in the following ships were yelling in anticipation, but suddenly the tone changed. There were cries of bewilderment. Pulling on the oar, Simon thought he noticed something different about the longship nearest to them. Was it lower in the water? And the gap between them—it was no longer narrowing, but widening.

The pursuing dragon's head rose sharply, as though it were a wingless beast trying to fly. The cries changed to a clamour of despair. The head stood right up, for a moment blacking out the moon. Then with a giant's gurgle, it slid beneath the water. Astern of it, the second ship was also tilting.

They had all stopped rowing. Brad looked across at Bos, whose teeth gleamed in a grin.

"That little reconnaissance you insisted on making . . . it didn't by any chance include coming down to the quay to loosen a timber or two?"

"Leave nothing to chance," Bos said. "It is the first thing a gladiator learns. Otherwise he does not live to learn more."

He released his oar and stood up, stretching out a hand. "A fair breeze, and from the right quarter. Let us get that sail up."

Glossary

This glossary can help you to pronounce and find out the meanings of words in this book that you may not know.

The words are listed in alphabetical order. Guide words at the top of each page tell you the first and last words on the page.

Each word is divided into syllables. The way to pronounce each word is given next. You can understand the pronunciation respelling by using the key below. A shorter key appears at the bottom of every other page.

When a word has more than one syllable, a dark accent mark (′) shows which syllable is stressed. In some words, a light accent mark (′) shows which syllable has a less heavy stress.

Information about the history, or etymology, of selected words is presented in brackets following the definition.

The following abbreviations are used in this glossary:

n. noun   *v.* verb   *adj.* adjective   *adv.* adverb   *prep.* preposition   *pl.* plural

Glossary entries were adapted from the *Macmillan School Dictionary* and the *Macmillan Dictionary*.

PRONUNCIATION KEY
Vowel Sounds

/a/	b**a**t	/ō/	r**o**pe, s**oa**p, s**o**, sn**ow**
/ā/	c**a**ke, r**ai**n, d**ay**	/ô/	s**aw**, s**o**ng, **au**to
/ä/	f**a**ther	/oi/	c**oi**n, b**oy**
/är/	c**ar**	/ôr/	f**or**k, **ore**, **oar**
/ãr/	d**are**, h**air**	/ou/	**ou**t, c**ow**
/e/	h**e**n, br**ea**d	/u/	s**u**n, s**o**n, t**ou**ch
/ē/	m**e**, m**ea**t, bab**y**, bel**ie**ve	/u̇/	b**oo**k, p**u**ll, c**ou**ld
/ėr/	t**er**m, f**ir**st, w**or**m, t**ur**n	/ü/	m**oo**n
/i/	b**i**b	/ū/	c**u**te, f**ew**, m**u**sic
/ī/	k**i**te, fl**y**, p**ie**, l**igh**t	/ə/	**a**bout, tak**e**n, penc**i**l, apr**o**n, helpf**u**l
/ir/	cl**ear**, ch**eer**, h**ere**		
/o/	t**o**p, w**a**tch	/ər/	lett**er**, doll**ar**, doct**or**

Consonant Sounds

/b/	**b**ear	/m/	**m**ap	/y/	**y**o-**y**o
/d/	**d**og	/n/	**n**est	/z/	**z**oo, egg**s**
/f/	**f**ish, **ph**one	/p/	**p**ig	/ch/	**ch**ain, ma**tch**
/g/	**g**oat	/r/	**r**ug, **wr**ong	/sh/	**sh**ow
/h/	**h**ouse, **wh**o	/s/	**c**ity, **s**eal	/th/	**th**in
/j/	**j**ar, **g**em, fu**dge**	/t/	**t**iger	/t͟h/	**th**ose
/k/	**c**ar, **k**ey	/v/	**v**an	/hw/	**wh**ere
/l/	**l**amb	/w/	**w**agon	/ng/	so**ng**

444

A

a·ban·don (ə ban′ dən) *v.* to go away from without intending to return.

ab·sent·ly (ab′ sənt lē) *adv.* not attentively; unconsciously.

ab·sorb (əb sôrb′) *v.* **1.** to soak up; **2.** to take up and retain.

ab·stract (ab′ strakt, ab strakt′) *adj.* relating to or designating a style of art that does not represent real objects directly, but often only the general characteristics of something.

abstract

ab·surd (ab sėrd′, ab zėrd′) *adj.* silly; ridiculous.

a·buse (*n.*, ə būs′; *v.*, ə būz′) *n.* the act of wrong or improper use; misuse. —*v.* **a·bused, a·bus·ing.** to misuse or use wrongly.

a·cad·e·my (ə kad′ ə mē) *n., pl.* **a·cad·e·mies.** an institution for learning; a school.

A·ca·pul·co (ak′ ə pül′ kō) a beach resort city in Mexico on the Pacific Ocean.

ac·com·pan·ist (ə kum′ pə nist) *n.* one who plays an instrument, or sings, to accompany a performer.

ac·com·plish (ə kom′ plish) *v.* to succeed in carrying out or completing; perform.

ac·cu·sa·tion (ak′ yə zā′ shən) *n.* **1.** the act of accusing. **2.** a statement claiming that someone did something, usually a misdeed.

ac·quaint·ance (ə kwānt′ əns) *n.* person whom one knows, but who is not a close friend. [Old French *acointer*, going back to Late Latin *adcognitāre* to make known, going back to Latin *ad* to + *cognitus* to have known + *antia* suffix.]

a·cryl·ic (ə kril′ ik) *n.* a chemical used in making fabrics and paints.

ad·o·les·cence (ad′ əl es′ əns) *n.* period or process of growing from puberty to adulthood.

af·fil·i·at·ed (ə fil′ ē ā′ tid) *adj.* associated together as members or supporters. [Medieval Latin *affiliatus*, past participle of *affiliare* to adopt, from *ad* to + *fīlius* son.]

ag·gres·sive (ə gres′ iv) *adj.* forceful; bold.

ag·o·ny (ag′ ə nē) *n., pl.* **ag·o·nies.** great pain or suffering of mind or body.

ail·ment (āl′ mənt) *n.* illness or affliction.

Al·bu·quer·que (al′ bə kėr′ kē) largest city in the state of New Mexico.

al·co·hol (al′ kə hôl′) *n.* **1.** intoxicating liquid produced by fermentation of grains and fruits. **2.** beverages containing this liquid.

Al·le·ghe·ny (al′ ə gā′ nē) **Al·le·ghe·nies. 1.** a mountain range extending from central Pennsylvania to western Virginia. **2.** a river in these mountains.

al·pac·a (al pak′ ə) *n.* a silky fabric, woven from the wool of an alpaca, an animal of South America that resembles a llama.

al·tered (ôl′ tərd) *adj.* made different; changed.

al·ter·na·tive (ôl tėr′ nə tiv) *n.* one of the things that may be chosen; choice.

445

al·tim·e·ter (al tim′ ə tər, al′ tə mē′ tər) *n.* an instrument for measuring altitude above the ground.

al·ti·tude (al′ tə tüd′, al′ tə tūd′) *n.* the elevation above a given point, especially the earth's surface.

am·a·teur (am′ ə chər, am′ ə tər) *n.* a person who does something for pleasure rather than as a profession or for money.

am·bi·tion (am bish′ ən) *n.* strong desire to succeed or to achieve something.

am·pu·tee (am′ pyə tē′) *n.* a person who has had a limb (leg or arm) removed.

an·a·lyze (an′ ə līz′) *v.* **an·a·lyzed, an·a·lyz·ing.** to examine carefully and in detail.

an·i·ma·tion (an′ ə mā′ shən) *n.* the process and technique of filming a movie to make drawings, puppets, and other inanimate objects appear alive. [Latin *animātus*, past participle of *animāre* to give life to.]

an·thra·cite (an′ thrə sīt′) *n.* a kind of coal that is very hard and shiny.

ap·pa·ri·tion (ap′ ə rish′ ən) *n.* a ghost, phantom, or other vision that comes unexpectedly or suddenly into view.

ar·chae·ol·o·gist (är′ kē ol′ ə jist) *n.* a scientist who studies the human past through excavation of former dwelling sites and the examination of tools, weapons, pottery, and other things found there.

ar·chi·tect (är′ kə tekt′) *n.* a person whose profession is to design, draw plans for, and supervise the construction of buildings or other structures.

ar·ro·gant (ār′ ə gənt) *adj.* characterized by or showing too much pride and a lack of respect for other people; conceited and haughty.

ar·ti·fi·cial (är′ tə fish′ əl) *adj.* made by people; not as in nature.

as·pect (as′ pekt) *n.* the way in which something can be viewed.

as·sem·ble (ə sem′ bəl) *v.* **as· sem·bled, as·sem·bling.** to gather; collect; come together.

as·sump·tion (ə sump′ shən) *n.* something that is taken for granted.

as·sure (ə shür′) *v.* **as·sured, as·sur·ing.** to make certain; guarantee; tell positively.

as·ton·ished (ə ston′ isht) *adj.* greatly surprised; amazed.

as·tound (ə stound′) *adj.* to surprise very much; amaze; astonish.

a·stride (ə strīd′) *prep.* with one leg on each side of.

au·di·tion (ô dish′ ən) *n.* a short performance to test the abilities of a singer, musician, actor, or other performer.

au·to·mat·i·cal·ly (ô′ tə mat′ ik lē) *adv.* acting, moving, or operating by itself.

av·a·lanche (a′ və lanch) *n.* the swift, sudden fall of something onto, and covering what was below. —*v.* **av·a·lanched, av·a·lanch·ing.** to fall, as in an avalanche.

avalanche

awe (ô) *v.* **awed, aw·ing.** to fill with wonder or fear.

az·ure (azh′ ər) *n.* a sky-blue color.

B

Bab·y·lo·ni·an (bab' ə lō' nē ən) a person who lived in Babylonia, an ancient kingdom in Mesopotamia.

back·stretch (bak' strech') *n.* the part of a racetrack farthest from the homestretch.

bal·lad (bal' əd) *n.* a song or poem that tells a story.

bar·bi·tu·rate (bär bich' ər it, bär bich' ə rāt') *n.* any of a group of drugs that is used to calm nerves and bring on sleep, usually habit-forming.

bar·ter (bär' tər) *v.* to trade goods for other goods without using money, usually involving bargaining to agree on the price.

bear·ings (bãr' ingz) *n. pl.* knowledge or understanding of one's position or direction.

beck·on (bek' ən) *v.* to signal or call to someone by a sign or gesture.

Bee·tho·ven, Lud·wig van (bā' tō vən, lüd' vig vän) 1770–1827, German composer

be·fall (bi fôl') *v.* **be·fell, be·fal·len, be·fal·ling.** to happen to.

ben·e·fit (ben' ə fit) *n.* a social or theatrical event held to raise money for some charity or cause.

Bern·hardt, Sar·ah (bèrn' härt', sãr' ə) 1844–1923, French actress.

bleak·ness (blēk' nis) *n.* the bareness or starkness of something.

boun·ty (boun' tē) *n., pl.* **boun·ties.** a reward, riches; wealth of something.

bow (bō) *v.* to bend or curve.

bran·dish (bran' dish) *v.* to wave, shake, or swing in a threatening way. [Old French *brandiss-*, a stem of *brandir* to brandish, going back to Anglo-Norman *brand* sword, from Old Norse *brandr* torch, sword.]

brisk (brisk) *adj.* quick and lively.

Brit·ish Co·lum·bi·a (brit' ish kə lum' bē ə) the westernmost province of Canada, on the Pacific Ocean.

buck·le (buk' əl) *v.* **buck·led, buck·ling.** to cause something to bulge or bend because of strain.

bur·den (bèrd' ən) *n.* something that is carried; something difficult to bear.

C

cairn (kãrn) *n.* a mound of stones piled up as a landmark or monument.

cal·cu·lat·ing (kal' kyə lā' ting) *adj.* given to careful or shrewd consideration, usually of one's own interests.

cal·is·then·ics (kal' is then' iks) *n., pl.* light gymnastic exercises used to develop strength and grace, and promote good health.

cal·o·rie (kal' ər ē) *n.* a unit of measurement of the energy-producing value of food.

cal·o·rim·e·ter (kal' ə rim' ə tər) *n.* a device for measuring the number of calories in a substance.

---

a b**a**t, ā c**a**ke, ä f**a**ther, är c**a**r, ãr d**a**re; e h**e**n, ē m**e**, èr t**e**rm; i b**i**b, ī k**i**te, ir cl**e**ar; o t**o**p, ō r**o**pe, ô s**a**w, oi c**o**in, ôr f**o**rk, ou **o**ut; u s**u**n, ù b**oo**k, ü m**oo**n, ū c**u**te; ə **a**bout, tak**e**n

cam·paign (kam pān') *n.* an organized series of actions carried on for a particular purpose.

candor (kan' dər) *n.* honesty; openness.

can·o·py (kan' ə pē) *n., pl.* **can·o·pies.** a covering of cloth or other material, hung or supported on poles over a bed, throne, person, entrance of a building, or other object.

ca·pa·ble (kā' pə bəl) *adj.* having or showing ability; efficient; competent; able.

Cape Horn (kāp hôrn) the southernmost tip of South America.

car·bo·hy·drate (kär' bō hī' drāt) *n.* an organic compound produced by plants and used by the human body for energy.

ca·reen·ing (kə rē' ning) *adj.* lurching or swaying from side to side.

car·go (kär' gō) *n., pl.* **car·goes** or **cargos.** the goods or merchandise carried by a ship, plane, or vehicle; payload.

car·i·bou (kār' ə bü) *n., pl.* **car·i·bous** or **car·i·bou.** a large type of deer that lives in the northern regions of the world. [French *caribou*; of Algonquian origin.]

cat·a·pult (kat' ə pult') *v.* **1.** to move quickly or suddenly; leap; spring. **2.** to hurl an object from one end of a lever by pressing on the other end.—*n.* machine that hurls something in this manner.

catapult

cen·ti·grade (sen' tə grād') *adj.* designating the temperature scale on which freezing is at zero degrees and boiling is at one hundred degrees.

cen·tral nerv·ous sys·tem (sen' trəl nèr' vəs sis' təm) the part of the nervous system composed of the brain and the spinal cord.

cen·tur·y (sen' chər ē) *n., pl.* **cen·tur·ies.** a period of one hundred years.

cer·e·mo·ni·al (sār' ə mō' nē əl) *adj.* used in connection with a ceremony or ritual.

cham·ber (chām' bər) *n.* an enclosed space.

chan·nel (chan' əl) *n.* a body of water used as a passage for boats or ships.

cher·ished (chār' isht) *adj.* held dear.

Cher·o·kee (chār' ə kē) a member of a group of North American Indians, once the largest in the southeastern U.S., now living mostly in Oklahoma.

Chil·e (chil' ē) a Spanish-speaking country on the southwestern coast of South America.

Chip·pe·wey·an (chip' ə wā' ən) *adj.* relating to an Indian group living in the region of northern Canada between Great Slave Lake and Hudson Bay.

Choc·taw (chok' tô) a member of a group of North American Indians formerly living in Mississippi, Alabama, and Louisiana, now living in Oklahoma.

cho·re·og·ra·pher (kôr' ē og' rə fər) *n.* a person who creates, arranges, or directs dance movement, as in ballet.

cir·cu·la·tion (sèr' kyə lā' shən) *n.* the movement of the blood to and from the heart through the blood vessels of the body.

civ·i·li·za·tion (siv′ ə li zā′ shən) *n.* the way of life of a particular people, place, or time.

co·caine (kō kān′, kō′ kān) *n.* a habit-forming drug obtained from the leaves of a South American shrub.

co·in·ci·dence (kō in′ si dəns) *n.* a remarkable occurrence of events at the same time and apparently by mere chance.

col·lab·o·ra·tor (kə lab′ ə rā′ tər) *n.* a person who works with another or others.

col·lide (kə līd′) *v.* **col·lid·ed, col·lid·ing.** to come together with force; crash.

com·mer·cial (kə mėr′ shəl) *adj.* of or relating to general business or trade.

com·mit·ment (kə mit′ mənt) *n.* an obligation or pledge.

com·par·a·tive·ly (kəm pār′ ə tiv lē) *adv.* in a way judged by comparison; relatively.

com·pe·tence (kom′ pə təns) *n.* ability; fitness.

com·pe·ti·tion (kom′ pə tish′ ən) *n.* the act of competing in a contest that tests or proves a person's skill or ability.

com·ple·ment (kom′ plə mənt) *v.* to make complete or balanced.

com·pound (kom′ pound′) *n.* an enclosed area containing buildings.

con·ceiv·a·bly (kən sē′ və blē) *adv.* possibly; realistically.

con·cen·trat·ed (kon′ sən trā′ tid) *adj.* describing something that has been made stronger or thicker.

con·di·tion (kən dish′ ən) *n.* something needed or required before something else can take place; stipulation.

con·dor (kon′ dər, kon′ dôr) *n.* a very large vulture with black and white feathers and an unfeathered head.

condor

con·fide (kən fīd′) *v.* **con·fid·ed, con·fid·ing.** to tell as a secret; trust with a personal matter.

con·fine·ment (kən fīn′ mənt) *n.* the state of being limited or restricted, usually to a particular place.

con·flict (kon′ flikt) *n.* a struggle or clash between opposing views, ideas, or interests.

con·front (kən frunt′) *v.* to face boldly.

co·ni·fer (kon′ ə fər, kō′ nə fər) *n.* a tree that bears cones.

con·science (kon′ shəns) *n.* a sense and memory of what is right and what is wrong.

con·scious·ness (kon′ shəs nis) *n.* state of being conscious; awareness.

con·spire (kən spīr′) *v.* **con·spired, con·spir·ing.** to plot. [Middle English *conspiren*, going back to Latin *conspirare* to breathe together, agree.]

con·stric·tion (kən strik′ shən) *n.* the act of constricting, squeezing, or compressing.

con·sult (kən sult′) *v.* to ask or look to for information or advice.

---

a **b**at, ā **c**ake, ä **f**ather, är **c**ar, ār **d**are; e **h**en, ē **m**e, ėr **t**erm; i **b**ib, ī **k**ite, ir **cl**ear; o **t**op, ō **r**ope, ô **s**aw, oi **c**oin, ôr **f**ork, ou **ou**t; u **s**un, ù **b**ook, ü **m**oon, ū **c**ute; ə **a**bout, tak**e**n

con·tem·po·rar·y (kən tem′ pə rãr ē) *adj.* current; modern.

con·tempt (kən tempt′) *n.* a feeling that a person or thing is low, mean, or worthless; scorn.

con·vert (kən vėrt′) *v.* to change in character, condition, or use; to exchange for something equal.

con·vey (kən vā′) *v.* to tell or communicate; send information.

con·vic·tion (kən vik′ shən) *n.* a firm belief or opinion.

co·or·di·na·tion (kō ôr′ də nā′ shən) *n.* the working well together, as of parts of the body.

cor·re·spon·dence (kôr′ ə spon′ dəns) *n.* communication by exchange of letters.

coun·ter·at·tack (koun′ tər ə tak′) *v.* to make an attack against an opponent's attack.

coy (koi) *adj.* shy or modest; bashful.

crack (krak) *n. Slang.* a less expensive and highly addictive form of cocaine.

crave (krāv) *v.* **craved, crav·ing.** to long or yearn for; desire eagerly.

cred·u·lous (krej′ ə ləs) *adj.* ready to believe or accept without proof.

Cree (krē) a member of a North American Indian group of northern and central Canada, now living mainly in Manitoba.

crest (krest) *n.* the highest point of a hill or mountain ridge.

crev·ice (krev′ is) *n.* a narrow crack in something, particularly a stone.

cri·sis (krī′ sis) *n., pl.* **cris·es** (krī′ sēz). a period of difficulty or danger.

crouch (krouch) *v.* to stoop low.

cru·cial (krü′ shəl) *adj.* very important; critical.

cul·ture (kul′ chər) *n.* the way of life of a group of people, including their customs, beliefs, and arts.

cun·ning (kun′ ing) *adj.* tricky; sly.

cur (kėr) *n.* a nasty, worthless person.

cur·lew (kėr′ lü) *n.* a wading bird with long legs, long slender beak, and brown feathers.

curlew

cur·rent (kėr′ ənt) *n.* **1.** a portion of a body of water or of air continuously flowing in approximately the same path. **2.** the flow of electricity in an electric circuit.

D

de·bate (di bāt′) *v.* **de·bat·ed, de·bat·ing.** to think about; consider alternatives.

dec·ade (dek′ əd) *n.* a period of ten years.

de·ceive (di sēv′) *v.* **de·ceived, de·ceiv·ing.** to make someone believe something that is false; fool.

de·cent (dē′ sənt) *adj.* fairly good; satisfactory.

de·ci·pher (di sī′ fər) *v.* to make out the meaning of; to uncode.

de·cline (di klīn′) *v.* **de·clined, de·clin·ing.** to fall into an inferior or poor condition.

ded·i·ca·tion (ded′ ə kā′ shən) *n.* devotion to a particular purpose or goal.

de·duce (di düs′, di dūs′) *v.* **de·duced, de·duc·ing.** to reach or draw a conclusion from something known or assumed.

de·fi·ant·ly (di fī′ ənt lē) *adv.* characterized by or showing resistance.

de·fy (di fī′) v. **de·fied, de·fy·ing.** to resist completely or successfully; withstand.

de·pen·dence (di pen′ dəns) n. the state of relying on something.

de·pos·it (di poz′ it) n. a natural layer of a mineral such as coal or oil. [Latin *depositus*, past participle of *deponere* to put down.]

deposit

de·pot (dē′ pō) n. a railroad station or bus terminal.

de·pres·sant (di pres′ ənt) n. a drug that slows down the central nervous system. Anesthetics, sedatives, and narcotics are depressants.

de·scend (di send′) v. to come down from an earlier source or ancestor.

des·per·ate (des′ pər it, des′ prit) adj. reckless because of hopelessness; rash.

des·tined (des′ tind) adj. something that is predetermined or fixed beforehand.

de·tach (di tach′) v. to unfasten and separate.

de·te·ri·o·rate (di tir′ ē ə rāt′) v. **de·te·ri·o·ra·ted, de·te·ri·o·rat·ing.** to lessen in quality or value; become worse.

de·tour (dē′ tür) n. a road used temporarily while the main road cannot be traveled. —v. to make or take a detour.

de·vise (di vīz′) v. **de·vised, de·vis·ing.** to think out; invent; plan.

de·vo·tion (di vō′ shən) n. strong attachment or affection; loyalty.

di·ag·nose (dī′ əg nōs′) v. **di·ag·nosed, di·ag·nos·ing.** to find out the nature of a disease or other harmful condition by careful examination and study of symptoms. [From Greek *diagnōsis*, from *diagignōskein* to distinguish, from *dia* through, apart + *gignōskein* to know.]

di·a·logue (dī′ ə lôg′, dī′ ə log′) n. the parts that are conversation in a movie, play, or novel.

dic·ta·tor·ship (dik′ tā′ tər ship′) n. a government or state ruled by a dictator, one who has absolute power and authority.

dig·ni·ty (dig′ nə tē) n., pl. **dig·ni·ties.** nobility of character or manner; stateliness, serenity, composure.

di·lap·i·dat·ed (di lap′ ə dā′ tid) adj. fallen into disrepair, decay, or ruin.

dil·i·gent·ly (dil′ ə jənt lē) adv. in a way that is careful and serious; attentively.

di·lute (di lüt′, dī lüt′) v. **di·lut·ed, di·lut·ing.** to thin or weaken by adding a liquid; to reduce the strength of.

dis·card (dis kärd′) v. to reject or give up as useless, worthless, or unwanted.

dis·cern (di sėrn) v. to separate or distinguish between things or ideas.

dis·con·cert·ed (dis′ kən sėr′ tid) adj. being upset or frustrated.

---

a **bat**, ā **cake**, ä **father**, är **car**, âr **dare**; e **hen**, ē **me**, ėr **term**; i **bib**, ī **kite**, ir **clear**; o **top**, ō **rope**, ô **saw**, oi **coin**, ôr **fork**, ou **out**; u **sun**, ù **book**, ü **moon**, ū **cute**; ə **about**, tak**e**n

dis·in·te·grate (dis in′ tə grāt′) *v.*
dis·in·te·grat·ed, dis·in·te·grat·ing.
to fall apart or be destroyed by breaking into parts. [From Latin *dis* apart +
integratus, past participle of *integrare*,
from *integer* whole.]

dis·man·tle (dis mant′ əl) *v.* **dis·man·tled,
dis·man·tling.** to pull down or take
apart.

dis·or·der (dis ôr′ dər) *n.* **1.** a physical
or mental sickness. **2.** lack of order;
confusion.

dis·rupt (dis rupt′) *v.* to throw into disorder or confusion; break up or apart.

dis·tinct (dis tingkt′) *adj.* clearly seen or
understood as different in quality or
kind.

di·vide (di vīd′) *n.* a raised area of land,
usually a mountain ridge, that separates two land areas drained by different river systems.

doc·u·men·ta·ry (dok′ yə men′ tər ē)
n., pl. **doc·u·men·ta·ries.** a film or
show whose subject deals with or is
supported by facts.

dog·ged·ly (dô′ gid lē) *adv.* in a stub-
born, nonyielding way; persevering.

dom·i·nate (dom′ ə nāt′) *v.* **dom·i·nat·ed,
dom·i·nat·ing.** to be more important
or striking than; stand out; monopolize.
[Latin *dominatus*, past participle of
dominari, from *dominus* master.]

dor·sal fin (dôr′ səl
fin′) a fin on or
near the back of
a fish.

dorsal fin

dread (dred) *n.* a fear or uneasiness that
something will or may happen.

drear·y (drir′ ē) *adj.* characterized by
sadness or gloom; dismal; depressing.

dumb·bell (dum′ bel′) *n.* a small bar
with weights on either end, held by
one hand and used for exercising.

du·pli·cate (dü′ pli kāt′, dū′ pli kāt′) *v.*
du·pli·cat·ed, du·pli·cat·ing. to
copy exactly; repeat.

E

ear·nest·ness (ėr′ nist nis) *n.* sincere or
serious feeling.

ec·o·nom·ic (ek′ ə nom′ ik, ē′ kə nom′
ik) *adj.* of or relating to money; making
good sense financially.

Ed·i·son, Thom·as Al·va (ed′ ə sən,
tom′ əs al′ və) 1847–1931, U.S. inventor.

ef·fi·cien·cy (i fish′ ən sē) *n., pl.*
ef·fi·cien·cies. the quality of bringing
about a desired effect with little waste.

e·lab·o·rate (i lab′
ər it) *adj.* highly
detailed or or-
namented.

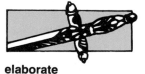

elaborate

e·lat·ed (i lā′ tid) *adj.* in high spirits;
joyful.

eld·er (el′ dər) *n.* an older, influential
member, as of a family or community.

el·o·quent (el′ ə kwənt) *n.* able to use
language expressively and effectively.

em·cee (em′ sē′) *n.* a master of ceremonies.

em·i·grate (em′ ə grāt′) *v.* **em·i·grat·
ed, em·i·grat·ing.** to leave one place
or country to live in another. [Latin
emigratus, past participle of *emigrare*,
from *e-* out + *migrare* to migrate.]

e·mo·tion (i mō′ shən) *n.* a strong
feeling.

em·pha·size (em′ fə sīz) *v.* **em·pha·
sized, em·pha·siz·ing.** to give emphasis to; stress.

em·pire (em′ pīr) *n.* a group of countries
or territories ruled or controlled by the
government of one country.

en·clo·sure (en klō′ zhər) *n.* something
that encloses, such as a wall or
building.

en·coun·ter (en koun′ tər) *v.* to meet
with; face; confront. —*n.* unexpected
or casual meeting.

en·dorse·ment (en dôrs′ mənt) *n.*
approval; support.

en·dure (en dür′, en dūr′) *v.* **en·dured,
en·dur·ing.** to tolerate, put up with,
or undergo.

en·thu·si·asm (en thü′ zē az′ əm) *n.*
eager or fervent interest; zeal.

en·vi·a·ble (en′ vē ə bəl) *adj.* worthy of
envy; desirable.

ep·i·sode (ep′ ə sōd′) *n.* installment of
a story that is presented in serial form,
as on television.

e·ra (ir′ ə, ãr′ ə) *n.* a period of time
marked by certain events, conditions,
ideas, persons, or things.

e·rect (i rekt′) *v.* to build; construct.

es·sen·tial (i sen′ shəl) *adj.* very important or necessary.

es·tab·lish (es tab′ lish) *v.* to determine,
set up, or define.

es·ti·mate (es′ tə māt′) *v.* **es·ti·ma·ted,
es·ti·ma·ting.** to form a judgment or
opinion of, often of a measurement.

et cet·er·a (et set′ ər ə) Latin phrase for
and so forth; and the rest; and others.

ev·i·dence (ev′ ə dəns) *n.* something
that serves to prove or disprove a
belief or conclusion; proof.

ev·i·dent·ly (ev′ ə dənt lē) *adv.* clearly;
apparently; obviously. [Middle English,
going back to Latin *evident*, from *e-*
out + *vident*, present participle of
vīdere to see.]

ex·as·per·ate (eg zas′ pə rāt′) *v.*
ex·as·per·at·ed, ex·as·per·at·ing.
to irritate greatly; provoke to anger.

ex·ca·vate (eks′ kə vāt′) *v.*
ex·ca·vat·ed, ex·ca·vat·ing. to
uncover by digging; unearth.

ex·cel (ek sel′) *v.* **ex·celled,
ex·cel·ling.** to do better than or be
greater than others; surpass others.

ex·cerpt (ek′ sérpt) *n.* a piece, passage,
or scene selected from a larger work.

ex·cess (ek′ ses, ek ses′) *adj.* more than
enough; an amount greater than what
is needed.

ex·haus·tion (eg zôs′ chən) *n.* a lack of
strength or energy; extreme fatigue.

ex·ile (eg′ zīl) *v.* **ex·iled, ex·il·ing.** to
send away from one's country or home
by law or decree.

ex·pres·sion (eks presh′ ən) *n.* a
particular look that reveals a person's
thoughts or feelings.

---

a b**a**t, ā c**a**ke, ä f**a**ther, är c**ar**, ãr d**are**; e h**e**n, ē m**e**, ėr t**er**m; i b**i**b, ī k**i**te,
ir cl**ear**; o t**o**p, ō r**o**pe, ô s**aw**, oi c**oi**n, ôr f**or**k, ou **ou**t; u s**u**n, ů b**oo**k, ŭ m**oo**n, ū c**u**te;
ə **a**bout, tak**e**n

ex·traor·di·nar·y (eks trôr′ də när′ ē, eks′ trə ôr′ də när′ ē) *adj.* very unusual; remarkable.

ex·ult (eg zult′) *v.* to rejoice greatly; be joyful and jubilant.

F

fal·ter (fôl′ tər) *v.* to act with hesitation; to stop short.

fas·ci·nate (fas′ ə nāt′) *v.* **fas·ci·nat·ed, fas·ci·nat·ing.** to attract by; captivate.

fat (fat) *n.* any of a group of oily or greasy substances found in animal tissues and some plants.

fa·tal (fā′ təl) *adj.* causing death; deadly.

fa·tigue (fə tēg′) *n.* loss of strength that is caused by hard work; tiredness.

fe·ro·cious (fə rō′ shəs) *adj.* savage; fierce.

fer·tile (fėrt′ əl) *adj.* able to produce crops or vegetation abundantly.

fil·ly (fil′ ē) *n., pl.* **fil· lies.** young female horse.

flank (flangk) *n.* the side of something.

flex·i·bil·i·ty (flek′ sə bil′ ə tē) *n.* the ability to bend without breaking.

foal (fōl) *n.* a young horse.

fo·cus (fō′ kəs) *n., pl.* **fo·cus·es** or **fo·ci** (fō′ sī). the central point of interest or importance.

fore·most (fôr′ mōst′) *adj.* first in position, rank, or importance.

fore·sight (fôr′ sīt′) *n.* care or thought for the future.

forge (fôrj) *v.* **forged, forg·ing.** to heat metal in a forge or furnace and then hammer into shape.

for·mal·i·ty (fôr mal′ ə te) *n., pl.* **for·mal·i·ties.** a proper or very polite way of behaving.

for·mi·da·ble (fôr′ mi də bəl) *adj.* difficult to deal with or do.

for·mu·la (fôr′ myə lə) *n., pl.* **for·mu·lae** or **for·mu·las.** a set method for doing something.

for·tress (fôr′ tris) *n.* a fortified place; stronghold; fort; castle. [Old French *forteresse* strong place, going back to Latin *fortis* strong.]

fortress

fran·tic (fran′ tik) *adj.* frenzied; anxious.

freight (frāt) *n.* goods transported by land, air, or water; cargo.

fre·quen·cy (frē′ kwən sē) *n.* the number of times something happens or takes place during a period of time; rate of occurrence.

frus·trate (frus′ trāt) *v.* **frus·trat·ed, frus·trat·ing.** to keep from doing or achieving something; thwart or disappoint.

fu·gi·tive (fū′ gə tiv) *n.* a person who is fleeing something or someone.

func·tion (fungk′ shən) *n.* the proper or natural action of something; purpose.

G

gal·ax·y (gal′ ək sē) *n., pl.* **gal·ax·ies.** any of the vast groupings of stars, dust, and gases scattered throughout the universe. [Old French *galaxie* the Milky Way, going back to Latin *galaxiās*, going back to Greek *galaxiās*, from *gala* milk.]

gear (gir) *n.* equipment used for a specific purpose.

gen·er·a·tion (jen' ə rā' shən) *n.* one step in the line of natural descent.

ge·o·met·ric (jē' ə met' rik) *adj.* made up of or decorated with straight lines, angles, circles, arcs, or similar forms. [Greek *gē* earth + *metron* measure, rule.]

gla·cier (glā' shər) *n.* a large mass of ice moving slowly over land, especially down a valley.

glum·ly (glum' lē) *adv.* sadly, sullenly.

god (god) *n.* a being in a mythology believed to have special powers over the lives and affairs of people.

god·dess (god' is) *n., pl.* **god·dess·es.** a female god.

grad·u·al·ly (graj' ü əl lē) *adv.* happening or changing slowly or by degrees.

gram (gram) *n.* a unit of weight equal to one twenty-eighth of an ounce.

Gram·my A·ward (gram' mē ə wôrd') an award given to individuals for notable achievement in the recording industry.

graph·ic (graf' ik) *adj.* **1.** vividly described; lifelike. **2.** of or relating to graphic arts.

grit (grit) *n.* strength of mind and spirit; courage. — *v.* **grit·ted, grit·ting.** to grind or tightly clamp together.

groom (grüm) *v.* to train or prepare someone for some purpose.

grudg·ing·ly (gruj' ing lē) *adv.* unwillingly.

gul·ly (gul' ē) *n., pl.* **gul·lies.** a ditch or channel cut into the earth by running water; small ravine.

H

hal·lu·cin·o·gen (hə lü' si nə jən') *n.* one of a group of drugs that causes one to see and hear things that are not real.

har·dy (här' dē) *adj.* strong, robust.

Har·lem (här' ləm) a section of New York City, in Manhattan, populated mainly by black and Hispanic residents.

hav·oc (hav' ək) *n.* great destruction; devastation; ruin.

hearth (härth) *n.* the floor of the fireplace, often extending beyond the opening.

her·ald (här' əld) *n.* a thing or person that announces, or is a sign of, something to come.

her·o·in (här' ō in) *n.* a drug made from morphine that is habit-forming and can be fatal if too much is taken.

hes·i·tate (hez' ə tāt') *v.* **hes·i·tat·ed, hes·i·tat·ing.** to wait or stop a moment.

hoist (hoist) *v.* to lift or pull up, especially by means of ropes or pulleys.

home·land (hōm' land') *n.* a region where people are forced to live by an order of law.

Hong Kong (hong' kong') a British crown colony located off the southeastern coast of the People's Republic of China.

horde (hôrd) *n.* a large group; swarm.

---

a b**a**t, ā c**a**ke, ä f**a**ther, är c**a**r, âr d**a**re; e h**e**n, ē m**e**, ėr t**e**rm; i b**i**b, ī k**i**te, ir cl**e**ar; o t**o**p, ō r**o**pe, ô s**a**w, oi c**o**in, ôr f**o**rk, ou **o**ut; u s**u**n, u̇ b**oo**k, ü m**oo**n, ū c**u**te; ə **a**bout, tak**e**n

ho·ri·zon (hə rī′ zən) *n.* **1.** line where the earth and sky seem to meet. **2.** the limit or range of knowledge.

hos·tile (hos′ təl, hos′ tīl) *adj.* feeling or showing hatred or dislike.

hy·per·bo·le (hī pėr′ bə lē) *n.* an extreme exaggeration, not meant to be taken literally, to give special emphasis to a statement.

I

i·den·ti·cal (ī den′ ti kəl) *adj.* exactly alike.

il·lu·mi·nate (i lü′ mə nāt′) *v.* **il·lu·mi·nat·ed, il·lu·mi·nat·ing.** to light up.

im·age (im′ ij) *n.* a picture or other likeness of a person or thing.

im·age·ry (im′ ij rē) *n.* pictures formed in the mind by memory or imagination.

im·bed·ded (im bed′ id) *adj.* set or enclosed in surrounding matter. Also, **em·bed·ded.**

im·mo·bi·lize (i mō′ bə līz′) *v.* **im·mo·bi·lized, im·mo·bi·liz·ing.** to make unmovable; to fix in place.

im·pass·a·ble (im pas′ ə bəl) *adj.* that cannot be passed or traveled over, across, or through.

im·pres·sion (im presh′ ən) *n.* **1.** an effect or influence produced on the mind, senses, or feelings. **2.** a feeling or judgment about something or someone.

In·ca (ing′ kə) a highly civilized South American Indian people who ruled a large empire in eastern South America.

Inca

in·ces·sant·ly (in ses′ ənt lē) *adv.* continuing without interruption.

in·ci·dent (in′ sə dənt) *n.* an event or act; a happening.

in·con·spic·u·ous (in′ kən spik′ ū əs) *adj.* not easily seen; not obvious.

in·de·ci·sive (in′ di sī′ səv) *adj.* unable to decide.

in·di·cate (in′ di kāt′) *v.* **in·di·cat·ed, in·di·cat·ing.** to direct attention to; point out; state briefly.

in·e·qual·i·ty (in′ i kwol′ ə tē) *n., pl.* **in·e·qual·i·ties.** the fact that two things are not equal.

in·fec·tion (in fek′ shən) *n.* a disease or condition caused by certain harmful germs entering the body.

in·flu·ence (in′ flü əns) *v.* **in·flu·enced, in·flu·enc·ing.** to change; affect.

in·hab·it·ant (in hab′ ə tənt) *n.* person that lives permanently in a place; resident.

in·her·it (in hãr′ it) *v.* to receive from a former owner at his or her death; come into possession of.

in·no·cent (in′ ə sənt) *adj.* free from guilt.

in·no·va·tive (in′ ə vā′ tiv) *adj.* tending to introduce new things.

in·scrip·tion (in skrip′ shən) *n.* a message or note written on something.

in·spire (in spīr′) *v.* **in·spired, in·spir·ing.** to have a stimulating effect or influence on.

in·stinc·tive·ly (in stingk′ tiv lē) *adv.* in a way done out of instinct; unprompted.

in·su·la·tion (in′ sə lā′ shən) *n.* a substance that prevents the passage of heat.

in·tact (in takt′) *adj.* whole; together.

in·tel·lec·tu·al (int′ əl ek′ chü əl) *n.* a person who likes to use his or her intellect.

in·tense (in tens′) *adj.* having or showing strong or earnest feeling.

in·ten·sive care (in ten′ siv kãr′) a unit of a hospital for very sick patients requiring thorough or concentrated care.

in·ten·tion (in ten′ shən) *n.* purpose; aim.

in·ter·cept (in′ tər sept′) *v.* to seize or stop on the way; to stop the progress of.

in·ter·pre·ta·tion (in tèr′ prə tā′ shən) *n.* an individual's understanding of something; a translation.

in·ter·val (in′ tər vəl) *n.* **1.** time or space between. **2. intervals** *Sports.* running exercise characterized by a series of sprints separated by resting walks; wind sprints.

in·va·sion (in vā′ zhən) *n.* the entrance of an armed force into a country or planet in order to rob or conquer.

in·vert·ed (in vėr′ tid) *adj.* turned upside down; inside out.

in·vest (in vest′) *v.* to give or devote time, effort, or the like for a specific purpose.

i·ron·ic (ī ron′ ik) *adj.* of, relating to, or characterized by irony, or an event or outcome of events opposite to what was, or might naturally have been, expected.

ir·rev·o·ca·ble (i rev′ ə kə bəl) *adj.* that cannot be revoked or recalled.

ir·ri·ga·tion (ir′ ri gā′ shən) *n.* the supplying of land with water by means of channels or streams, usually manmade.

irrigation

J

jazz (jaz) *n.* music of a style originated by American blacks late in the nineteenth century, characterized by improvisation and syncopation, or the stressing of certain beats.

joint (joint) *n.* the place or part where two bones meet, usually able to move freely.

ju·bi·lant (jü′ bə lənt) *adj.* joyfully happy or triumphant; exultant.

ju·ry (jür′ ē) *adj. Nautical.* temporary; for use in an emergency; makeshift.

K

ketch (kech) *n., pl.* **ketch·es.** a sailing ship with two masts.

key·board (kē′ bôrd′) *n.* an arrangement or set of keys, as in a piano or typewriter.

ki·lo·gram (kil′ ə gram′) *n.* a unit of measurement of mass and weight equal to one thousand grams or 2.2046 pounds.

L

la·bor (lā′ bôr) *n.* physical or mental effort; work; toil; a specific task.

a b**a**t, ā c**a**ke, ä f**a**ther, ãr c**ar**, ãr d**are**; e h**e**n, ē m**e**, ėr t**er**m; i b**i**b, ī k**i**te, ir cl**ear**; o t**o**p, ō r**o**pe, ô s**aw**, oi c**oi**n, ôr f**or**k, ou **ou**t; u s**u**n, u̇ b**oo**k, ü m**oo**n, ū c**u**te; ə **a**bout, tak**e**n

lair (lãr) *n.* a home or resting place, especially of a wild animal.

land·mark (land′ märk′) *n.* an object in a landscape that is familiar and serves as a guide.

land·scape (land′ skãp′) *n.* a stretch or expanse of scenery that can be viewed from one point or place.

lap (lap) *n.* one length or circuit of something, such as a racetrack.

lat·i·tude (lat′ ə tüd, lat′ ə tūd′) *n.* the distance north or south of the equator, expressed in degrees, with 0° at the equator.

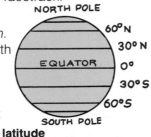

latitude

lee (lē) *n.* **1.** shelter or protection. **2.** the sheltered or protected side of something.

leg·end (lej′ ənd) *n.* a story passed down through the years that is not regarded as historically true, but is usually based on some facts.

lei·sure·ly (lē′ zhər lē, lezh′ ər lē) *adv.* in an unhurried or relaxed way.

lev·el·head·ed (lev′ əl hed′ id) *adj.* having or showing common sense and good judgment.

lev·er (lev′ ər, lē′ vər) *n.* a bar, handle, or piece that is moved to operate, control, or adjust a mechanism.

lime·stone (līm′ stōn′) *n.* a rock consisting chiefly of calcium carbonate, used for building, and for making lime.

lin·e·ar (lin′ ē ər) *adj.* consisting of or making use of lines.

lit·ter (lit′ ər) *n.* a group of animals born at the same time.

lla·ma (lä′ mə) *n.* a South American animal related to the camel, having a thick woolly coat, and used as a pack animal.

lo·ca·tion (lō kā′ shən) *n.* the place where something is or might be established; site.

log·i·cal (loj′ i kəl) *adj.* in agreement with logic; reasonable; a natural consequence.

loom (lüm) *v.* to appear or rise over as a large threatening shape.

LSD *n.* a drug that produces hallucinations and temporary changes in personality. [Abbreviation for **ly**sergic acid **d**iethylamide.]

lunge (lunj) *v.* **lunged, lung·ing.** any sudden forward movement.

lurch (lèrch) *v.* **1.** to move jerkily and unsteadily; **2.** to sway suddenly from side to side.

M

main·tain (mān tān′) *v.* to keep as is or hold on to.

ma·jes·tic (mə jes′ tik) *adj.* having or showing great dignity, splendor, or grandeur.

ma·neu·ver (mə nü′ vər) *v.* to move or manage skillfully or cleverly.

ma·nip·u·late (mə nip′ yə lāt′) *v.* **ma·nip·u·lat·ed, ma·nip·u·lat·ing.** to manage or work with the hands. [French *manipulation* handling, going back to Latin *manipulus* handful.]

man·u·al (man′ ū əl) *adj.* relating to, done by, or involving the use of the hands.

mar·a·thon (mãr′ ə thon′) *n.* a foot race of 26 miles and 385 yards.

ma·son·ry (mā′ sən rē) *n.* something built of stone, concrete block, or brick.

mast·head (mast′ hed) *n.* the highest part of the mast of a ship.

ma·ture (mə chür′, mə tür′, mə chūr) *v.* **ma·tured, ma·tur·ing.** to become fully grown or developed; reach maturity.

mech·a·nism (mek′ ə niz′ əm) *n.* the working parts, or arrangement of parts, of a machine.

mem·o·ra·ble (mem′ ər ə bəl) *adj.* worthy of remembrance; not to be forgotten.

men·ac·ing (men′ ə sing) *adj.* threatening; dangerous.

merge (mėrj) *v.* **merged, merg·ing.** to unite so as to become one.

me·te·or·ite (mē′ tē ə rīt′) *n.* matter from space that has fallen, ablaze with heat, to earth.

me·thod·i·cal·ly (mə thod′ ik lē) *adv.* performed, carried on, or arranged in a systematic or orderly manner.

mind-al·ter·ing (mīnd′ ôl′ tər ing) *adj.* something that changes or distorts the way one would think about or perceive reality when not under its influence.

mi·rage (mi räzh′) *n.* an optical illusion caused by the bending of light rays by layers of air having different densities and temperatures.

mo·not·o·ny (mə not′ ən ē) *n.* a tiresome sameness; lack of variety. [Greek *monotoniā* sameness of tone, going back to *monos* single, alone + *tonos* sound.]

mon·u·ment (mon′ yə mənt) *n.* a building, arch, statue, or other structure set up in memory of a person or event.

monument

mor·phine (môr′ fēn) *n.* a powerful, habit-forming drug made from opium and used to relieve pain.

mo·ti·va·tion (mō′ tə vā′ shən) *n.* the drive or incentive that leads a person or animal to behave in some way.

Mount O·lym·pus (mount′ ō lim′ pəs) a mountain in Greece that, in Greek mythology, was the home of the twelve major gods.

mul·ti·tal·ent·ed (mul′ ti tal′ ən tid) *adj.* having many talents, or natural abilities and aptitudes.

mum·my (mum′ mē) *n., pl.* **mum·mies.** a dead body embalmed and wrapped in cloth for preservation, especially as done by the ancient Egyptians.

mu·ral (mūr′ əl) *n.* a large picture painted on a wall or ceiling.

mute·ly (mūt′ lē) *adv.* without speaking.

N

Ndeb·e·le (ən deb′ ə lē) a group of people who live in southern Africa.

ne·go·ti·ate (ni gō′ shē āt′) *v.* **ne·go·ti·at·ed, ne·go·ti·at·ing.** to succeed in going or passing over.

---

a bat, ā cake, ä father, är car, âr dare; e hen, ē me, ér term; i bib, ī kite, ir clear; o top, ō rope, ô saw, oi coin, ôr fork, ou out; u sun, u̇ book, ü moon, ū cute; ə about, taken

New Zea·land (nü zē′ lənd) an island country in the South Pacific, east of Australia.

no·ble (nō′ bəl) *n.* distinguished by high birth, rank, or title; aristocrat.

no·mad (nō′ mad) *n.* a member of a group that moves from place to place for food or land on which to graze their livestock.

nov·ice (nov′ is) *n.* a person who is new to an occupation, activity, or the like.

nu·tri·tion (nü trish′ ən) *n.* the process by which the body gets nutrients.

O

ob·jec·tive (əb jek′ tiv) *adj.* not affected or influenced by personal feelings or opinions; without bias.

ob·lit·er·ate (ə blit′ ə rāt′) *v.* **ob·lit·er·at·ed, ob·lit·er·at·ing.** to remove all traces of; erase.

ob·sess (əb ses′) *v.* to excessively trouble with a particular idea; preoccupy; haunt.

ob·sta·cle (ob′ stə kəl) *n.* a person or thing that opposes, stands in the way, or blocks progress.

oc·cur·rence (ə kėr′ əns) *n.* something that occurs or happens; incident.

o·men (ō′ mən) *n.* a sign or event that is supposed to foretell good or bad luck.

om·i·nous (om′ ə nəs) *adj.* threatening, foreboding.

op·ti·mism (op′ tə miz′ əm) *n.* tendency to hope for or expect the best.

or·deal (ôr dēl′) *n.* a very difficult test or painful experience.

out·come (out′ kum′) *n.* result; consequence.

out·go·ing (out′ gō′ ing) *adj.* sociable, open, and talkative.

out·land·ish (out lan′ dish) *adj.* strange, unfamiliar, or odd.

out·raged (out′ rājd′) *adj.* greatly angered.

o·va·tion (ō vā′ shən) *n.* an enthusiastic burst of applause or other approval.

o·ver·come (ō′ vər kum′) *v.* **o·ver·came, o·ver·com·ing.** to get the better of; conquer.

o·ver·whelm (ō′ vər hwelm′, ō′ vər welm′) *v.* to overcome completely; overpower or crush; cover or bury completely.

P

pace (pās) *n.* the rate of speed in walking or running.

Pan·a·ma (pan′ ə mä′) a country on the Isthmus of Panama, on either side of the Canal Zone.

Panama

pan·ic (pan′ ik) *n.* a terrible, often uncontrollable fear that can spread suddenly through a crowd.

par·al·lel (pār′ ə lel) *adj.* going in the same direction and always being the same distance apart.

pas·tel (pas tel′) *adj.* having a pale, soft shade.

pa·thet·ic (pə thet′ ik) *adj.* arousing pity, sadness, or sympathy.

per·il (pār′ əl) *n.* danger.

per·ma·nent (pėr′ mə nənt′) *adj.* lasting or intended to last indefinitely without change; enduring. [Latin *permanēns*, present participle of *permanēre* to continue, endure.]

per·sist·ent (pėr sis' tənt) *adj.* continuing firmly and steadily in spite of opposition or difficulty; persevering.

per·suade (pėr swād') *v.* **per·suad·ed, per·suad·ing.** to convince or cause someone to do or believe something.

phan·tom (fan' təm) *n.* something that appears to be real but is not; ghost; apparition.

phi·los·o·phy (fə los' ə fē) *n.* a person's principles and beliefs.

phy·sique (fi zēk') *n.* the structure, development, or appearance of the body. [French *physique* physical, going back to Latin *physicus* natural, going back to Greek *physikos*, from *physis* nature.]

pitch (pich) *n., pl.* **pitch·es.** a downward slope.

piv·ot (piv' ət) *v.* to turn around on, or as if on, a pivot.

Pi·zar·ro, Don Fran·cis·co (pi zär' ō, don' fran sis' kō) 1471? 1541, Spanish conquerer of the Incas, founder of Lima.

pluck (pluk) *v.* to pull out or off; pick.

plum·met (plum' it) *v.* to fall or drop straight downward.

plun·der (plun' dər) *v.* to loot or rob, as during a war; to take by force.

pol·i·cy (pol' ə sē) *n., pl.* **pol·i·cies.** a guiding principle that helps determine what decision to make.

port (pôrt) *n.* the left side of a boat or ship as one faces the front.

port·hole (pôrt' hōl') *n.* a small, usually circular, opening in the side of a boat or ship to let in air and light.

porthole

pos·ses·sion (pə zesh' ən) *n.* the act or fact of holding or owning.

pos·ture (pos' chər) *n.* the way of carrying or holding the head and body; carriage.

po·tent (pō' tənt) *adj.* having force, strength, or power.

prai·rie (prãr' ē) *n.* a large, level or gently rolling grassland without trees.

pre·cise (pri sīs') *adj.* very accurate; exact.

pre·fer (pri fėr') *v.* **pre·ferred, pre·fer·ring.** to like better than; choose above others.

prej·u·dice (prej' ə dis) *n.* unwarranted dislike or intolerance of a particular group, such as members of a race or religion.

pre·miere (pri mir', prim yīr') *n.* the first formal public performance or presentation.

pre·oc·cu·pa·tion (prē ok' yə pā' shən) *n.* the state of having all of one's attention taken up by something or someone.

pri·ma·ri·ly (prī mãr' ə lē) *adv.* chiefly; principally.

prin·ci·ple (prin' sə pəl) *n.* basic rule or belief.

---

a bat, ā cake, ä father, är car, ãr dare; e hen, ē me, ėr term; i bib, ī kite, ir clear; o top, ō rope, ô saw, oi coin, ôr fork, ou out; u sun, ù book, ü moon, ū cute; ə about, taken

prob·a·bil·i·ty (prob′ ə bil′ ə tē) *n.* **prob·a·bil·i·ties.** likelihood; the ratio of the number of occurrences of a particular outcome to the total number of possible outcomes.

pro·fes·sion (prə fesh′ ən) *n.* an occupation or job that requires special education and training.

pro·file (prō′ fīl) *n.* **1.** a side view, especially of a human face or head. **2.** a brief biographical sketch.

profile

pro·gres·sive re·lax·a·tion (prə gres′ iv rē′ lak sā′ shən) a learned method of relaxation by comparison with tension.

pro·mote (prə mōt′) *v.* **pro·mot·ed, pro·mot·ing.** to aid in the growth, development, or progress of.

prop·er·ty (prop′ ər tē) *n., pl.* **prop·er·ties.** a special quality of a person or thing.

pro·tein (prō′ tēn) *n.* one of several organic compounds that are the essential constituents of living cells.

prow (prou) *n.* the front part of the ship; bow.

psy·chol·o·gist (sī kol′ ə jist) *n.* a person who is trained in psychology, or the study of the mind and human behavior.

pul·ley (pul′ ē) *n., pl.* **pul·lies.** a grooved wheel over which a rope or chain is pulled, used to lift heavy loads.

pulley

pur·sue (pər sü′) *v.* **pur·sued, pur·su·ing.** to strive for or seek.

R

ral·ly (ral′ ē) *v.* **ral·lied, ral·ly·ing.** to bring together; gather or assemble.

ran·som (ran′ səm) *n.* money or goods paid to free someone. [Old French *raencon* price paid for the release of a captive, from Latin *rēdemptiō* a buying back.]

ra·ti·o (rā′ shē ō′) *n.* a relative comparison between the value or degree of two numbers.

re·cede (ri sēd′) *v.* **re·ced·ed, re·ced·ing.** to move back or away.

re·con·nais·sance (ri kon′ ə səns) *n.* a mission or action to obtain information.

ref·uge (ref′ ūj) *n.* a place providing shelter, protection, or safety.

ref·u·gee (ref′ ū jē′) *n.* person who flees to safety or refuge, especially one who leaves his or her home or homeland because of persecution, war, or danger, and seeks safety in another place.

rel·ic (rel′ ik) *n.* thing from the past, such as an object or custom, that has survived the passage of time; remnant.

re·lieved (ri lēvd′) *adj.* freed from discomfort or pain.

ren·o·vate (ren′ ə vāt′) *v.* **ren·o·vat·ed, ren·o·vat·ing.** to repair and make like new.

rep·ri·mand (rep′ rə mand′) *n.* a sharp reproof, especially one formally or officially given.

re·sist (ri zist′) *v.* to keep from yielding to; abstain from.

res·o·lute·ly (rez′ ə lüt′ lē) *adv.* with strong determination.

rev·er·ence (rev′ ər əns, rev′ rəns) *n.* a feeling of deep respect and affection.

ridge (rij) *n.* **1.** a long and narrow chain of hills or mountains. **2.** the top edge of this chain.

rig (rig) *v.* **rigged, rig·ging.** to fit a boat or ship with masts, sails, spars, lines, and the like.

rit·u·al (rich′ ü əl) *n.* set form for the performance of religious or other ceremonies.

rud·der (rud′ ər) *n.* a vertical piece of metal or wood, hinged to the stern, or rear, of a boat and used for steering.

ru·ins (rü′ inz) *n. pl.* the remains of something destroyed or decayed.

run (run) *n.* a group of fish assembling and ascending a stream to spawn.

rune (rün) *n.* a letter or character used in ancient Germanic writing, especially in Scandinavia and England.

rune

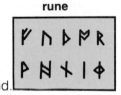

ruth·less (rüth′ lls) *adj.* without pity, mercy, or compassion.

S

sa·ga (sä′ gə) *n.* a long story about adventurous or heroic deeds and passed down from generation to generation.

sar·cas·ti·cal·ly (sär kas′ tik lē) *adv.* in a way that is intended to hurt or make fun of.

scent (sent) *n.* a characteristic smell of an animal or human.

schol·ar·ship (skol′ ər ship′) *n.* a grant of financial aid given to a student to help him or her continue a course of study.

scythe (sīth) *n.* an implement consisting of a long curved blade atttached at an angle to a long bent handle, used for mowing, cutting, or reaping.

sear·ing (sir′ ing) *adj.* burning; scorching.

se·clud·ed (si klü′ did) *adj.* kept apart or removed from others.

Shake·speare, Wil·liam (shāk′ spir′, wil′ yəm) 1564–1616, English poet and dramatist.

sheer (shir) *adj.* **1.** total; utter. **2.** thin; nearly transparent. **3.** straight up or straight down.

sib·ling ri·val·ry (sib′ ling rī′ vəl rē) competition between siblings, or brothers and sisters.

sin·is·ter (sin′ is tər) *adj.* threatening or suggesting evil. [Latin *sinister* left; referring to the belief of people in ancient times that the *left* side was unlucky.]

site (sīt) *n.* place where something happened.

sky·way (skī′ wā′) *n.* an elevated road.

slab (slab) *n.* a broad, flat, and usually thick piece of some material.

sla·lom (slä′ ləm) *n.* a zigzag ski race down a course marked by poles.

---

a **b**at, ā **c**ake, ä **f**ather, är **c**ar, âr **d**are; e **h**en, ē **m**e, ėr **t**erm; i **b**ib, ī **k**ite, ir **cl**ear; o **t**op, ō **r**ope, ô **s**aw, oi **c**oin, ôr **f**ork, ou **o**ut; u **s**un, ů **b**ook, ü **m**oon, ū **c**ute; ə **a**bout, tak**e**n

slith·er (slith′ ər) v. to move along with a sliding or gliding motion.

smelt·ed (smel′ tid) adj. melted.

smith·y (smith′ ē) n., pl. **smith·ies.** the workshop of a blacksmith.

snick·er (snik′ ər) v. a sly laugh, usually expressing scorn or disrespect.

sol·emn (sol′ əm) adj. serious and earnest; grave.

so·lic·it (sə lis′ it) v. to seek to obtain; to ask for.

so·lo (sō′ lō) adj. made, or done, by one person alone.

som·ber (som′ bər) adj. dark and gloomy.

souf·flé (sü flā′) n. a puffy, rounded baked dish.

soul mu·sic (sōl′ mū′ zik) music originated by black Americans in the middle twentieth century with origins in jazz, blues, swing, and rock and roll.

spin·dle whorl (spind′ əl hwôrl) a ball-like wheel used in spinning wool.

spit (spit) n. a slender rod on which meat is roasted over a fire.

spon·son (spon′ sən) n. an air-filled compartment on the side of a seaplane to stabilize it.

spon·sor (spon′ sər) n. a person who assumes responsibility or support for another person or thing.

sprint (sprint) n. a short race at full speed.

sta·bil·i·ty (stə bil′ ə tē) n. the state or condition of being stable; steadiness.

stance (stans) n. a manner or way of standing.

sta·tion·mas·ter (stā′ shən mas′ tər) n. the person in charge of a railroad or bus station.

sta·tis·tics (stə tis′ tiks) n. pl. numerical data, or facts, that have been collected and are used as information about a particular subject.

sta·tus (stat′ əs, stā′ təs) n. the position or rank of someone with respect to other people.

stern (stėrn) n. the rear of a boat or ship. [Middle English for *rudder*, going back to Germanic *stieren* to steer.]

stim·u·lant (stim′ ū lənt) n. a drug or chemical that speeds up the activity of the central nervous system.

sto·ry·board (stôr′ ē bôrd′) n. a panel or series of panels on which rough drawings are attached, depicting the progress of scenes in a comic strip, advertisement, or movie, used for planning.

storyboard

strait (strāt) n. a narrow waterway or channel connecting two larger bodies of water.

stren·u·ous (stren′ ū əs) adj. requiring great effort.

stride (strīd) n. a long, sweeping step.

surge (sėrj) n. a sudden increase or onset. —v. **surged, surg·ing.** to increase, rise or swell suddenly, as waves.

sus·pense (sə spens′) n. the worry or tension caused by an undecided or doubtful situation.

sym·pa·thy (sim′ pə thē) n., pl. **sym·pa·thies.** sorrow for unhappiness or suffering of another or others.

T

taunt (tônt) *v.* to provoke or tease.

taut (tôt) *adj.* tightly drawn or stretched; not slack or loose.

tech·nique (tek nēk′) *n.* a method or manner of bringing about a desired result.

three-di·men·sion·al (thrē′ di men′ shən əl) *adj.* giving the illusion of, or having depth. Also, **3-D.**

trans·fer (trans fėr′, trans′ fər) *v.* **trans·ferred, trans·fer·ring.** to remove from one person or place to another.

trans·form (trans fôrm′) *v.* to change in shape, form, or appearance.

treach·er·ous (trech′ ər əs) *adj.* dangerous; hazardous.

U

un·daunt·ed (un dôn′ tid) *adj.* not discouraged or frightened; fearless.

u·nique (ū nēk′) *adj.* having no equal; unmatched.

V

van·i·ty (van′ i tē) *n.* a very high opinion of oneself or of one's achievements; conceit.

venge·ance (ven′ jəns) *n.* the act of causing injury to another person in return for an injury or wrong.

vi·cious (vish′ əs) *adj.* fierce; savage.

vig·il (vij′ əl) *n.* the act of remaining awake to guard or observe something.

vig·or (vig′ ər) *n.* healthy strength.

Vi·king (vī′ king) a member of the seafaring raiders from Scandinavia from the eighth to the eleventh centuries who made long voyages to the New World.

Viking

vin·di·cate (vin′ də kāt′) *v.* **vin·di·cat·ed, vin·di·cat·ing.** to show to be just or reasonable; justify.

vis·u·o·mo·tor be·hav·ior re·hears·al (vi′ zhü ō′ mō′ tər bə hāv′ yər rē hėrs′ əl) mental rehearsal of a physical activity to enhance one's ability. Also, **VMBR.**

vi·tal·i·ty (vī tal′ ə tē) *n.* physical and mental energy; vigor. [Latin *vītālıs* relating to life, from *vīta* life.]

vow (vou) *n.* solemn promise or pledge.

W

Wa·tut·si (wä tü′ sē) a group in Africa known for their tallness. Also, **Watusi.**

wist·ful (wist′ fəl) *adj.* sadly longing; yearning.

---

a b**a**t, ā c**a**ke, ä f**a**ther, är c**a**r, ãr d**a**re; e h**e**n, ē m**e**, ėr t**e**rm; i b**i**b, ī k**i**te, ir cl**ear**; o t**o**p, ō r**o**pe, ô s**a**w, oi c**oi**n, ôr f**o**rk, ou **ou**t; u s**u**n, ů b**oo**k, ü m**oo**n, ū c**u**te; ə **a**bout, tak**e**n

This section of *Noble Pursuits* includes a review of letters and the sounds they stand for. Good readers know that letters in a word are clues. Looking carefully at these letters is one way to figure out how to say a word. Some words may look new, but once you say them you may discover that you already know them.

Lessons

Word Work

Beginning Sounds

Letters stand for sounds at the beginning of words.

A. Copy the sentences below. Fill in the missing letters. Choose the letters from those in the box. Be sure the words make sense in the sentence.

b d g l m p qu t v w y z

I was __ery __isappointed. A __eek camping, hoping to see a __oose, and we never saw one. We had __aited __atiently by the __ake where the __ark ranger said they came. "Weren't they hungry?" I __used. "Didn't they need to __ench their thirst?" I __earned to see one in the __ild. It would be so much more satisfying than __azing at one in a __oo.

"__erhaps next __ear," my __other said, as we drove home.

"__aybe," I __uttered and __ozed in the __ack seat. In a __ittle __own, the __ateway to the __ountains, we stopped suddenly. I __ooked up __uickly. And there, as __ig as __ife, was a moose, ambling across the road with a funny __ait. It __igzagged up a __irt road and __ isappeared into the __oods.

Some beginning sounds can be spelled more than one way.

B. Number your paper from 1 to 8. Read each group of words below. Write the two words from each group that begin with the same sound.

1. circus
   kin
   cue

2. heavy
   who
   weaver

3. jiggle
   giggle
   gypsy

4. wreath
   wealth
   reach

5. kennel
   knobby
   noodle

6. fatal
   poise
   physics

7. cyclone
   canter
   session

8. cycle
   kindle
   somber

Ending Sounds

Letters stand for sounds at the end of words.

A. Copy the sentences below. Fill in the missing letters. Use the letters below.

b   d   l   m   p   n   x   dge   g   t

    Everyone at the antique car show was asked to be a ju__. "Pick your favorite," a ma__ with a ba__ sai__.

    "Tha__ one's too dra__," though__ Lena. "Wow, look at those si__ beauties over there! Which one of the__ is my idea__?" she wondered. And the__ she saw it—an old Model T. On to__ of the hoo__ was a sign saying *Elizabeth.* It was decorated with a spri__ of lilac. Lena marked her ballo__ and turned towar__ the gate.

Some ending sounds can be spelled more than one way.

B. Copy the sentences below. Fill in the missing letters. Choose the letters from those in the box.

f   ff   ph   k   c   ck   s   ss

1. Doug had to pi__ his way carefully acro__ the rocks.
2. The lighthouse ahead looked like a fortre__ on the cli__.
3. The light warned ship__ of the ree__ hidden by the water.
4. In earlier times, many vessel__ had met a tragi__ end on this blea__ point.
5. With a cli__, Doug too__ a photogra__ of the lighthouse, then headed ba__ to the paved path.

Short Vowel Sounds

There are five short vowel sounds. Some short vowel sounds can be spelled more than one way.

a	e	i	o	u
d<u>a</u>b	th<u>e</u>ft	fl<u>i</u>nt	cl<u>o</u>p	f<u>u</u>nd
	thr<u>ea</u>d		w<u>a</u>tt	w<u>o</u>n
				r<u>ou</u>gh

Number your paper from 1 to 7. Complete each sentence below with a word that has the same vowel sound as the underlined word. Write the word on your paper. Underline the letter or letters that spell the short vowel sound.

1. With a <u>swish</u>, something flew out of the _____ fireplace.
   stone   brick   high

2. A <u>bat</u> _____ around the room.
   flew   raced   flapped

3. I wanted to crawl _____ the <u>rug</u>.
   beneath   under   through

4. "_____ for yourself," I muttered to Dad under my <u>breath</u>.
   Fend   Save   Watch

5. "<u>Watch</u> out!" he cried, grabbing a _____ and swinging it.
   mop   broom   rake

6. "It could be _____ getting it out, <u>Son</u>," Dad called. "Open the door."
   hard   slow   tough

7. Not soon <u>enough</u>, the bat _____ through the door and out into the night.
   tore   rushed   flew

Word Work

Consonant Clusters with *l* and *r*

> Consonant clusters are made up of two or more letters whose sounds blend together.

Read the poem below. Notice the underlined words.

Flutes and clarinets,
Not harps or violins,
Drums and slide trombones,
Not horns or saxophones.
Do you see why? I know you're smart.
Look at the consonant clusters at the start.

Number your paper from 1 to 13. Read each word clue below. Write your answer, using one of the consonant clusters in the box.

bl	cl	fl	gl	pl	sl
br	cr	dr	fr	gr	pr	tr

1. I am a mixture of rain and hail or snow. __eet
2. I am a high, flat expanse of land. __ateau
3. I can make your laundry whites whiter! __each
4. I am a fine mass of bubbles. __oth
5. I am rough or raw. __ude
6. I am a brief shower of snow. __urry
7. I am an acknowledgment of respect. __ibute
8. I am tiny rough pieces, usually sand or small stones. __it
9. Ho hum! You're me when you're sleepy, very sleepy. __owsy
10. I am a small valley. __en
11. I am self-respect. __ide
12. I am a woman getting married. __ide
13. I am not graceful. __umsy

Consonant Clusters with *s*

> Consonant clusters can be two or three letters whose sounds blend together.

Many consonant clusters begin with *s.* Look for consonant clusters as you read the story below.

Instead of a haunted house for Halloween this year, the scouts made The Frightful Swamp. Mrs. Smith was the specialist who planned this spectacular success. You walked through it without shoes or stockings on: bare feet squishing through the soft slime. Nothing was in the mud, but you never knew for sure. Spider webs caught your face. Eerie screeches and squeaks rang in your ears. Reeds and long grasses scratched past your arms. A bat swept close to your head. Scrawny creatures sprang out, making you scream in mock fright. Other small crawly things skittered across the spotlights. They cast strange shadows everywhere. At the end, an alligator snapped its jaws open and shut. Sometimes it seemed nearly to snag a victim. An evil-sounding laugh followed you out into the starry still night. A small pool of warm water and a stack of sweet-smelling towels were there for washing and drying your feet.

Number your paper from 1 to 11. Write the consonant clusters below. Next to each, write the word or words from the story that begin with the cluster.

1. sc	2. sn	3. sw	4. squ	5. sk	6. sp
7. scr	8. str	9. sm	10. st	11. spr	

Ending Consonant Clusters

> Consonant clusters can come at the beginning or at the end of words. Some important ending consonant clusters are listed below.
>
> ld   nd   nk   sk   mp   ft   lt   nt   st

Number your paper from 1 to 12. Write each sentence below. Find one consonant cluster that will complete both incomplete words in the sentence. Use the consonant clusters in the box.

1. Sara and Ron tried to thi__ of a good pra__ to play on Anne for April Fool's Day.
2. That last try made Ella the school's long ju__ cha__.
3. I won fir__ place in the conte__.
4. A bitter co__ wind blew across the open fie__.
5. Shopping for a ma__ to complete my costume was a ta__ I rather enjoyed.
6. I finally fou__ the poetry book I wanted to le__ Pat.
7. A narrow cle__ ran down the le__ side of the canyon wall.
8. The flowers on that pla__ have a particularly sweet sce__.
9. Mike fe__ warm once that old qui__ was wrapped around him.
10. May had to fe__ for herself as she climbed up the ledge; but once she was there, she gave me a ha__.
11. It's an o__ folk tale but I never tire of hearing it to__.
12. I dete__ hearing my brother boa__.

Short Vowel Sounds

Some short vowel sounds can be spelled more than one way.

ô	u̇
false	nook
raw	bull
cross	could
caught	

Number your paper from 1 to 6. Complete each sentence below with a word that has the same vowel sound as the underlined word. Write the word on your paper. Underline the letter or letters that spell the vowel sound.

1. The butcher _____ softly toward the meat locker, wondering what had caused the loud noise.

   walked   strolled   tiptoed

2. He _____ quietly. "Maybe I should call the police," he thought.

   crawled   stopped   stood

3. Suddenly he went to a _____ basket and looked inside.

   bushel   large   crude

4. He saw a _____ black nose.

   small   tiny   cute

5. It was like a cartoon: a dog with a string of _____ at its feet.

   meat   sausage   pork

6. "It's all my_____," the butcher said, "I left the back door open."

   mistake   error   fault

Long Vowel Sounds

> Many words that end in *e* have a long vowel sound.

Read the poem below. Notice the vowel sound in each underlined word.

Cods to codes and cans to canes.
    Pins to pines and plans to planes.
How's it done? Can't you see?
    The changes come from adding *e*.

The magic *e* changes the short vowel sound to a long vowel sound. The missing word in each sentence below can be discovered by adding the magic *e* to one of the other words in the sentence. Number your paper from 1 to 8. Write the complete sentences.

1. There was enough cloth in the warehouse to _____ the entire city.
2. Here's a good _____ for our camp; we can sit on that log to eat our meals.
3. Mom was mad about the mess we _____ .
4. A brown bear cub was in the meadow this morning licking the cow's salt _____ .
5. The lumberyard gave us materials to _____ in building the stage sets.
6. We had to quit when it got dark even though the game was not _____ over.
7. The rider's back was as straight as a rod as she _____ around the ring.
8. Sal bought a bicycle at the sporting goods _____ last week.

Long *a* Vowel Sound

> The long *a* vowel sound can be spelled more than one way.
>
> d<u>a</u>t<u>e</u>   sl<u>eigh</u>   m<u>ai</u>l   b<u>ay</u>

Read the poem below. As you read, notice the long *a* vowel sound in each underlined word.

> The <u>rain</u> <u>today</u> stopped the <u>game</u>—
>   at the <u>eighth</u> inning.
> It <u>came</u> down hard and spoiled the <u>play</u>—
>   while we were winning.
>   Should we <u>stay</u> and <u>wait</u> it out?
>   "<u>Nay</u>," the coaches said.
>   "You've <u>played</u> enough. We'd <u>say</u> you won."
> We went home grinning.

Number your paper from 1 to 8. Read each group of words below. Write the two words in each group that have the long *a* vowel sound.

1. payment	2. fasten	3. nasty	4. sleigh
upstage	vague	tease	slack
alone	earth	haystack	slat
peacock	neighbor	afraid	slain

5. repay	6. shapeless	7. axle	8. came
recall	freight	tailor	canoe
remain	foal	grayish	canal
repeat	neither	cleanse	chain

Long e Vowel Sound

> The long e vowel sound can be spelled more than one way.
> wh**ee**l   w**ea**k   coz**y**   sh**e**   chi**e**f

A. Number your paper from 1 to 12. Write each word below. Then underline the letter or letters that stand for the long e vowel sound.

1. strategy
2. energy
3. lease
4. fiend
5. sleepless
6. yield
7. referee
8. cedar
9. canteen
10. beacon
11. recently
12. foresee

B. Number your paper from 1 to 6. Find the word or words with the long e vowel sound in each sentence below. Write them on your paper. Underline the letter or letters that stand for this sound.

1. I headed east on my bicycle to meet Nancy for an early swim.
2. The street was bumpy but I pedaled quickly and easily.
3. Suddenly I was lying in the middle of the street, my bicycle on top of me.
4. Though I had tried to keep free of the bumps, I had hit one and had gone head over heels.
5. I lay there for a brief moment, realizing I seemed to be okay.
6. When I got to the beach, the lifeguard told me that warm sea water would clean the scratches on my knees.

Long *i* Vowel Sound

> The long *i* vowel sound can be spelled more than one way.
>
> pri<u>me</u>   fr<u>igh</u>t   tr<u>y</u>   l<u>ie</u>

The beach is narrow when the water is <u>high</u>
   But it's <u>wide</u> and <u>nice</u> when it's low.
     It's a good place to <u>lie</u> and a good place to play
     and a good place to walk and to look for some shells.
The <u>tide</u> is controlled by the moon in the <u>sky</u>.
   As it pulls on the oceans below.

The underlined words in the poem show different letters that stand for the long *i* vowel sound: *igh, ie, y,* and *i-e.*

Number your paper from 1 to 26. Read the story below. Then write each word that has the long *i* vowel sound. Underline the letter or letters that stand for the long *i* vowel sound.

   "Well," smiled Dad at dinnertime, as he loosened his necktie. "What would you think of a trip to see a petrified forest this summer?"
   "That sounds delightful!" said Mom. "But if we drive, it will take a mighty long time to get there."
   "You're right," Dad replied. "We could fly. But the sights along the way are almost as nice as the forest itself. We'll see highlands and lowlands, city skylines and rolling farmlands, dry deserts and green hillsides. If we apply ourselves to the task and organize the trip well, we'll be able to devise a route that offers plenty of adventure. Let's speak with my brother Mike before we decide. He's been there twice, so we can rely on his advice."

Word Work

Long *o* Vowel Sound

The long *o* vowel sound can be spelled more than one way.
> rope   poach   zero   show

Read the poem below.

"You can't sing a note,"
  said the bird to the toad.
"You can't float on the wind,
  or go south when it's cold."
"Oh, but I croak from my throat with a musical trill
  And I hop down the road—
    and know when to sit still."

A. Number your paper from 1 to 10. Write the words from the poem that have the long *o* vowel sound. Underline the letter or letters that stand for the long *o* vowel sound.

B. Number your paper from 1 to 12. Read each group of words below. Write the two words from each group that have a long *o* vowel sound.

1. oppose	2. audio	3. conceal	4. vowel
trod	growth	foal	cod
peacock	policy	ordeal	seagoing
furrow	pouch	potato	owing
5. wholesome	6. soapsuds	7. tower	8. rose
auction	hopeful	golden	overgrown
pinto	onto	lowly	occupation
coil	froth	coop	other
9. hero	10. mouse	11. broth	12. outfield
couch	coach	problem	boast
rejoice	poised	approach	drone
glowing	lope	globe	ground

The Unusual *u*

> There are two short *u* vowel sounds and two long *u* vowel sounds. Each is spelled in more than one way.

Read the words in the box. Look at the underlined letters. Listen for the sounds the underlined letters stand for.

Short Vowels		Long Vowels	
u	u̇	ü	ū
sk<u>u</u>nk	w<u>oo</u>d	z<u>oo</u>	conf<u>u</u>se
s<u>o</u>n	p<u>u</u>t		f<u>ew</u>
r<u>ou</u>gh	sh<u>ou</u>ld		<u>u</u>nit

Number your paper from 1 to 8. Read each key word below. Then find a word in the row that has the same vowel sound. Write the word on your paper.

1. **tooth**   brook   goose   enough
2. **view**   cousin   usher   menu
3. **could**   bull   cloud   unit
4. **tough**   sudden   fuel   amount
5. **cute**   stood   pulley   unique
6. **ton**   few   ugly   total
7. **wool**   cushion   clock   soon
8. **boot**   wooden   igloo   summer

Short and Long Vowel Sounds

A. Read the two underlined words in each sentence below. Notice that they look almost the same but sound different. Write the headings *Short Vowel* and *Long Vowel* on your paper. List each underlined word under the correct heading.

1. Tonight we would dine on clams she would dig, Alice told us.
2. She claimed to know where the best clams could be found.
3. I carried the shovel Alice had brought for us to use.
4. We went to the head of Sad Cove and soon had a heap of clams.
5. Our shoes and socks were soaked, but we were triumphant.

B. The underlined word in each sentence below is shown divided into syllables at the end of the sentence. Number your paper from 1 to 6. Write each underlined word, leaving a space between the syllables. Underline each syllable with a short vowel sound once and each syllable with a long vowel sound twice.

1. Martin thought we were crazy to get up at sunrise. (cra zy)
2. My sister is a redhead. (red head)
3. From the airplane the coastline looked just as it does on the map. (coast line)
4. Louis knows the rules and will explain them. (ex plain)
5. The gram and the pound are both units of weight. (u nits)
6. "Follow that red car!" the woman said to the taxi driver. (fol low)

Beginning Consonant Digraphs

> Two or three consonants that stand for one sound are called consonant digraphs.

Read the words below. Look at the underlined letters. They are consonant digraphs.

chart	shine	white	thick	there

Notice that the letters *th* can stand for two different sounds. Number your paper from 1 to 7. Add a consonant digraph to complete each word below. Write the complete word on the paper. Be sure it makes sense in the sentence.

1. I wondered __y anyone would __oose to spend a week camping in the woods.
2. "It's fun," Robin said __en __e asked me to go. "It's quiet and peaceful."
3. The birds' __irping woke me every morning at 4:30. __is is peaceful?
4. Splitting firewood and hiking so far __at my legs __ake is fun?
5. I must have walked a __ousand miles, I __ought last year.
6. Robin just asked if I'd like to go with __em again.
7. "You bet I would! I can't wait to hear __ose __ispering pines—and I bet I'll be the __ampion wood __opper."

Ending Consonant Digraphs

> Consonant digraphs can come at the end of words.

The words below have ending consonant digraphs.

> song   fre<u>sh</u>   mun<u>ch</u>   nor<u>th</u>   scra<u>tch</u>

Read the story below.

What a day it seemed for flying my new kite! It was a beauty: a bright silver fish with two strings. Whit has one like it, and he said he'd teach me how to make it really dance.

I did pretty well until it started to dive. And dive it did. It landed with a crash—no, a splash—in the park lake. Of course, it got caught on a branch stuck in the mud, out of reach. My arms are long, but I couldn't stretch them that far. I tugged gently on the kite strings; the kite wouldn't budge.

Whit got a stick, thinking we could push the kite free with it or loosen the branch from the mud. We each tried but had no luck.

We'd just sat down on a nearby bench to think when a sea gull landed on the branch and began to tug at my kite. Did he think it was a mammoth fish? Suddenly the string became untangled and the gull flew off, taking my kite along. I held my breath as he carried it a few feet and then dropped it. I dashed to the water's edge to haul it in.

My kite is okay. I'll have to patch a small hole; but it will take wing again—and dance with more grace, I hope, next time.

Write each word below. Next to each word write the words from the story that end with the same sound and are spelled in the same way.

1. di<u>sh</u>   **2.** tru<u>th</u>   **3.** ri<u>ng</u>   **4.** swi<u>tch</u>   **5.** bea<u>ch</u>

Syllables

Some words can be divided into parts called syllables.
You can hear a vowel sound in every syllable.

Sometimes two or more vowel letters stand for one vowel sound. For example, in the word *cloak* you see two vowels, but you hear only one vowel sound. The word *cloak* has one syllable. The word *oasis* has three syllables; it has three vowel sounds.

A. Number your paper from 1 to 20. Read each word below. The number of vowel sounds is the same as the number of syllables. How many syllables does each word have? Write your answers.

1. destiny	2. bareback	3. paralyze	4. engage
5. headdress	6. examination	7. presentation	8. slain
9. straight	10. ideal	11. unidentified	12. ivory
13. institution	14. righteous	15. imaginative	16. pout
17. rotate	18. nonfiction	19. predicament	20. wreath

When you say a word that has more than one syllable, you stress, or emphasize, one syllable more than another. In a dictionary or glossary, the stressed syllable is followed by an accent mark (').

cat' a log   re view'

B. Number your paper from 1 to 15. Read each word below. Which syllable is stressed: the first, second, third, or fourth? Write your answers.

1. nature	2. cascade	3. vigorous
4. collide	5. constitution	6. majestic
7. souvenir	8. varnish	9. interference
10. outfield	11. sacrifice	12. terrific
13. relieve	14. emerald	15. division

Schwa

> The schwa is a special vowel sound. It can be spelled with *a*, *e*, *i*, *o*, or *u*. The schwa vowel sound is often heard in the unstressed syllable of a word.

Read the words below. The underlined letters stand for the schwa vowel sound.

compass   item   ultimate   method   cheerful

The schwa vowel sound can also be at the beginning of a word, as in *oppose,* or in the middle of a word, as in *fascinate.* Number your paper from 1 to 8. Write each underlined word below. Underline the vowel that stands for the schwa vowel sound.

1. What a majestic sight it was: the planet Oarrfus.
2. It was the only other civilized planet in the universe.
3. It seems so long ago that I had applied to be a student agent on Oarrfus.
4. I had no idea I would actually be chosen.
5. Yet here I was, one of a dozen students headed for the first alien colony on Oarrfus.
6. The trip out had been uneventful, but I felt nervous now.
7. A great deal of hard work lay ahead of us.
8. The spaceship landed gently upon Oarrfus's landing pad and our adventure began.

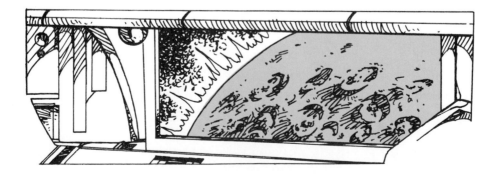

Vowel Combinations

> Some vowel combinations make the same sound but are spelled with different letters.
>
> jo**y**   n**ow**
> s**oi**l   h**ou**se

A. Write the words *joy* and *now* at the top of your paper. Under each word, write the six words from the list below that have the same vowel sound.

annoyance	snowplow	ouch	oilwell
scowl	broiler	moisture	drowning
pounded	pout	toystore	disloyal

B. *Ou* and *ow* do not always stand for the vowel sound you hear in *now*. Read the words below. Only eight of them have the vowel sound you hear in *now*. Which eight are they? Write them on your paper.

clown	recount	tomorrow	doubt	conscious
fourteen	growl	souvenir	trouble	cloudy
knowledge	rowboat	outstanding	browse	nightgown

C. Number your paper from 1 to 8. Read the word clues below. Each answer will be a word you wrote in part B.

1. I am overcast, I am _____ .
2. No circus is complete without me, I am a _____ .
3. I am uncertainty, I am _____ .
4. Not a loud roar, I am a low _____ .
5. I am superior, I am _____ .
6. I'm not ready to buy. I just want to _____ .
7. I narrate, I _____ .
8. A long dress with silver stars would be a real _____ .

Vowel + *r*

The letter *r* changes the sound of the vowel it follows.

Read the underlined words below. Notice the vowel sounds.

<u>Jam</u> and <u>jar</u>
<u>Mane</u> and <u>mare</u>
<u>Pain</u> and <u>pair</u>
<u>Held</u> and <u>herd</u>
<u>Bid</u> and <u>bird</u>
<u>Code</u> and <u>core</u>
<u>Lunch</u> and <u>lurch</u>

Look again. Read each pair. How do their vowel sounds compare?

A. Number your paper from 1 to 5. From each list below write the two words that rhyme.

1	2	3	4	5
worm	squirt	barn	bread	frost
warm	hurt	burn	beard	burst
germ	hut	tern	world	twist
harm	grit	then	twirled	thirst

B. Number your paper from 1 to 5. From each list below write the two words in which *r* changes the vowel sound.

1	2	3	4	5
careful	raid	worsen	parka	crude
firmest	compare	furry	granite	darn
muskrat	illustrate	rascal	apricot	jerk
strain	staircase	already	airplane	unreal

r-Controlled Vowels

> Some *r*-controlled vowel sounds can be spelled in different ways.

Read the two groups of words below. Listen for vowel sounds that are the same in each group.

1. disappeared	career	sphere
2. adorned	keyboard	seashore

A. Pick a word from the box above that has the same vowel sound as the underlined word. Write the word to complete each sentence below.

1. Marc will play the French horn; Holly will be at the ___ .
2. Sandy has a clear idea what her ___ will be: a veterinarian.
3. I know I left my glasses here, but they seem to have ___ .
4. Nora wore a long purple dress; a big hat with a plume ___ her head.
5. When I peered through the telescope I could see Mars, a giant red ___ , almost close enough to touch.
6. I knew the ___ was near when I heard the roar of the surf.

> The letter *r* can follow and change the schwa vowel sound.

B. Number your paper from 1 to 6. Write the words from the list below that end with the sound you hear at the end of *fever*.

ajar	differ	interior	quaver	unclear
visor	singular	hot-air	deer	cedar

487

Short and Long Vowel Sounds

> The letters *a, e, i, o, u,* and sometimes *y* can be used alone or together to spell short or long vowel sounds.

Idioms are groups of words that have meanings that are not the same as the meanings those words usually have. Number your paper from 1 to 8. Copy the sentences below. Choose a word from the box that completes the idiom in each sentence. The word you choose should have the same vowel sound as the underlined word.

c<u>a</u>t	cr<u>o</u>codile	cr<u>o</u>w	f<u>i</u>sh
g<u>oo</u>se	m<u>o</u>nkey	w<u>ea</u>sel	wh<u>a</u>le

1. Let's not _____ around; we'll get the job done if we <u>just</u> get to it.
2. I thought Chuck <u>did</u> a good job in the school play, but he said he felt like a _____ out of water up there on the stage.
3. As the _____ flies it was only a short distance, but Pat chose to take the winding path and <u>roam</u> through the woods.
4. "Don't _____ out of coming," Sue teased <u>me</u>. "Skiing is fun."
5. At first it seemed like a wild _____ chase, but we finally did see a pair of <u>loons</u> on the pond.
6. That <u>sail</u> was great fun! I had a _____ of a time.
7. It was a big disappointment, but Gene did <u>not</u> cry _____ tears when he lost the race.
8. Who let the _____ out of the <u>bag</u> and told June about the surprise party?

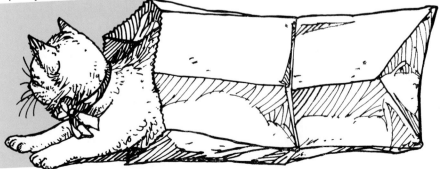

Syllables and Short Vowel Sounds

Learning to divide words into syllables can help you read new words. When you come to a difficult word in your reading, you can work on one small part at a time.

Read these one-syllable words.

stack   stem   still   stone   stuck

Now read these words.

cactus   costume   classic

How many vowel sounds are in each word?
How many syllables does each word have?
Below are the same words divided into syllables.

cac tus   cos tume   clas sic

Notice that a vowel comes between two consonants in the first syllable of each word. Do you hear a short or a long vowel sound?

> When two consonants stand between two vowels, the word is usually divided between the consonants. The vowel in the first syllable is often short.

Number your paper from 1 to 24. Write each word, leaving a space between the syllables.

1. thunder
2. engine
3. fatten
4. biscuit
5. capsule
6. invade
7. custom
8. distance
9. plunder
10. glimmer
11. terrain
12. offense
13. dismal
14. clamber
15. vendor
16. missile
17. marrow
18. contest
19. fragment
20. rampart
21. collide
22. grammar
23. villain
24. contents

Syllables and Long Vowel Sounds

Read the poem below.

> My eyes are <u>hazel</u>, some folks say.
> Others think that they are gray.
> In fact, I've <u>noticed</u> the color <u>wavers</u>.
> I'm not sure which one I <u>favor</u>.
> I can't change it anyway.

Read the underlined words above. How many vowel sounds does each have? How many syllables?

This is how the words are divided into syllables.

ha zel   no ticed   wa vers   fa vor

Notice that a vowel is at the end of the first syllable of each word. Do you hear a short or a long vowel sound?

> When one consonant stands between two vowels, the consonant usually goes with the second syllable.
> The vowel in the first syllable is often long.

A. Number your paper from 1 to 16. Write each word below, leaving a space between the syllables.

1. stifle	2. pilot	3. rotate	4. hazy
5. tidy	6. ideal	7. croquet	8. digest
9. final	10. fatal	11. unique	12. female
13. human	14. future	15. station	16. moment

B. Number your paper from 1 to 5. Find five words below that have a long vowel sound in the first syllable. Write them, leaving a space between the syllables.

flavor	pretzel	victim	music	upon
program	cascade	spider	stubby	meter

Syllables, Consonant Digraphs, and Consonant Clusters

Read Marta's chore list. Look for consonant digraphs and consonant clusters.

<u>Chore List</u>

plant flowers	fix left roller skate
polish black shoes	sweep kitchen floor
write thank you letter	get book from library
make present for Grandpa	draw trail map
find kite string	write speech
stack scrap paper	clean doghouse
make mask and shield	buy whistle

A. Look at the underlined letters in the list above.

 1. Remember that consonant digraphs are two or three letters that stand for one sound. List the consonant digraphs.
 2. In a consonant cluster, the separate sounds of the consonants blend together. List the consonant clusters.

Look out for these letter combinations when you are dividing a word into syllables.

> In most cases, do not divide words between the letters in a consonant digraph or in a consonant cluster.

B. Number your paper from 1 to 12. Write the words below on your paper. Underline each consonant digraph or consonant cluster. Then draw a line between the syllables.

1. migrate	2. betray	3. lengthen
4. abstract	5. swiftness	6. author
7. vibrate	8. fragrance	9. strongly
10. splashing	11. supreme	12. brother

Syllables and Prefixes

Read the following sentence.

David <u>disliked</u> the city buses, but he loved riding the <u>subway</u>.

Look again at the underlined words. Notice that each has a prefix.
How many vowel sounds does each word have?
How many syllables?

This is how those words are divided.

dis liked   sub way

> In a word with a prefix, the prefix is usually a separate syllable.

Number your paper from 1 to 30. Write the words below. Underline the prefix in each word. Then draw a line between the syllables.

1. import	11. outfield	21. misplay
2. restrain	12. tricycle	22. disable
3. precede	13. reenter	23. uncertain
4. unearth	14. disagree	24. malnutrition
5. dispose	15. improve	25. befriend
6. invade	16. midair	26. outnumber
7. submarine	17. insight	27. subcontract
8. nonprofit	18. unafraid	28. implant
9. postwar	19. overtake	29. post season
10. misspell	20. reunite	30. pregame

Syllables and Suffixes

Read the following limerick.

There once was an <u>organist</u> named Nate,
Who first played when he was just eight.
    He gave concerts <u>weekly</u>
    And played not at all <u>meekly</u>,
With <u>loudness</u> and an alarming, fast rate.

Look again at the underlined words. Notice that each has a suffix.
How many vowel sounds does each word have?
How many syllables?

This is how those words are divided into syllables.

or gan ist   week ly   meek ly   loud ness

In a word with a suffix, the suffix is usually a separate
syllable.

Number your paper from 1 to 30. Write the words below. Underline
the suffix in each word. Draw a line between the syllables.

1. blindness	11. greenish	21. plentiful
2. gleeful	12. basketful	22. earthen
3. heroic	13. hasty	23. championship
4. waiter	14. violinist	24. tension
5. achievement	15. attention	25. ruthless
6. southward	16. forlornly	26. glorious
7. joyous	17. sleepless	27. historic
8. counselor	18. artist	28. amazement
9. meaningless	19. instructor	29. golden
10. loyalty	20. distinctly	30. sensitively

Stressed Syllables

When the first vowel in a word is followed by a double consonant, the first syllable is usually accented. In most two-syllable words, the first syllable is accented.

flus′ ter	shal′ low	traf′ fic
for′ mal	gyp′ sy	ras′ cal

Read the story below. Number your paper from 1 to 24. Write the underlined words. Divide each word into syllables. Put an accent mark after the stressed syllable. REMEMBER: In most, but not all, two-syllable words the first syllable is accented.

Most of Joan's friends had a pet: a <u>puppy</u> or a dog, a <u>kitten</u> or a cat, a <u>rabbit</u>, fish, or <u>even</u> a <u>pony</u>. Joan had a bird: a <u>parrot</u> named <u>Penny</u>. It had <u>brightly</u> colored <u>feathers</u>—red and <u>yellow</u> and blue and green—and was a nice pet, Joan thought, <u>except</u> when a friend was visiting. Then Penny embarrassed Joan by <u>saying</u>, "I'm <u>hungry</u>!" This <u>often</u> made Joan's friends tease her. "What's the <u>matter</u>, Penny, doesn't Joan feed you?" Joan knew they were <u>only</u> teasing, and she didn't <u>really</u> mind. But she did want to break Penny's habit.

Last night after <u>dinner</u> she filled Penny's seed dish to overflowing. Then she cut twelve <u>paper</u> cups to fill full of seed. She put them on the <u>bottom</u> of Penny' cage. She watched Penny. Penny looked at the seed <u>mostly</u> covering the bottom of the cage. Joan asked, "<u>Enough</u> food, Penny?"

Penny stared at Joan. Joan asked again, "Enough?"

Penny squawked, "Enough." Joan took all the seed out of the cage and refilled the seed dish to its <u>normal</u> level. Penny <u>rarely</u> said "I'm hungry" again. She did say "Enough!"

494

Stressed Syllables and Long Vowels

Read the poem below.

Water <u>Music</u>

The <u>ocean's</u> roar is a long, loud snore,
  It's a <u>lullaby</u> at night.
But this babbling creek doesn't let me sleep.
  I'm <u>awake</u> at the earliest light.

Look at the underlined words. Here is how those words are divided.

mu sic   o cean's   lul la by   a wake

Which syllable of each word has a long vowel sound?
Which syllable is accented?

Syllables with long vowel sounds are often accented. Another syllable in the word may have the primary accent, however. For example, when you say the word *lullaby*, you accent the first syllable most even though the third syllable has the long vowel sound. The third syllable has a secondary accent.

Number your paper from 1 to 16. Write each word. Divide it into syllables. Underline the syllables with a long vowel sound.
Put an accent mark after the syllable that has the primary accent.

1. aimless	2. afraid	3. conceal	4. cascade
5. dispose	6. fatal	7. gleeful	8. human
9. lovely	10. occupy	11. oppose	12. unite
13. sightless	14. supreme	15. timely	16. lengthwise

Stressed Syllables and Base Words

> In a word that has a prefix or suffix, the accent is usually on or within the base word.

Read the words below

> mo′ tor ist   mis lead′   pre pay′

What are the base words? Notice that the base words *lead* and *pay* are accented. Notice that the first syllable of the base word *motor* is accented.

Number your paper from 1 to 12. Write the underlined word or words in each sentence below, leaving spaces between the syllables. Put an accent mark after the syllable that is stressed. Then write the base word.

1. My dog Mac tends to <u>misbehave</u>.
2. He has chased every cat in the <u>neighborhood</u> and dug in most of the gardens.
3. Most people like him but think he's just a mite too <u>playful</u>.
4. I wasn't sure about Mr. Kaplan next door; I thought he <u>truly disliked</u> Mac.
5. That is, I wasn't sure until the day the sidewalks along our street were <u>replaced</u>.
6. Mac got <u>untied</u> and dashed though the wet concrete.
7. Mr. Kaplan saw it happen and called, "He's <u>hopeless</u>, Sarah."
8. I nodded in <u>agreement</u> as he walked into his house.
9. He <u>returned</u> with a broad flat mason's trowel.
10. He <u>carefully</u> smoothed out the surface of the sidewalk.
11. "Mac's a good dog," Mr. Kaplan said. "He's just <u>energetic</u>."
12. You might say the incident cemented my <u>friendship</u> with Mr. Kaplan.